Tales of
dark-skinned women

Race, gender and global culture

Gargi Bhattacharyya
University of Birmingham

First published in 1998 by UCL Press

UCL Press Limited
1 Gunpowder Square
London EC4A 3DE
UK

and

1900 Frost Road, Suite 101
Bristol
Pennsylvania 19007–1598
USA

The name of University College London (UCL) is a
registered trade mark used by UCL Press with the
consent of the owner.

British Library Cataloguing-in-Publication Data
A CIP catalogue record for this book is available from
the British Library.

**Library of Congress Cataloging-in-Publication Data are
available**

ISBNs: 1–85728–611–1 HB
       1–85728–612–X PB

Typeset by Graphicraft Typesetters Ltd., Hong Kong
Printed by T.J. International Ltd., Padstow, UK

WITHDRAWN

Tales of dark-skinned women

Race and representation

A series edited by John Solomos, Michael Keith and David Goldberg

Race and representation is a series of books designed to open up new ways of thinking about race, racism and ethnicity in contemporary societies. International and multidisciplinary in focus, it aims to establish a dialogue between contending theoretical and political perspectives and to provide a forum for the most innovative contemporary work in the field.

Also in the series:

New ethnicities and urban culture by Les Back

Liberation and purity: Race, new religious movements and the ethics of postmodernity by Chetan Bhatt

Contents

Series editor's preface

There is today wide agreement that questions about race, racism and ethnicity are at the heart of contemporary social and political changes in many societies. It seems that almost everybody is talking about the role of racial and ethnic categorisation in the construction of social and political identities. There is, however, little clarity about how to analyze the transformations that are currently going on. *Race and representation* is a series that is focused on the need to provide a forum for some of the best and most challenging work in this field. It seeks to build on recent theoretical advances by providing an arena for new and challenging conceptual and empirical studies on the changing morphology of race and racism in contemporary societies. The need for studies of this kind is evident in the complex varieties of racial and ethnic conflict that have emerged in a variety of societies in recent years and in the changing expressions of racism and forms of racial identity.

One of the most notable developments in recent years has been the re-evaluation of the relationship between race and gender in the construction of understandings of race and ethnicity. Much of this work has sought to explore the complex variety of forms that racial and ethnic identities take, the meanings attached to gender and sexuality, and the changing visual forms of the representation of difference. It is in this wider context that Gargi Bhattacharyya's *Tales of dark-skinned women* needs to be located. Writing from a perspective shaped by cultural studies she weaves together a series of stories that seek to uncover how it is that race and ethnicity gain meaning as ways of fixing and naturalizing the difference between belongingness and otherness. Following the example of writers such as Patricia Williams among others Bhattacharyya uses the story form as a way of alluding to a wide variety of issues while simultaneously making the work accessible. Moving easily between general storytelling, theoretical debates and very specific social trends and realities the author seeks to draw the reader into an analysis of race, gender and identity that challenges commonly held assumptions. Precisely because of the style of this volume it is impossible to fit it into any narrow pigeonhole, but its key concerns can be seen as linked in one way or another to the question of how corporeal properties, and most fetishistically, skin colour, come to furnish an epidermal schema not only for anchoring difference but for distinguishing the pure from the impure. A recurrent theme that runs through the stories is the argument that to the extent that the body comes to signify difference so too does it become a site for strategies of normalization and discipline. *Tales of dark-skinned women* is a nuanced and sensitive exploration of these issues and it illustrates the complex mechanisms that are at work in shaping racial images and myths.

Bhattacharyya's experimental writing distinguishes this volume from most other forms of writing in this area. It eschews the format of most academic texts and monographs and seeks to explore its main concerns through a series of interlinked stories. It is precisely because of this style that it is an exciting and imaginative attempt to re-think the certainties of much of the recent theorizing in this field. The constant movement between storyline and very concrete specificities about racial imagery and politics creates the possibility for a dialogue between academic and wider socio-political concerns about the changing boundaries of racial and ethnic identities.

John Solomos
University of Southampton
April 1998

Acknowledgements

Thank you to MCA Music for the words to "Girl from Ipanema" and to Tim O'Sullivan for telling me how to get permissions for the song; to Newham Monitoring Project, Institute of Race Relations, Campaign Against Racism and Fascism and Inquest for additional information; to Heidi Mirza and Chris Gittings for publishing earlier versions of some of these stories and keeping straight faces; to John Solomos and Michael Keith for (sometimes) treating me like a grown-up; to my colleagues and students at the Department of Cultural Studies and Sociology; and most especially my surrogate family, Mark Erickson, John Gabriel, Yvonne Jacobs and Marie Walsh for the office banter; to Joe Kelleher for being such a patient audience, despite my showing off; to Stan Butt (who I hope never reads this) for making me look like the quiet one; to Manju and Dilip, I guess for everything, including their naughtiness; and most of all to Sonali, whose best adventures are still to come.

CHAPTER 1

Beginning

This is the beginning of a long trail of stories – a trail which will lead us twice around the world, in both directions, touching everywhere, but stopping nowhere. These are the tales of a fabulous, dangerous, downright bloodcurdling place, the West; and, to tell this story, we need to hear about the range of Western fantasy and the places and peoples which bore the scars of these fictions.

Our trail begins with Scheherazade, storyteller extraordinaire. Her story leads on to a tale about all stories and the reasons why we think stories are important. This sets the scene for our own tale – a tale about a land of suffering, greatly in need of narrative healing.

In the tales to follow, we will have call to remember the potency of stories, of various sorts. We will come to see, as fairytale audiences always do, that an appreciation of the logic of fantasy can smooth our understandings of the everyday, and, in reverse, a remembrance of mundane pains is the only route to the heart of a story. Above all, we will hear that both the serious business of social analysis and the frivolous business of distraction require a similar attentiveness. Good stories help us to practise the necessary concentration, stretch our capacities for patience and possibility, help us to process a world which is not easily or immediately understood. Stories promise to teach us an attitude to learning.

But this is all to come. For now, you must only listen, and the shape of the tale will start to appear.

Once there was a woman called Scheherazade. She told stories to keep alive, to save her people, to keep it going.

And of course, the main story is her.

The two brothers, Schahzenan and Schahriar, have discovered that their wives and queens sleep with their slaves and servants – despite giving the appearance of being respectable women. At first, both brothers resolve to renounce the world and travel until they find someone unhappier than themselves. But on their journey they are seduced by the mistress of a jealous genie who imprisons his lover to ensure her chastity. Elated by this experience, the brothers decide that this is proof of woman's devious and lascivious nature and that they are no more fools than other men. Relieved, they return to their lives and Schahriar begins his new life.

In his new life, Schahriar resolves to be no woman's fool. He orders his vizier to bring him the daughter of his general to marry, and next morning he orders her execution. The next night he does the same with someone else's daughter. And the next and the next and the next, until the land lives in terror. Scheherazade is the talented daughter of the grand vizier and she offers herself as wife to the king in order to halt the bloodshed. Her method of salvation is stories.

She is dealing with an absolute and unreasonable power. The caliph is already convinced that women are lesser, treacherous, contaminated. The heterosexual imperative which signifies his potency in all areas (to himself at least) pushes him into sex with women, compulsively, fearfully. Managing the fear means killing the girls. Our heroine volunteers for this bedroom duty which has always led to death. Her self-assigned task is to distract the king. If she can distract him with her stories, the framing story will shift. If she keeps on talking, woman will mean different things. She becomes voice and mind, a thing above the sex-hungry flesh of the king's imagination.

Scheherezade talks her way to safety and saves her people into the bargain. She tells us nothing about herself, although she tells many tales, a countless number, until she is free. No clues about what kind of woman she is – only her dutiful-daughter advert at the start of the story. But whatever she is, her skin is dark. And that is where our story starts.

Where is she from?

This is a mixed-up set of stories; what we are talking about here is not some founding text or key work of enduring truth. No-one is quite sure where these stories came from. Despite attempts to collect and translate definitive versions, popular wisdom recognizes stories from many sources as belonging to the title *Arabian nights*. Sindbad and Aladdin belong in this collection now – tracing their origins to other sources cannot disrupt the long history of feverish fantasy which links these tales to those of the ladies of Baghdad and the other textually authenticated episodes. The angry forewords denouncing the failings of orientalist scholarship in relation to this story series can never hit their target; it is much too late to reclaim one version as *the* version, and, more importantly, who is interested in authentication here? Listen to a scholar, one who understands the violences of the West.

> The stories of the *Nights* are of various ethnic origins, Indian, Persian, and Arabic. In the process of telling and retelling, they were modified to conform to the general life and the customs of the Arab society that adapted them and to the particular conditions of that society at a

particular time. They were also modified, as in my own experience, to suit the role of the story-teller or the demand of the occasion. But different as their ethnic origins may be, these stories reveal a basic homogeneity resulting from the process of dissemination and assimilation under Islamic hegemony, a homogeneity or distinctive synthesis that marks the cultural and artistic history of Islam.[1]

As the twentieth century draws to a close and the most powerful and violent concoct new fears to justify their brutality, it makes sense to remember the long, varied and exceptionally multicultured history of Islam.[2] One version of literary scholarship ties the work known in "the West" as *Tales from one thousand and one nights* to a geography and historical moment named "Islam". Now that so many stories are told about the monolithic and frighteningly humourless and sexless character of this thing, Islam, it is worth remembering that these fragments also belong to this tradition. The account which follows does not dispute this parentage. But it does work on a different version of family, one which acknowledges the messy links of hidden sex and out-of-town blood as well as the official family tree.

1. Haddawy (1992): xi.
2. In relation to this, David Stannard describes the content of a songbook produced by the 77th Tactical Fighter Squad of the US Airforce, during the Gulf War, in which "personifications of entire Arabic and Islamic peoples as racially inferior, maggot-infested women whose mass destruction by Americans is equated with brutal, violent sex". (Stannard (1992): 253). For now, it is enough to note the violence; we will hear more about the sexualization later.

All commentators agree that, in its written form, the *Arabian nights* remains cut through with the traces of the oral practices from which it comes. Kernels of various individual tales can be traced to the story-telling traditions of different places – some to several places. Consideration of the echoes of form and concern spread the tales' origins further still. The names of the chief characters seem to be Iranian; the frame story can be traced to India; the names within the tales are Arabic. We know that, in its written form, there were two translations from Persian into Arabic in the eighth century; that the ninth and tenth centuries saw new collections which included other stories current at the time; that in the twelfth century Egyptian tales were added; that the version we inherit, more or less, can be traced to the sixteenth century and includes earlier tales plus stories from Islamic counter-crusades and tales from further east, brought to the Middle East by the Mongols. Given this history, who is brave enough to name the origin of the tales? Better to accept this global mix-up as part of our own confusion.

In their incarnation via the West, it is inevitable that the Arabia of the tales is that of orientalist fantasy. This is unspecifically not the West – easily North Africa and Asia, and most probably beyond – and my attraction to the stories is their status as archetypally "foreign", not from anywhere in particular, but emphatically not the work and property of white men. Even in the collections of white men, the discomforts of this foreignness show through; maybe these stories are bad for you, much too distracting, enticing, from somewhere else. One editor worries about the focus on entertainment "to the total exclusion of moral and didactic teaching" (Baskett in

Galland 1995); other commentators on the progress of the tales in the West berate the *Nights* for being too feminine and feminizing, fit for women and children, but potentially weakening to the intellects of adult men (Galland 1995: xvii). Unlike the dubious discipline of literary study, these stories are too much like fun to be good for you. Mixing in with the hothouse cultivations of anthroporn and travel writing and bedding down with the poor cousins of literary culture, fairytales and folklore, the *Nights* retain their deeply marked foreignness however much translation, appropriation and misunderstanding take place around them. Perhaps it is these confused processes which confirm the epithet "foreign"? It is the many levels of inauthenticity – from being dangerously fantastic, to being from many places, to being fragmentary and multi-authored, to being different things to different people and changing shape in repetition – which make sure we know what the name means. "Entertainments", "Arabia", "nights" – every part beyond the reasonable and reasoned world of white men in modernity.

> While the history of textual scholarship in the West has been, since the Renaissance, increasingly one of keen accuracy and authenticity, its counterpart in the East, especially in the case of the *Nights*, has been one of error and corruption, at the hands of Eastern and Western scholars alike, the result of ignorance and contempt.[3]

As we shall see, the storytelling of white men has taken certain forms, with their own particular pleas-

3. Haddawy (1992): xv.

ures and prohibitions. The development of technologies of writing and reproduction, most obviously
print, has contributed to the naturalization of this
one form of narrative, the way the white men tell it.[4]
As the big theorists say, the concept of reiterability
has a special status in Western cultures: this is what
makes truth, the ability to repeat and check.[5] The
error-filled and corrupt pleasures of the *Nights*, on
the other hand, in any inauthentic version from orientalist translation to half-remembered half-embellished
bedtime story, offer another way of telling the story
and making sense of the world.

The white men who translated pretended not to
understand this alternative set of claims about the
world. To them, as we will go on to see, foreign was
scary, but it was necessary and had its own place
and logic in the worldview of the white men. They
are talking supplement, not alternative. These stories
are supposed to supply the thrill of the other and the
reassurance of the known, that special buzz we call
"exotic". The exotic cannot work unless its audience
believes that it presents something like truth, in the
terms they understand. If you can see that it is a
trick, a fantasy, just make-believe, the fun is spoilt.
Instead of seeing the tales as a strategy of narrative
collected from many times and places, the key orientalist translators of the *Nights* presented "their" work
as part of the important business of learning about
the mysterious East. However unlikely, this was supposed to be social science.[6] "Time and again, Galland,
Lane, or Burton claimed that these tales were much

---

4. See Chartier (1989).
5. See, famously, "Signature, event, context" in Derrida (1982).
6. For more on this, see Kabbani (1994): ch. 2.

more accurate than any travel account and took pains to translate them as such."[7]

Of course, this is partly about making the translation of strange and unusable stories into a respectable job for a white man. When Said writes his seminal work on the career the East became, he is describing a process in which white men learned to pass off unlikely stories as hard knowledge. Orientalism, as he explains it, gives birth to a region called the Orient, new-found supplement to the West. For the supplement to do its job, whole legions of white men must now devote their time to telling these stories with a straight face. The *Nights* get included in this collection of potentially useful fictions, because this is their best chance of respectability. This produces whole bookshelves of dubious scholarship, with fictions built on fictions, without reference to anything which may disrupt the story.

> ... amongst themselves Orientalists treat each other's work in the same citationary way. Burton, for example, would deal with the *Arabian Nights* or with Egypt indirectly, *through* Lane's work, by citing his predecessor, challenging him even though he was granting him very great authority. Nerval's own voyage to the Orient was by way of Lamartine's, and the latter's by way of Chateaubriand. In short, as a form of growing knowledge Orientalism resorted mainly to citations of predecessor scholars in the field for its nutriment. Even when new materials came his way, the Orientalist judged them by borrowing from predecessors (as scholars so

---

7. Haddawy (1992): xxi.

often do) their perspectives, ideologies and guid-
ing theses. . . . From these complex rewritings the
actualities of the modern Orient were systematically excluded, especially when gifted pilgrims
like Nerval and Flaubert preferred Lane's des-
criptions to what their eyes and minds showed
them immediately.[8]

The strange happenings of the *Nights* are passed off
as some kind of accurate depiction of what the East is
like – in the footnotes if not in the main story – and,
of course, this is part of that wider process which
concocts fictions as part of political domination. Who
would deny this? All those regions which have been
"orientalized" by wealthier and more militarized powers
have indeed come to suffer through these fictions. But
apart from all this, there is still the story.

Framing the stories as victims and props to the
orientalist conspiracy misses what I like about them,
something which bypasses issues of authenticity and
correct translation altogether. However the stories of
the *Nights* are collected and translated, the framing
conceit remains the same. A country is ravaged by
an implacable and irrational power and a young
woman demonstrates that even the most irrational
and violent of rulers can be distracted by entertainment; and in the gap of this distraction unimagined
change becomes possible. The glamour of Scheherazade is her ability to see another story hidden in the
despair of today.

She, unlike her father, was convinced that she
had exceptional power and could stop the killing.

8. Said (1978): 176–7.

She would cure the troubled king's soul simply by talking to him about things that had happened to others. She would take him to faraway lands to observe foreign ways, so he could get closer to the strangeness within himself. She would help him see his prison, his obsessive hatred of women. Scheherazade was sure that if she could bring the king to see himself, he would want to change and to love more.[9]

Storytelling

More recent storytellers have also entered into contracts with implacable powers. In a world where some people face disparagement for irrational yet inescapable reasons, once more the test has been to shift the thinking of the king. When some bodies (dark-skinned, female) mean violence and disorder (all-round bad times) somehow the story has to shift. This is a story about all those attempts to shift the focus from weak flesh to citizenship. To go from being someone's thing to being your own person.

The stories take several shapes.

First, there are the stories which explain what the bodies of dark-skinned women have meant . . .

These are the stories of a past which has lasted forever. This is the place of that inescapable constraint, history. The place where we encounter our ancestors and understand ourselves. For us, the past comes to mark the limit of the present, and we are destined to relive the old stories again and again.

Secondly, there are the stories about dark women now . . .

9.   Mernissi (1994): 15.

These are the stories which tell about the complexities of the present, which try to give us some distance on the lives we lead, some way of seeing afresh the ways we take for granted.

Thirdly, there are the stories which wish for new meanings . . .

These are the exciting stories which tell of possibility as well as constriction. In these stories, the past and present blur out of view and the future appears clean and untouched. Here, no-one knows the ending.

Each set of stories assumes the others. Although each story stands alone, the framing story reveals how they melt into each other. The storyteller demands respect because only she can hold the different stories in one narrative, chart the connection and development between them. The storyteller promises to reveal the hidden meanings of the everyday; we see strange things, she explains what is going on. This ability shows that she herself is more than we can see. Her talents cannot be comprehended by just looking. Understanding the story also means learning to appreciate the hidden talents and possibilities of the teller. To understand we must learn to listen and wait.

Storytelling is one of those all-time-everywhere cultural practices which has become associated with the backward glance of tradition and the compensatory rituals of the socially marginalized. As a source of education and entertainment, stories are a cheap option: requiring no outlay or staging equipment, no training or professional qualification, no more than the ability to make it through to the end. This is the most everyday of cultural forms, so mundane that we hardly notice the presence of most examples. But, people keep doing it. Even when they have access to the frenzied information sources of the rich world in the twentieth century, people don't give up stories. Storytelling plays some part in our lives.[10]

> Through her fairy tale, the grandma brings the past into the present as a transformative and interruptive force. This very action defines the efficacy of the fairy tale as post-mythic – something related to myth but beyond it, a narrative that extracts and liberates, disassembles and re-assembles the substance and fragments of myth in order to create passageways between time and space. . . .[11]

In another part of the world, many years after Scheherazade told her tales to her dangerous husband, another story begins.

Violence against black men

"What the learned Sharazad provides in an entertaining form is the accumulated wisdom of her civilization, which, delivered in the right manner, can correct the mislearnings of a far more limited individual experience."[12]

10. "Stories are part of ordering, for we create them to make sense of our circumstances, to re-weave the human fabric. And as we create and recreate our stories we make and remake both the facts of which they tell, and ourselves." Law (1994): 52. For some very diverse alternative views on the place of storytelling in modernity, see Benjamin (1992): "The storyteller"; Warner (1995); Williams (1991).
11. Seremetakis (1994): 219.
12. Malti-Douglas (1991): 25.

This is a story of that mystical place, the West. The land of tricksters and travellers, fantastic tales of fabulous creatures. There is plenty to astound here: monstrous cruelty, mischief and magic, genies, princesses and a host of scary bad guys. These fairytales amaze and entertain, but hidden within their distracting plots lies the true history of the West. From this the reader can gather the brutal and the beautiful which make up the occidental mind. Pretty fictions more than anything can reveal the essence of the West.

Long ago and far away, in another time and place, there was a people who lived in great fear and suffering. The scourge which afflicted them wrecked their lives, leaving them twitching and sleepless, mistrusting each other and themselves. Unable to protect themselves, the people turned against each other, forgetting their kinship and seeing only enemies.

The rifts of fear tore families apart: splitting sister from brother, parent from child, like from like. To each other, the women told of their pain.

"Our brothers are so vulnerable to violence. The king kills another of our number each day, to protect the people, he says. Instead of seeing the value of their lives, he sees vermin to be destroyed, criminals to be controlled, threats to be restrained."

"The country is awash with blood, but it seems that only we can see. Everywhere the stories are of rising crime, law and order, the loss of respect and the need to arm the police and build bigger tougher scarier prisons. How else can the country be safe in such dangerous times?"

"But we know that the police are the enemy and prisons are also killers. Crime hurts (hurts us most, still poorest, most vulnerable, most attacked), but law and order is no defence. Some take up weapons, patrol the streets, talk about policing our own communities; but no-one trusts the state. Haven't we been tasting their justice for a thousand years?"

In the land of our story plenty of families have suffered plenty of pain.

On 3 March 1991 Rodney King is stopped for a driving offence and in the course of his arrest by an estimated 21 police officers Rodney King suffers "a split inner lip, a partially paralyzed face, nine skull fractures, a broken cheek bone, a shattered eye socket, and a broken leg".[13]

Although this beating was recorded on video by a bystander, the jury in 98 per cent white Simi Valley (chosen as location of the trial so that the accused officers would not suffer unfair treatment from adverse publicity) found all accused not guilty of this assault.

On 29 September 1994 Norman Washington Manning, known as Bunson, died mysteriously in Long Lartin prison in Evesham. It seemed that Norman had been stabbed and beaten in his cell by white prisoners, after a previous attack in the chapel. The reported source of the white inmates' anger was Norman's participation in a Black History group in the prison.

Long Lartin is a high-security prison. It is not possible to enter wings unless the security doors are opened by prison officers. The corridors and landings are monitored by CCTV. However, the camera positioned only a few metres from where Norman was killed mysteriously was said to have no film in it.

Norman's killers must have been covered in blood. Somehow prison officers allowed them to return to

13.   From Baker (1993): 42.

their own wings, where they washed and changed their clothes, later boasting about what they had done.

Initially the Crown Prosecution Service insisted that they could not pursue a prosecution, because of insufficient evidence. However, after a year and a half of campaigning, public pressure forced the CPS to reopen the case. In November 1997 Frederick Lowe was found guilty of the murder of Norman Washington Manning. He was sentenced to serve another life sentence concurrently with his existing life sentences. His wealthy co-defendant, Bruce Knowles, was found not guilty. No prison officers have been charged in relation to this killing.[14]

On 16 December 1994 Shiji Lapite, 34-year-old father of two, died in mysterious circumstances after being arrested in Stoke Newington, London. At the inquest the two officers involved, PC Paul Wright and PC Andrew McCallum, denied using unreasonable force. At the inquest Wright said of Lapite, "He was immensely strong. I was in fear for my life and PC McCallum's life" (*Telegraph*, 26 January 1996: 1–2).

McCallum added, "Mr Lapite was the strongest and most violent man I have ever come across" (Ibid.).

A pathologist had counted 45 separate injuries to Lapite's body, including bruising to his neck and larynx, substantial skin loss, gravel in his eyes and face, a fractured voicebox and a small haemorrhage to his brain. The coroner, Stephen Chan, questioned Wright: "You had just a graze to your elbow. There appears to be a great disparity of injuries to say the least between you and the deceased. Do you have any explanation for that?"

14. Information from Norman Washington Manning Memorial Campaign.

Wright made no reply. As the *Caribbean Times* suggested, "They thought it would be enough to conjure up a figure straight from colonial fantasy – a giant, super-human black man, high on drugs and totally unrestrained." (*Caribbean Times*, 3 February 1996: 1)

On 25 January 1996 the inquest jury returned a unanimous verdict of unlawful killing. The officers involved are still working. No-one has been prosecuted for Shiji's killing.[15]

On 19 September 1994 Shkander Singh died mysteriously in a police cell in Glasgow. The 37-year-old father of three was arrested after a disturbance in an arts centre. He died from heart failure after he had been heard shouting, crying and banging in his cell. His turban was found floating in the toilet and his hair was wet. There was bruising on his arms, wrists and hands. Despite Shkander's distress, police officers had judged him to be feigning illness. The Sheriff supervising the inquiry recommended that Strathclyde police tighten up their procedures and that guards should send for medical assistance in every case of apparent illness. The family still do not know how Shkander died.[16]

In May 1995 Brian Douglas died after being arrested in Clapham, south London. Douglas was stopped because of the way his car was being driven. The officers involved, PC Mark Tuffey and PC Paul Harrison, claimed that Brian was armed with CS gas and a knife and that they acted in self-defence. Civilian witnesses denied seeing the CS gas canister. Tuffey

15. Information from Newham Monitoring Project and Campaign Against Racism and Fascism.
16. Information from Institute of Race Relations.

and Harrison could not explain the seven fractures on Douglas's skull which pathologists reported. Witnesses claimed that Douglas had been hit at least twice over the head with the new US-style longer baton which had been issued to PC Tuffey a few months earlier.

Brian Douglas died in hospital five days after his arrest. After his arrest on 3 May he was taken to Kennington police station in south London. There he was examined four times by a police surgeon, who said Brian was suffering from excess alcohol or drugs. Fifteen hours after his arrest he was finally taken to hospital, where he was found to have no general co-ordination, a half-paralyzed face and slurred speech. He died from haemorrhages and a fractured skull.

The inquest into Brian Douglas's death recorded a verdict of death by misadventure. The officers involved continue to work. No-one has been prosecuted for Brian's killing.[17]

On 8 December 1995 Alton Manning, a young man from Birmingham, died mysteriously in Blakenhurst prison, Redditch. Blakenhurst is a Group 4 prison, one of the new type of privately run prisons which is not directly under Home Office jurisdiction. For four years before his death, Alton had complained of harassment by police and prison authorities, changing solicitors many times in his attempts to get justice. On the day of his death Alton had spoken to his mother on the telephone, telling her that he had sent back a money order to her, because she "had more need of it than me". Later that night he was dead.

Friends and family say that Alton expected to die. Witness reports suggest that up to seven prison officers

17. Additional information from Inquest.

were involved in the restraint procedure which led to Alton's death. His sister managed to take photographs of his body, which show extensive injuries, particularly to his head. However, prison authorities maintained that Alton did not die as a result of violence; instead they suggested that he choked on his food or had heart failure. The family suspected otherwise, and a public campaign demanded that the truth be made known.

In September 1996 the CPS leaked its decision not to prosecute to a journalist – before informing the family. Apparently, the testimony of inmates had less credibility than that of prison officers, and on this basis there was insufficient evidence to pursue the case. The prison officers involved continue to work.[18]

In December 1995 Wayne Douglas was found dead in his cell at Brixton police station in south London less than one hour after his arrest. Witnesses reported that 15 police officers, including WPCs, were involved in the beating Douglas received before his arrest. Local residents reported that the police dragged Douglas away from the road and into a children's playground; one woman recalled what she saw:

> They layed [sic] into that young man like a hungry pack of animals. They were using the most disgusting racist language. They called him every abusive name you can think of. The worst one had a Scottish accent. There was another witness who they chased away. They were trying to baton him as well. (*Caribbean Times*, 16 December 1995: 3)

18. Information from Justice for Alton Manning Campaign.

In August 1996 the CPS decided against instigating criminal proceedings.

On 21 February 1996 21-year-old Amer Rafiq was arrested in Rusholme, Manchester, during Eid celebrations. His family later found him in hospital – his left eye had to be removed as a result of damage.

In recent years police have targeted Eid celebrations in Rusholme, using dogs, horses and riot squads to disperse crowds. The report of the Police Complaints Authority (PCA) showed that the socket of Amer's eye was shattered inside the police van by a "wham ram", an item used to break down doors. The police van apparently took 30 minutes to take Amer from Wilmslow Road to Platt Lane police station, only 5 minutes away. No account has been given of what occurred in the extra 25 minutes.

In August 1996 a PCA document was leaked to the press which recommended that no officer should be prosecuted for the assault on Amer. The family waited a month to be informed officially of this decision.[19]

On 16 March 1996 Ibrahima Sey died while being arrested in Forest Gate, east London. Between 4 and 5 am Ibrahima was arrested at his home in Manor Park and taken to Ilford police station. He went calmly after giving his two children into the care of family friends. His friend Paa was allowed to accompany him to the station.

At the station Ibrahima was dragged into the back yard of the station and Paa was told to leave. Ibrahima was pushed to the ground and police officers knelt on top of him, handcuffed his hands behind his back and applied a neckhold. Ibrahima recited verses from the Koran. Paa heard Ibrahima shout,

19. Additional information from Amer Rafiq Defence Campaign.

"See what they are doing to me" several times, but was prevented from intervening. Instead he was taken to an interview room to wait. Five hours later, Paa was informed that his friend was dead.

Ibrahima Sey was 29 years old and the father of two small children, a five-week-old baby and a daughter of five. He was a former member of the Gambian football team. Despite this, the police post mortem found that Ibrahima died of "hypertensive heart disease following a period of exertion". Ibrahima's family protested that he had no history of heart disease.

Police admit that CS gas was used on Ibrahima, but will not say at what point in his arrest. However, Paa was present until Ibrahima was handcuffed. CS gas must therefore have been used after this, when Ibrahima was already restrained.

CS gas had been in use only since 1 March 1996 for everyday police work. Training trials were interrupted in June 1995 when a police officer suffered 50 per cent burns to his eyes. He and two other police trainers are now suing Northamptonshire police for damages for injuries incurred while demonstrating CS spray. This has not stopped the adoption of the spray in 20 police areas across Britain, by over 2,000 officers.

On 28 August 1996 Michael Howard, the Home Secretary, approved the use of CS gas by police forces nationwide. Two forces, Hertfordshire and Surrey, have withdrawn the spray after trials because of concern about safety. The officers involved in Ibrahima's death continue to work.[20]

20.   Information from Ibrahima Sey Memorial Campaign, Newham Monitoring Project and Campaign Against Racism and Fascism.

In August 1996 another young man died while in the custody of east London police. Ahmed El Gammal, a 33-year-old Egyptian PhD student and part-time lecturer, was arrested and taken to Leyton police station. A forensic medical examiner declared Ahmed fit for detention, but five hours later he was dead. The post mortem found that he had died of acute coronary thrombosis.

At first police claimed that Ahmed had been found breaking and entering into the home of a vicar. Later they withdrew this allegation. The officers involved in Ahmed's death continue to work.[21]

Cases of deaths in custody, police shootings in disputed circumstances, and police ill-treatment continued to be reported. Victims included Frank Arzuega, an unarmed 15-year-old Puerto Rican, who was shot dead in January by an officer from the New York City Police Department (nypd) while sitting in the back seat of a suspected stolen car; Hong Il Kim, a Korean man who died in February after being shot several times by four California police officers at the end of a car chase; and Aswan Watson, an unarmed black man who died after being shot 18 times by nypd officers while sitting in a parked car in June. In April, a police video showed two sheriff's deputies from Riverside County Sheriff's Department, California, beating Mexican immigrants Leticia Gonzalez and Enrique Funez-Flores after a car chase.[22]

---

21. Information from Campaign Against Racism and Fascism.
22. Extract from Amnesty International Report 1997.

In August 1997, Abner Louima, a Haitian man, was arrested outside a New York nightclub. While in police custody Louima was attacked by as many as five white officers. During this assault Louima was sodomized with a toilet plunger which was then forced into his mouth, breaking two of his teeth. Louima later required hospital treatment for a punctured bladder and intestines. After the attack, Louima was denied medical treatment for 90 minutes, because officers were waiting for a new shift to begin rather than pay overtime to a departing officer. Officer Justin Volpe and Officer Charles Schwartz were arrested and charged with first-degree assault. However, key evidence such as the plunger have disappeared and, as always, witness testimony from other police officers is sparse.[23]

Of course, there had always been plenty of violence. But now things seemed worse, death after death, overwhelming evidence of brutality and still no accountability. There was only the sketchiest attempt to cover up. Somehow it didn't matter that people knew, because the killers seemed immune from prosecution. Killing black people was justifiable in these circumstances.

We had feared the police forever – hadn't we been losing our loved ones to them for generations?[24] But our neighbours could not understand. They heard about the increases in crime, the prevalence of violence, the threats to police officers, and they agreed that the answer was to kick back hard. Only tough

---

23. Information from "Brutal 'Laws of Flatbush' wreck New York mayor's war on crime", Edward Helmore, in *The Observer*, 17 August 1997.
24. See Anderson & Killingray (1991); Anderson & Killingray (1992); Cashmore & McLaughlin (1991).

policing could make society safe again; and if there were casualties, well, then that was the risk criminals took. However much we protested, they were adamant that the police would not attack without good reason. To them, we were never innocent; and that tinge of guilt justified the most brutal of punishments.

The king played on this climate of fear, promising to protect those who already believed that we were the source of danger. The police grew strong, armed, above the law; and people applauded. When another of our number died, we heard only of their criminal record, alleged violence, inhuman nature – and then nothing. They were not even trying to make examples out of us. The remains of the dead were not displayed at the city walls. After the first flurry of embarrassed excuses, each killing disappeared from view, already accepted as a necessary cost of fighting crime.

The king didn't need to share his thirst for blood. Crazed with the madness of the inbred, he saw only dangerous dark flesh. Excessive and inhuman bodies. To himself, the king promised to wipe these people out; their women are good for sex, but they can't raise families. Let the women live, for the pleasure of the court, but kill their men to ensure their obedience. At night the king dreams of being smothered by sweet dark flesh, endless bodies piled up around him. He wakes with half-remembered images, twisted in sweat-damp sheets.

Under the orders of the king the deaths went on.

People stopped crying. Instead they devoted their energies to weaving spells and muttering curses; kicking back where they could against the evil devouring their numbers. There were public protests and secret societies, relearnings of old magic, and plans to escape to a new place or an ancestral home. No-one could tell where it would end. Until our heroine arrives.

One day the daughter of the king's bodyguard and accountant decided that enough was enough. Like her predecessor she was learned and beautiful, accomplished in all things. She asked her father, "Grant me an audience with the king. It will do us all good."

Of course, her father was scared: "This is not a man of reason, daughter. Your clever arguments will not save our people, nor will your girlish charms protect you from his irrational violence. As a father I cannot allow you to run towards your own death."

"Trust me, father. I know what I am doing. Of course, I cannot reason with this man. He will never see me as his equal, so there can be no appeal to reason. I plan to use what we have learned to do best – distract. Even if he never learns the error of his behaviour, I hope that I will make him forget to continue his bloodthirsty plan."

The father knew his daughter. Once an idea was in her head, nothing could shake it out again. With a heavy heart, he conveyed his daughter's request to the king. The king was amused. "Yes", he said, "Bring her to me. Let me see this flower of your community. I have often wondered what potentials lie unrealized among your people." The king chuckled with the anticipation of this educational spectacle.

Back at home the father relayed this troubling acceptance to his daughter. "He means to hurt you, daughter. I have seen his ways. I know his thoughtless habits."

"Fear not, father. Perhaps he doesn't know what he means. It is time to make the story our own."

The girl collected her prettiest clothes and went to the palace with her father. At court her face shone brightly, still bright with hope. Even the jaded courtiers silently wished her well, praying that she would escape the violent end which she seemed to embrace. Surprised at himself, the king was taken with her looks. "Come closer, girl, I hear you have a request for me."

The girl kept her head and remained composed: "On the contrary, your highness, I have come with a gift. For many years I have practised my storytelling – now at last I have learned the story of our times. I have come to share this with you, ruler of our age."

The king was certain of his power. No-one challenged him. He met no resistance. The girl's audacity amused him, and he could afford to be amused. "And what price do you demand for this great service?"

"No price, your highness. I only ask that you spare our sons and brothers until you have heard my tale."

Of course, the king agreed.

Settling down, the girl began her tale.

This is a story about the power of stories. It is also a warning that those who live by the tale will, in time, fall prey to their own narrative. If you spend your energy creating monsters, don't be surprised when they eat you up. It is a story about storytellers, about how people who tell tales about others are really talking about themselves. Most of all it is about how all good stories end with everyone getting their comeuppance.

But this is all to come. First, let us go back to thinking about why we love to tell stories.

The politics of representation

For many years we have been the people of stories and pictures. The meanings of the world have been told in tales which we people. The stories of power are narrated by others, but in the realm of entertainment and spectacle we are the most seen.

In more recent times, stories have come out of our mouths: sometimes the ventriloquized tales of white men, sometimes stories of our own invention, from our pasts and futures.

In different places people ascribed different meanings to these stories. The voice they heard was different; the picture they saw or imagined was not the same.

In the lands of the New World, many people began to speak, loudly, excitedly, all their stories charging up against each other. The most demanding nation on earth? In the crevices of this babble, the first people of these places tried to edge in their version before it was too late. The people brought there against their will gathered to relate their particular stories. The people who found themselves there through accidents of history at last began to tell their own tales.

In the decaying land of the old world, it was no longer possible to tell one story of the nation.[25] Of course, some people tried, pretending to be bigger than they were, not afraid to use violence in their attempts to make their stories real. But even the old world was changing, in ways that no amount of kicking and killing could hide completely. Before, the narrative of how the world was could be told by rich white men; their richness and whiteness made them great, and so their actions became history. The rest of the world suspected that this was not all that was going on; after all, where were their lives in all this?

25. See Back & Nayak (1993).

But the stories of great men were so loud and so widespread that it was hard to hear anything else: the books were full of them, in classrooms children learned to chant their achievements, the statues in the street reminded passers-by that this was the only story in town. But things change. The rest of the world whispered to their children that there were other stories, not only the ones they learned in school.

As time went by the children of the rest of the world grew up to tell the stories of their whispered bedtimes out loud. The stories of great men went on; they owned the forces of amplification after all. But they were not the only stories anymore. Now all sorts of others had tales to tell. People who worked because they had to, the previously silent wives and daughters and sisters of the great men and the women who did their work for them, even the people who had had their land and freedom stolen, those whom the great men said were less than human – all of these people started to tell their stories.

Now everyone understood how important the stories were. Yes, some people had money and power, the machines and the weapons to get their own way, but the stories also mattered. The stories we heard and believed changed what happened in the world.

Negative stereotypes

The rest of the world learned this by listening to the stories of great men. Their children came home from school crying and kicking, hating their parents for their powerlessness. In the loudly trumpeted tales of great men's achievement, the rest of the world listened carefully for any recognition of their existence.

They did not yet hope for acknowledgement of their contribution, just some confirmation that they were in the story, that they were part of what happened. And when they looked and listened they found that they were indeed in the stories, but what they saw and heard made them as bitter as their children. Here were tales of misshapen savages and child-like natives, grateful workers and weak and wanton women. In the tales of the great men, the rest of the world looked like a source of entertainment and pity. Not invisible, exactly, but nothing to be proud of.[26]

The secret was that, along with their self-congratulation, the great men liked to talk about the rest of the world. The great men's stories were full of characters nothing like themselves; the rest of the world was more talked about than the great men themselves. But none of these stories had anything good to say. Just a thousand-and-one volumes of close-packed abuse.

After centuries of being badmouthed by rulers, masters, employers, the rest of the world decided to change the story completely. What was needed was a set of stories which would stop their children's tears and raise their own spirits. Taking the stories of great men as their cue, the rest of the world set about changing all the endings.

If the stories you believe define your range of possibility, then you have to change the story to be something else. In the stories of great men work had no value and so people who worked were less than those who employed or had no need of a wage. In

26. Plenty has been said about this sad recognition and its consequences. A few examples include Sennett & Cobb (1993); Pieterse (1992); Rowbotham (1973).

the old stories being poor was a punishment for working and the wealth of those who did not need to work was a reward for their special talents and extra cleverness. The confinement and subjugation of women was determined by nature; and was therefore unquestionable and unavoidable. The formerly colonized and enslaved had limited capacities and, although this was sad, it was also the way of the world. These repeated stories crossed over and reinforced each other, until the lives of the rest of the world seemed to be tied down to almost nothing at all. The great men rode plots of achievement and adventure, while the rest of the world were stuck tight in their destinies of disrespect. Telling the story the great men's way meant erasing the work and contribution of the rest of the world. Of course, when you rubbed out all the people underneath, it looked as if the great men could fly.

This story had many effects: bringing good luck to the great men and bad to the rest. And as long as everyone believed in it, life perpetuated the story. Of course, the great men had other things on their side; they had wealth and controlled the livelihoods of those without, they had strength and used it on those less strong, they controlled the army and police force and the whole suspect machinery of the state, and those who didn't were cowed into obedience. But somehow, despite all this, the great men relied on their stories to make things go smoothly.[27]

27. In the hoo-ha over the importance of stories, much was made of this phenomenon named hegemony. After Gramsci, many suggested that our rulers did not rule by force alone. Instead they used the machinery of culture to gain popular acquiescence, while maintaining the machinery of violence as back up. See Gramsci (1971).

As long as the great men believed their own stories, they felt justified in using violence to maintain their privilege; after all, this was the right and natural order. As long as the rest of the world believed at least some of the great men's stories, they remained feeling sad and powerless, unable to imagine routes out of social structures which accorded them no value. Worse still, they could make no connection between themselves and others; their belief colluded in the wiping-out of others' achievements and they saw potential allies through the devaluing eyes of great men. All the wonderful things which could be done never ever got done.

Or was that part of the story?

Either way, times were bad, indeed.

But, of course, no story is absolute. There had always been some dissent. Other people had told their own stories in whispered voices and cursed the great men for their lies and violence. People had tried to live through other kinds of stories, taking risks, battling against odds. Even the great men's massive machinery of privilege could not silence everyone everywhere all the time.

Positive images

At certain moments the great men grew too complacent, they forgot that they could not really fly, they believed their own propaganda too completely. In these moments, new possibilities arose. The whispered voices of dissent carried a little further, the rest of the world started to doubt a little more. After a while, no matter how loudly the great men shouted, everyone realized that there were other stories to tell and hear. And it was in these moments that the rest of the world chose to change all the endings.

Workers talked about the pain and necessity of their work, about the double-bind of their value. They talked about making wealth for great men who bled them dry, building great nations which denied them citizenship or self-respect or comfort in their old age.

Women talked about the capacities they were not allowed to develop, the hidden services they provided for great men, the skills they had which were used but not valued.

The formerly colonized and enslaved reversed the story to question the claim to humanity of their barbarous rulers. They excavated histories which did not exist in the stories of great men, revealing worlds which had been destroyed and violence which had been forgotten.

All of the newly remembered stories showed that these sufferings did not belong to the sufferer alone. The flight of the great men depended on the hidden supplement of work, of home, of elsewhere; the height the great men gained was built on the backs of these other disregarded people. Each step erased its conditions of possibility. That was the secret magic of the great men's stories. In all the adventurous grandeur of high leaps and big buildings, long treks and deep thoughts, no gaps were left to ask how the great men got there. Who worked the machines of their fabulous technologies? Who bore and raised the offspring of their talented dynasties? Who rowed them to the brink of their gobsmacking discoveries? The terms of the great men's stories did not allow these questions. But the stories of the rest of the world did.

Of course, the stories did not change on their own. Battles were won against the great men and hand-in-hand with this the stories shifted. The fighting of battles partly depended on other stories becoming believable, but also, as they were won, the possible narratives of the world expanded. As the rest of the world grew into their own political battles and ways of doing things, more and more people could spend time thinking up new stories. Whole new ways of life emerged as it became possible to study about ourselves, even make a living discussing the hidden stories of our people. The hard work of political change freed others to think in different ways.

In the new stories, the rest of the world regained their history. Instead of being born into a victimage determined by nature, they rediscovered themselves as the offspring of rich heritages which had been stolen from them. Those who worked learned that workers had always resisted brutalization and fought for their right to humanity. It was only the ruthless actions of the great men through the ages which erased these stories of struggle. Once they were remembered the stories about waged poverty as destiny made no sense. People forgot how they ever believed such a story.

Instead they believed new stories; in these workers were resilient against terrible odds, their lives stealing back a myriad of values denied by their employers. Against the theft and dishonesty of the already wealthy, the lives of those who worked became admirable, the epitome of human achievement in difficult circumstances. Of course, no-one wanted to be poor, but still the cultures of working life took on a certain glamour. Because of the new stories the names associated with work stopped being sources of shame and sometimes even became desirable.[28]

28.   On a version of working-class envy see Hebdige (1979).

The stories about women changed even more dramatically. Again, old histories were rediscovered: people with the name "woman" who had lived unrecognizable lives, people who had changed or chosen or adapted their gender names, women who had battled against confinement and propriety. Sometimes these figures had appeared in the stories of great men, but only as dangerous monsters. In the old stories they appeared as signs of women's inherent weakness; their agency was erased. The new stories showed that the name "woman" could mean all manner of things.

Most importantly for our story, those who had been enslaved and colonized learned a whole new set of stories about themselves. Like the others, they learned that subjugation was not their destiny, just a temporary disempowerment brought about by their enemies. Contrary to what was said by great men, they were not perpetual children, devious shirkers, cannibalistic savages; just people whose freedom had been stolen by strangers. They, too, had their hidden histories of resistance: everyday rituals of survival and downright refusals to give up, buckle down, live a less-than-human life. The new stories let their children remember the lost civilizations of their ancestors. Instead of being confined to an endless misery of less-than-whiteness, those who had been enslaved and colonized now understood the unimaginable evil of their persecutors. Out of this understanding came chapter after chapter of new possibility; explorations of all the pleasurable talents which the great men had denied existed.[29]

29. For an account of one aspect of this change see Wilson (1994).

The new stories made people feel better. The great men didn't look so great any more. The rest of the world could look them in the eye and laugh about their former delusions. But new stories didn't change everything.

Postmodern knowingness

The point about telling new stories or even believing old ones is that you believe that the important things can be told. You think that the ways of the world can be made appreciable to frail old humanity. Before, we all learned the stories of great men as truth; this was the way the world was, and we were just born unlucky, in the wrong body in the wrong place at the time. This kind of widespread belief, among both us and them, affected how we all lived and dreamed. The stories which we thought were truth delimited our imagined possibilities.

This is the argument which says that some stories are downright dangerous. They hurt our sense of self when we hear them and remember them, and opportunities to revamp and rebuild ourselves are damaged by the wide circulation of these stories. We can call this moment of thinking the debate about negative stereotypes, or the dangers of Eurocentrism, or the hegemony of privileged peoples; but whatever the angle, each critique calls for a change in the narrative.

The answer becomes chapter two. Changing the narrative is about reinventing possibility. Things have been bad and we all need a pep-talk; so the new stories look on the bright side and stress achievement, beauty, potential. Once they are told, we all work hard at believing them, against our learned-long-ago habits. The idea is that we will believe in this depiction of ourselves as rare and multi-talented creatures, and that this belief will help to increase the range and scope of our talents. Emulating the great men, we try to learn how to talk ourselves up and impose our stories on the world.[30]

The move from chapter one to chapter two happens differently in different times for different groups of people; but it is always a version of that heady mixture of a change in consciousness plus a change in material conditions. I don't mean that people get more cash and then feel better about themselves (although this could be one version of the story). What I am talking about is that through some mysterious mechanism of mutual determination the shape of the world and the shape of the stories allow each other to shift, each determining the possibility of change in the other. How this happens and what it might mean is a subject filling many shelves of books.[31] For now it is enough to remember that there has been a struggle to get to chapter two.

Chapter two of the story – the new story which gives us back our self-esteem – normally leaves out the shift in material conditions part of what is happening. After all, the new story is about making everything possible; reliance on material shifts, however hazy and mutual, feels like a limitation. We could call this kind of chapter two the move to positive images, or, if we were being flash, the challenge to hegemony. This new story starts to be told because of rumbling changes in the world, and the idea is

30. For a range of discussion on this tactic, see Ten.8 (1992).
31. For an accessible account of some of these debates, see Eagleton (1991).

that if you can just keep the story rolling the other changes will rumble on as well. It is a gladdeningly, maddeningly optimistic story which says that if we just believe enough everything will come to us.

This kind of chapter two does not disregard other types of political work or ways of making change, it just says that we can start with the stories. Changing the stories is meant to make the other stuff possible, because organization and agency and power are all about consciousness, how you think about yourself and other people and the relation between you. So if we can just shift what we believe, everything else will start to fall into place. This is obviously good news for teachers and artists, because now that kind of airy-fairy work has social value; it's not leisure activities for great men, it's at the forefront of the struggle for justice. But it's also good news for polit-icos, because now we don't have to wait around for the time to be right. Instead, we make the time right by doing all this story work, reminding people how to believe in themselves. The move into chapter two is some exciting time, I can tell you.[32]

Sadly, that bubble of excessive hope bursts almost immediately. Lots of things changed with the new stories and our children certainly grew up feeling better about themselves, but the longed-for rumble of greater and ongoing changes never transpired. Instead, life went on being a struggle. We went on ducking and diving, better equipped than before, but still under attack. People started to wonder if their faith in stories had been misplaced. Maybe other kinds of work should have happened first?

32. A famous example of this time of debate and excitement is Hall & Jacques (1989).

The return of the rest of the world

Into this arena stepped another even newer/even older set of stories. This time the breadth of the story seemed wider, so that we saw more but also felt much smaller. Most of us were less in thrall to the great men down our streets than before. Yes, they terrorized us, but they could never regain their lost giant status. As they grew smaller, we suddenly found that we could see around them. The rest of the world was coming into view and we began again to see that all our lives were in thrall to powers far larger than ourselves. After we had exposed the claptrap powers of our Wizard of Oz rulers, we realized that the real power lay elsewhere.

In the new world of diminished great men, but continuing evils, this trip-net of power became known as globalization. No-one was sure whether this was an old or a new phenomenon, or a good or a bad thing.[33]

But everyone could tell that it made our enemies harder to place. We had learned to see through the fictions of the great men of our immediate acquaintance; what we had not learned to see was where the new powers lay.

In lots of ways, it was those who worked for a living who had been talking about this for longest. Way back when, it is the "workers of the *world*" who are called upon to unite. Capital develops as a global business, so those who get their name from being waged have been connected with the rest of the world for a long time. The labour movement of

33. See Hall (1991) for an account of old and new, bad and good, aspects of globalization.

another time recognized this, and called for international solidarity in the pursuit of their demands; if capital is globalized, resistance must be too.

At best, this led to labour movement support for anti-colonial struggle and a refusal to view the great men as allies against dangerous black people abroad.[34] In its best traditions, the white working class has organized with a global perspective. Sadly, in its worst it has become transfixed again by the spectacle of its own great men and fallen for the fiction of national interest.[35]

Of course, for us, dark-skinned rest of the world who already lived dispersed and internationalized lives, global also felt familiar. Yes, we had our particular national and location-specific struggles; but who ever thought that these things happened to us alone? Understanding our own position always required us to recognize our kin in other places.[36]

So, sadly, it was the white girls who learned global thinking most belatedly. In the most recent and powerful version of chapter two, the daughters of great men have thought about the name "woman". When the women of the great men's lands rallied together against their body-defined fate, too often they assumed that the name "woman" had universal

34. See Saville (1988) on some aspects of labour movement internationalism.
35. For an account of trade union racism see Miles & Phizacklea (1981).
36. Gayatri Chakravorty Spivak tells about seeing on TV an African-American woman who remembers being one of the first black children to attend struggling-to-stay white schools in the Ocean Hill–Brownsville School District in 1968. She says, "We became Third World. We became international." Spivak in Pieterse & Parekh (1995): 188.

application. Women were everywhere and everywhere downtrodden; so surely their concerns were those of all women.

The power of this universal claim certainly added strength to the white girls' claims. The broad sweep got plenty of other white girls on side; who wouldn't want to become part of a global movement? And for some people, good things happened. But the others who were different kinds of women were rarely these people, and soon the fighting started.[37]

After an eternity of fighting and splitting and re-deployment and retreat, people started to agree that "woman" was not a unified name and that it covered a range of needs and experiences. Being one kind of woman didn't mean that you were automatically connected to all other kinds. Sometimes women from different places did not understand or recognize each other, let alone want the same things.

> This is not the tired nationalist claim that only the native can know the scene. The point that I am trying to make is that, in order to learn enough about Third World women and to develop a different readership, the immense heterogeneity of the field must be appreciated, and the First World feminist must learn to stop feeling privileged *as a woman*.[38]

That statement, and others like it from other people, stops the party. Of course, some people still savour the anachronistic pleasures of being tourists and

37. A favourite example of this recognition of difference among women is Moraga & Anzaldua (1981).
38. "French feminism in an international frame", in Spivak (1987): 136.

missionaries. But the sensible people realized that one story would not do for everyone. Chapter two rested on the assumption that people would recognize their own names in the new story and see that this story was about them. Changing the world involved changing your beliefs about yourself and changing belief meant reconstructing knowledge, thinking differently about who you were.

The new stories of chapter two took the disparaged names worn by the rest of the world and collected sagas of achievement for each name. Listening to this could make you feel better only if you connected one of these names of new-found achievement with yourself. So those who worked for a living uncovered lost histories of labour and saw themselves in these centuries of struggle. Those named "woman" uncovered the violences visited upon that name and the resistances that heralded – and each tale of survival joined the canon of what had been done by women in the name of women, so that all those named "woman" could take heart and ownership of these deeds. However diverse the stories of women, all contributed to this resource. Although those who had been enslaved and colonized used a variety of names for themselves, not always recognizing each other as part of their own story, there were still similar collections assembled.

And somehow, in all this effort to remember ourselves, we forgot everything else. Our perspectives pared down to our immediate experience; this was the authentic thing which must be told. In the process, the good globalizing habits of other times were lost, just as our enemies became more intangibly global. Before we knew it, we were telling tales which sounded uncannily like the great men.

It was time for some hard questions.

"What does it mean when the tools of a racist patriarchy are used to examine the fruits of that same patriarchy? It means that only the narrowest perimeters of change are possible and allowable."[39]

Somehow, even in the brand new stories, the bad old stories kept cropping up. Of course, the new stories were inevitably a response to the old ones. However often new beginnings were promised, the recognition that something new was needed came from the sad times before. Even in the new story, the choices always harked back to these things which had happened before. Nothing could start just now, born new without the baggage of history.

People realized this, but some still warned against the temptations of obedience. Too many continued to long for love from the great men. Now that they had their own stories they felt sure that the great men would recognize their value and close kinship; the years apart would be overcome in an instant and everyone would see that great was the lost family name. If we overcame negative stereotypes, it was so that the great men would stop thinking ill of us. If we developed positive images, it was so the great men would be convinced of our worth. However much we talked of self-love, it was hard to stop looking to the great men for approval, or judging ourselves through their imagined eyes. The warnings were against these hidden addictions to the old order, to people who could not or would not make the leap into belief in the new story.

"*For the master's tools will never dismantle the master's house.* They may allow us temporarily to

39.   Lorde (1984): 110–11.

beat him at his own game, but they will never enable us to bring about genuine change. And this fact is only threatening to those women who still define the master's house as their only source of support."[40]

Two things happened: the narrative constraints of answering the accusations of great men began to feel hopelessly limiting, the kind of game you could never win; and people started to learn that some things could not be told in stories.

Apart from pictures

After a while, people realized that words and pictures would never be good or bad, but always mixed and various. The belief that the world could be fixed in place by the right story belonged to the dull old days of the great men. The great men had relied on particular ways of seeing and telling to secure their place in the world. Now, as they tried to shake off the bad smell of the great men's ways, the rest of the world found themselves with only the great men as models.

All of the new stories had assumed that the tools of the great men were the right tools in the wrong hands; change hands and their powers would become forces for good, not evil.

If the ways of the great men had their problems, the question became one of how the world could change. No-one wanted to give up on changing consciousness, because belief still seemed the most malleable aspect of agency. The structures shaping our lives felt immovable, but the way we thought about

40. Ibid.: 112.

them seemed more negotiable. But somehow that investment in shifting belief as a way of shifting society always led back to debates about representation. The word-and-picture strategies of great men still defined the arena of activity. However cleverly everyone argued about the drawbacks, the slip-ups, the loopholes, representation remained the only game in town. How could we imagine thinking or doing without it?

"How do we organise our perceptions of the world? Recent discussion of this age-old question have centered around the function of visual conventions as the primary means by which we perceive and transmit our understanding of the world around us."[41]

Perhaps this bind of representation was our destiny, a legacy from a past which we could no longer remember? As long as representation was double – both a picturing and a standing-in for – our enfranchizement rested on our ability to manipulate its terms.

There is a fundamental reason for thinking about popular politics in terms of pictures. Ever since classical city states began the traditions that still underlie contemporary political organization, an integral component of political practice has been the faculty of sight. This has been exploited in different ways over the years, so there's a history of looking in which the *visualization* of the public, the public domain, and of political practice, has developed and changed. Visualization is the means by which direct .or "primitive"

41. Gilman (1986): 223.

democracy can be enlarged and complicated to become representative democracy; it's the foundation of contemporary political process, and is therefore among the most important tasks that popular media have undertaken, a task made more rather than less crucial by the fact that representative and direct democracy are not the same thing, and that things have changed since the disappearance of a physical space in which the public could congregate, gaze upon, and so govern, its collective self.[42]

Hidden in all the talk about new stories was the underlying but resilient belief that if you could develop a more open system of representation as picturing, you would, through this, initiate more open systems of representation in political process. Of course, this meant that the new stories emulated the ways of the great men, because who was more politically enfranchized than them? Even when we had learned the limits of this approach, we were caught between unlikely alternatives.

There seemed to be no way out of the dilemma: tell tales or keep silent, both ways you lost. Knowledge remained mysterious, life remained frightening. Narrative held little relation to truth, but also could not be easily distinguished from it. We agreed to keep going, because stopping seemed no better. All sorts of stories went on being told.

It is more than ever crucial for different peoples to form complex concrete images of one another, as well as of the relationships of knowledge

42. Hartley (1992): 5.

and power that connect them. But no sovereign scientific method or ethical stance can guarantee the truth of such images. They are constituted – the critique of colonial modes of representation has shown at least this much – in specific historical relations of dominance and dialogue.[43]

So all our attempts at being good and knowing more ended up producing more stories; all as full of fantasy as the dangerous narratives we criticized. Time to pay more attention to the tales.

"Our understanding of the problems of 'real' women cannot lie outside the 'imagined' constructs in and through which 'women' emerge as subjects. Negotiating with these mediations and simulacra we seek to arrive at an understanding of the issues at stake."[44]

To understand these dilemmas fully, you must hear the tale of the four dark women. Only then will you see the troubled range of our lives.

The tale of the four dark women

Once a king in a great land assembled his courtiers and asked this question. "My people look different to me – these days when I visit the residential quarter of the city, I see fresh kinds of people in the street. Who are these people and what do their lives mean?"

The king often raised these questions. He knew little of the people he governed and he relied heavily

43. Clifford (1995): 259.
44. Rajan (1993): 10.

on his court to keep him informed. The court saw their role more honestly, and fed the king tales to keep him amused and distracted. This time, however, the question was more direct. The king himself had noticed some difference among his people; and now he demanded an outside opinion. "Call on the people to answer this question – I want to hear their answers for myself."

And because the king was all-powerful, everyone obeyed, and the doors of the court were thrown open to the public.

After days of annoyance and boredom, at last four women arrived with a tale to entertain the fretful king. The king was pleased: "Yes, yes, these people will know what I want – they are the colours of my new subjects"; and the court noticed that, despite their varied features, bodies, costumes, all these women wore some shade of brown skin, some tone between bitter chocolate and sweet honey.

"We embody fresh options for our communities. Daughters of our time, our paths are not those of our mothers. Their histories haunt us, but still, we live differently. Each of us is an incarnation of the new people you have encountered in your kingdom – differently coloured, differently shaped, unfamiliar creatures reshaping familiar roles. This is who we are."

The first woman stepped forward, and the court sighed with desire. This one was a beauty, by anyone's standards. Big-eyed, long-legged, no weight at all. "I am a model", she began, "unlike my foremothers, I am considered a beauty. I make my living as an ideal of femininity – but my story will make you question the value of beauty."

The next woman stepped forward, and this time the court gasped at her immense strength. Beside the flabby effects of easy court living, the woman's body glowed with the potential of the human form. Around the room, courtiers sucked in their bellies and re-arranged their clothes. "I am an athlete", she began. "Although my foremothers were renowned for their physical prowess and resilience, they received few rewards for their capacities. Unlike them, I am acclaimed for my feats of strength and endurance. I make my living as an example of what the human body can achieve – but my story will make you question the value of human flesh."

Unlike her predecessors, the third woman appeared quite ordinary: sure of herself, but not one to turn heads. It was only when she began to speak that the sound of her voice prickled the court into attention. "I am a newsreader", she said. "My foremothers collected plenty of wisdom, but their voices were seldom heard. Unlike them, I am entrusted to speak the truths of the contemporary world. I make my living by sharing information – but my story will make you question the value of knowledge."

By the time the fourth woman came forward, the court knew what to expect. This one was harder to categorize, it was true. When they looked at her to see her secret, she seemed to change before their eyes, becoming all manner of people all at once. They wanted to look, but no-one was sure what it was that they saw. "I am an entertainer", she said. "My foremothers provided plenty of diversion, but their hard-learned skills commanded no respect. I, on the other hand, am a singer, a dancer, a thinker, an all-round pukka artiste. By your gasps I see you are impressed, and perhaps a little excited? But my story will make you question the value of pleasure."

And the court settled down to hear the tales to come.

So ends the first section of our tale. All players acknowledge the power of stories, but the source of this power remains mysterious. In the section to follow, we will hear some attempts to uncover the power of stories, to unwrap their magical workings. Of course, in the process, fresh tales get told and more yarns are spun.

Further reading

There are many editions of *The Arabian nights*; an accessible recent translation is by Husain Haddawy.

The most famous account of intrusive Western fantasies remains *Orientalism* by Edward Said.

For more thoughts on the various politics of representation, see "The whites of their eyes: racist ideologies and the media", by Stuart Hall in *Silver linings*, by George Bridges and Rosalind Brunt; *Policing the crisis*, by S. Hall et al.; *The decolonization of imagination*, by Jan Nederveen Pieterse and Bhikhu Parekh.

CHAPTER 2

The next few stories

The first lesson of storytelling is that nothing is straightforward – so, of course, the tale of the four dark women does not reach its conclusions quickly. Instead we embark on a long and winding tale, sometimes losing sight of the four sisters altogether.

This second section of our tale slips away from the women towards a more general tale about tales. Here we hear tales which advise the listener on the duties of their role: how do we appreciate the significance of details while also remaining open to the quirks of the larger story, how can we apprehend without pushing to own?

To help the lesson, we hear of that famously bad audience, the West, and the unfortunate consequences of its lazy habits. The wish to own through your eyes collapses sensual apprehension into an adjunct of power, just another back-up to the nasty ways of the world. And, of course, you miss all the magical things which are really going on.

In this section of our tale, we learn how many of the dark women's troubles stem from these misapprehensions about where truth and value lie.

Here our girl storyteller, Scheherazade-come-lately, sucks up her breath and concentrates on the difficult business of pulling her audience into a tale they are not yet equipped to hear. What follows is that boring but necessary section which sets the scene, identifies the characters, tells the audience what it needs to know before the story really starts. The storyteller has to set the audience up for a long wait.

Before I tell the story of these four sisters, you must hear another tale. This next tale will explain the stories which follow – without it you will never understand the curse which haunts the four sisters, because these are the stories which explain the strange significances of their bodies and skins.

Tall and tan and young and lovely: evocations of girls' skin

Once, long ago, many lifetimes from here, people sang a song about the delicious poignancy of looking at a young girl's skin.

> Tall and tan and young and lovely, the girl from Ipanema goes walking, and as she passes each one she passes goes "Ah".
>
> When she walks it's like a samba that swings so cool and sways so gently that when she passes each one she passes says "Ah".
>
> Oh But he watches so sadly. How can he tell her he loves her? Yes he would give his heart gladly.
>
> But each day as she walks to the sea, she looks straight ahead not at he.
>
> Tall and tan and young and lovely, the girl from Ipanema goes walking, and when she passes he smiles, but she doesn't see.[1]

The song is about looking and longing – not a torch song but an easier lust, supermarket aisles, holiday camp entertainment, coffee bar kitsch. Whatever the story, the form places the narrative strictly in the realm of the everyday, tongue-tied rather than sublime.

1.   "The girl from Ipanema", Jobim–deMoraes–Gimbel, from Getz/Gilberto, MGM Records, 1964.

The story is about responses to that tall and tan and young and lovely girl; but the response is unspeakable. No more than "Ah". I guess we all know what it means, or think we do. Because our response is already contained in the description "tall and tan and young and lovely": a pretty explicit evocation. Of course, you still have to get what this means – and particularly respond to the cue of "tan" – but there is plenty of guidance towards the relevant factors. Only what is important to our response, what we need to be told to identify with that "ah", gets said.

So what we are told is that her outline is "tall", her substance is "tan" and that these attributes are characterized as "young and lovely". That should be enough for us to get the picture of this soft brown femininity, pushing the right buttons to elicit the involuntary "ah" of the song.

In case that isn't enough, the song also lets us know how she moves that lovely young flesh, swaying gently to an underlying rhythm – a more substantial back-up to the covering "tan". To the English-speaking world who adopt a translated version of the song, the girl is definitely *exotic*. And the particular distance and attraction of that term marks the "ah" of our response.

We, the appreciative audience, watch, wait, smile, sigh, to our heart's content. She, object of our attentions, walks by, oblivious. We have the eyes; she has the skin and the flesh. Somehow we live in the same space.

That is at the heart of our entire story, the long history behind those strange missed meetings, the confusing interplay between the exotic and the everyday. All those dark-skinned girls who wander around our streets and lives and are partly mundane Britain and partly something else altogether.

So our model is the girl from Ipanema in Birmingham City Centre. Tropical fruit on the underground. Hothouse flowers at rainy bus-stops. The end of the twentieth century when nobody is at home.

The story of trying to understand

There is another story about people trying to understand the world in which they live. These are the hard-working well-meaning book-reading note-taking people who believe education is a privilege and study hard to make the most of theirs. Their best teachers tell them that colonial histories shape contemporary understandings – that that is our commonsense understanding – and that learning must start from this assumption.[2] If you want to know about the meanings of skin and bodies, this is the history to learn. Only then can you understand what is evoked in the song and explain the mechanism giving rise to the "ah".

Listen to the tale of a well-meaning teacher and you will see.

I work in the most well-meaning sections of higher education. My department designs courses to address the puzzles of living, to resonate with the everyday lives of students, to teach things which matter; we often fail, but try hard. Because the world is changing, we, too, have to keep changing tack.

Nowadays the race course which I co-teach comes back again and again to issues of whiteness, the construction of those invisible powers, the anxieties of

2.   See Solomos & Back (1996).

dominance; like everyone else we've been trying to shift the focus from a pathologizing scrutiny of blackness. This makes particular sense as the students are largely white. Better to make them look at themselves than perpetuate the racial zoo. Maybe.

But we still work through debates around the representation of blackness. The commonsenses around race still revolve around visibility in this country, Britain, and her sisters; so we teach through these expectations. Everyday consciousness is, supposedly, what we are interested in. One result of this is that we all happily identify languages of racialization and collect a whole array of ways in which popular representations have done black people down. Pretty soon we've all got our denunciation of the degrading white gaze down pat and quickly pounce on the evil racism of all images of anyone except the racially privileged. Later on the smart ones return to this and berate us for having such a static view of the world. Everything is always changing, of course. If it wasn't it would be time to lie down and die.

But how are we going to learn anything?

At least assuming a static world lets us start to think about how representations might work.

I used to teach English literature – with a great deal of confusion. One of the reasons why I gave it up was that I was so unsure what we were supposed to be learning. Not "the best that had been thought and said" – the EngLit I went to learn about was already too knowing for that easy invocation of the inherent value of high culture – but surely, something of worth.[3] Otherwise, why bother? Instead of

3. The idea that culture is enobling comes here from Arnold (1960): 70.

becoming clearer, my ideas about literary education became more confused.

At the first opportunity I stepped sideways into the non-discipline of cultural studies. Although I should know better, I am still drawn by the promise of "relevance"; "Look", said the hoarding for cultural studies, "you might be a sad academic, but here you can study the ways in which people actually live." The lure of populism was too much and I burnt my novels.

Once in cultural studies I looked around and realized that much of the discussion mirrored that in English; even the key books overlapped. Some version of the mystery grouping "literary theory" was shaping ways of thinking even without the literature.

This was happening all over: throughout the humanities and social sciences everyone was talking signs, interpretation, meaning.

I've got a few ideas about what this means and how it comes about.

My most self-congratulatory theory places interpretation at the centre of all study, particularly of the social. Learning about the construction of meaning becomes the central focus of all social science and humanities education. Literary theory wins a following because it offers a set of tools for this endeavour. All that talk about language and its mysterious workings might seem obscure, abstract, without any grounding in anything which actually happens ("reality", "people's lives", economy, politics, history), but, if we study hard, this stuff can teach us general skills which can be transferred to the case-study of our choice. Story books are good practice precisely because they are self-contained, formal, not open-ended like real life. The version of literary

education put forward in this version o*f*
for the social sciences suggests that stor*i*
training before encountering the confusions *o*
day life. Reading literature is a safe way of lear*n*
how to deal with the really hard stuff.

Textual analysis as argument/persuasive way of talking

Studying literature is a way of learning to shape your argument around the available proof. Believe nothing without proof; isn't that the world we are living in? Reality is what can be demonstrated: convincing interpretation displays its object. Turn your example to the light and show how obvious and inevitable your reading is. If I want you to start thinking like me, I have to offer you a practice case, something to let you work out how I got to this place of belief. This game works best with words and pictures. For us these things most easily allow us to see what we mean. Point to them and it seems obvious. The obviousness of visual perception proves your point for you.

But other senses can reveal the shape of an argument, surely?

If I tell you about a girl-scent, will that work?

That smell conjures up a body, the flesh of reality. Involuntarily my body responds to that sensation which is not a representation. A suggestion, maybe, an evocation, a reminder; but not any kind of picture. Even if you see me twitch to that memory, that is no kind of proof. This sensory trace might evoke a disturbingly vivid recollection for me, but you don't have access to that immediacy.

education put forward in this version of literary theory for the social sciences suggests that stories are a good training before encountering the confusions of everyday life. Reading literature is a safe way of learning how to deal with the really hard stuff.

Textual analysis as argument/persuasive way of talking

Studying literature is a way of learning to shape your argument around the available proof. Believe nothing without proof; isn't that the world we are living in? Reality is what can be demonstrated: convincing interpretation displays its object. Turn your example to the light and show how obvious and inevitable your reading is. If I want you to start thinking like me, I have to offer you a practice case, something to let you work out how I got to this place of belief. This game works best with words and pictures. For us these things most easily allow us to see what we mean. Point to them and it seems obvious. The obviousness of visual perception proves your point for you.

But other senses can reveal the shape of an argument, surely?

If I tell you about a girl-scent, will that work?

That smell conjures up a body, the flesh of reality. Involuntarily my body responds to that sensation which is not a representation. A suggestion, maybe, an evocation, a reminder; but not any kind of picture. Even if you see me twitch to that memory, that is no kind of proof. This sensory trace might evoke a disturbingly vivid recollection for me, but you don't have access to that immediacy.

Instead, I have to tell you what it is like. The smell of green mango. Sharp and acidic, with a promise of some later sweetness. An almost rancid edge; the organic as threat rather than an easy nature. Ambiguously edible as if you could put out your tongue, but it might burn.

"There is also a tactility of smells. Each smell generates its own textures and surfaces. No smell is encountered alone."[4]

Of course, this is all lies. No body smells of green mango. I might wish they did, but that is my own sad incorporation into exoticist fantasy. What I'm interested in here is the extent to which my narration shapes your response to the example. The point at which you buy into my response and don't need to be persuaded any more. What does it take for this argument to work? How do examples work as rhetoric? With smell I have to tell you how to respond to a sensation which isn't there; but don't words and pictures require similar guidance if I am going to persuade you to think like me?

Listen to another story about understanding and believing; another tale from our well-meaning teacher.

The story of the illustrative example

The first volume of *Capital* opens with the announcement: "Our investigation must . . . begin with an analysis of a commodity."[5]

Focusing on the commodity is presented as a way into understanding the whole mysterious web of

4. Seremetakis (1994): 218.
5. Marx (1983): vol. 1, 43.

capital's workings. The commodity is the exemplary product of this system; the story of the commodity is inevitably the story of its production. This part both stands in for and summons the whole. Familiar stuff.

The opening of *Capital* says that if you devote enough attention to the right detail of a system, the knowledge you gain will reach far beyond that particular detail. It's that idea I want to proceed with. The Marx of *Capital* presents this as the obvious way of going about things: "The wealth of those societies in which the capitalist mode of production prevails presents itself as 'an immense accumulation of commodities', its unit being a single commodity. Our investigation must therefore begin with the analysis of a commodity."[6]

There isn't much room for doubt here; this is clearly the place to start. The commodity is obviously the exemplary text of capitalism, so a close and attentive reading of its comings to meaning will give us an insight into the whole crazy system.

I want to take this as a more general model for attempts at social knowledge. If you want to know about the world it soon becomes clear that you can't look at everything at once. No enquiry can take an overview of social relations as its initial starting-point; because then you would know the answers before the questions. You would already know what the world was like. So you concentrate on a detail in order to illuminate its context of production: narrate the story of this point properly and you will narrate the story of its world.

I'm pretending for now that all social science is based on a version of textual analysis; I'm not sure if

6. Ibid.: 13.

this is always the case, but it's enough to recognize how widespread this way of learning things is for us. We've probably all at one time or another focused on some detail in order to extrapolate a larger story; I'm not really suggesting any more than that for now.

What *Capital* suggests is, of course, a little more than this. *Capital* assumes that there are exemplary texts which can be identified; this goes back to assuming that you have an overview before you start. Otherwise how can you spot the right text as exemplar?

I'm not making any particular claims, positive or negative, for Marxist epistemology. I'm using *Capital* as a way of making a point because of the special resonances that piece of writing has for all of us, whether we like it or not.

Admittedly, I'm relying on a certain authority effect from using Marx. This is, after all, pretty much the biggest secular book when it comes to learning and doing. However, this piece isn't about championing Marxism and its continuing relevance. I have my own uncomfortable allegiance to Marxism; but that isn't what I'm talking about here. Instead, what I'm doing is using the starting-point of *Capital* to think about techniques of learning. Think about the shape of the argument, not its content for now.

Capital is a story in which understanding comes from identifying the phenomena which typify a system and subjecting them to scrutiny. Unpack the processes by which these phenomena come to social meaning and the unspoken dynamics of human life are revealed. Understanding comes from proper interpretation of significant details. Tell the story of the commodity in the right way and you tell the story of all our lives. Or of all our economic lives.

Something like this has always been the promise of EngLit courses: read this poem and learn about the world. I'm trying to unlearn my scepticism about this because I'm starting to see the same shape in other kinds of study. Most people nowadays are a bit careful about suggesting that they know the answers before they start the enquiry. If nothing else, all that mud-slinging around postmodernism has caused this shift in attitudes to study. So we start small, identify the limits of our sample, case-study, location; and wait until later to make our claims about bigger truths. Those final fun paragraphs where you can talk about the implications of your work.

I don't think there is anything wrong with this. No point studying if you have to invent the wheel every time; making connections and identifying transferable knowledges is what learning is about, surely? What I'm not doing is slamming anyone's oppressive will to mastery and metanarrative, not even my own; I am saying that the nastiest kinds of "intellectual debate" have effects on how everyone goes about learning.[7]

What shifts for us, perhaps, is the sense of certainty about where to focus your enquiring attentions? In the story of *Capital* the commodity is unquestionably the unit of capitalist economic relations; there is no doubt that that system will be illuminated through that detail. Things get harder if you can't name your

7. I don't think it is worth citing the bookshelves of work on postmodernism, or the reams of rudeness which say that no such thing exists; these can be found easily by anyone with access to a computerized library catalogue. I am only saying that this unproductive name-calling has changed how all of us think about knowledge and learning.

system, let alone identify the magical unit of its workings. So that's us; all those who must believe social life to be multiply structured in mysterious ways. Don't kid yourselves that you have a choice.

Lots of thinking around "race" and "gender" has revolved around discussions of representation, as if what you see is the significant detail which facilitates analysis. This can seem like an obvious choice. To our commonsenses "race" and "gender" are about what is physically conspicuous; this stuff is all about picturing anyway. So if the categories are constituted through the visual and its recreation, representation is the obvious place to learn about these things. So the reasoning goes.

There is, of course, a more substantial background to the concentration of issues of representation in relation to certain topics. Women's politics and black politics in the West at least have pressed words and pictures into the mainstream of how we think about what shapes the world. What gets said about the constitution of gender and "race" is seen to have enormous consequences for how people live. "Culture" is where a lot of the dirty work of power takes place.

I take it that we have all already learned this lesson, so well that it has become second nature, something we mouth in our sleep. I know that it is something like the taking on board of these ways of thinking which has led to everyone suddenly doing courses on representation, culture, image. Even the real-world wallahs feel like they ought to know about interpretation these days. The real world is also about the mysteries of signification, the pleasures of storytelling.

But acknowledging that systems of representation have significant social effects – perhaps particularly in relation to "race" and "gender" – doesn't help us to identify a starting-point for enquiry. There doesn't seem to be an exemplary text, no one thing which exemplifies these systems.

As a result of this, attempts to learn about "race" and "gender" can seem quite random. It can be hard to decide which the most important and illuminating examples might be, or even to prioritize between examples. Think about it too much and pretty soon everything seems scarily packed with the traces of a racialized and gender-divided world. Of course this is equally true of the world of *Capital*: the capitalist economy inscribes all parts of life. What is different is the way in which the commodity can be identified as the thing which embodies the processes of capital. Without that key thing to focus on, you're left with a world of random examples. Just walking around the world evokes girls' skin again and again, until that is all you can see.

The tales that follow tell of two ways of seeing this.

The story of politics

This is a well-known story about seeing dark women.

Once there was a land which feared for its future. Life grew harder and many of the people believed that their enemies lived among them. Scared of unrest, the wise men of the court proclaimed that the trouble in the land had come with the dark-skinned people. Eager for explanations, many of the fair-skinned people believed; and, elated by this success, the wise men of the court grew more confident. They concocted a plan to remove the weakest among the dark-skinned people from the land, to persuade the restless majority that they were solving the problem.

Reeling from the effects of this public scapegoating, the dark-skinned people developed strategies to protect themselves. This is a tale about this resistance.

Of course this is one of those suspicious flauntings of political credentials that we are all familiar with; and I am always deeply embarrassed to resort to this kind of thing, admitting the limits of narrative enchantment, a sign that you must listen because it is good for you. *But*, how else will you know that this is an important and serious story, not just entertainment.

So – in this troubled land far way, the most troubled people planned their counter-attack. The court were trying to deport them as if this was a cure for society's ills. In response they must persuade their neighbours that they had a claim here and that the trouble lay elsewhere. As others had said, the struggle was for hearts and minds. The argument is that you have to know how words and pictures work in order to mount any kind of campaign; you have to know how to use the building blocks of popular rhetoric, how to tell the right story for the right audience.

All the campaigns against deportation tried to make visible hidden violences by the state. The wise men of the court hated immigrants, but were still embarrassed to disclose what their hatred meant for these people's lives. That all happened by stealth, at night, quickly, quietly, to people with no public voice. So in the dreams of resistance the main objective was to make a noise, to get ourselves heard. In terms of storytelling, this meant mobilizing popular mythologies at the same time as trying to challenge them.

Many of the people fighting the threat of deportation through public campaigns have been women escaping domestic violence.[8] British immigration policy being what it is, the majority of cases have involved Asian, African or African–Caribbean women.[9] Campaigning has to take account of the connotations of these girls' skins.

The wise men of the court knew that they could make deportation work by invoking a faceless mass of threatening overstayers, the swamping horde of long-established white imagination. In response, the campaigns against deportation had to resurrect the individual.

Come closer into the story. Think about what you can do. You make leaflets which use headshots in the manner of women's magazines and portraiture. You go for eye-contact, heartstrings; lone woman, perhaps with children, victimized by a faceless state.

Inevitably this echoes wider mythologies about helpless black women (perhaps more Asian than African–Caribbean); black men as absent, feckless, abusive; black families unable to ensure the safety of their children. The pictures can mean vulnerable in the worst kinds of way; and, in part, the campaign relies on this being the case. This vulnerability can slip into suggesting the legendary sexual availability of dark-skinned women; and for the individuals fighting

8. The British Home Office says it keeps no figures on the numbers of women deported as a result of escaping domestic violence. Southall Black Sisters has collected information which suggests that between January 1994 and July 1995, 755 black and migrant women were threatened with deportation because of marriage breakdown and 512 of these were women fleeing domestic violence.
9. Standard accounts point to the explicitly racist basis of British immigration law. For an accessible summary, see Joint Council for the Welfare of Immigrants (1995).

their deportation, there is a regular stream of bizarre sexual proposals and offers of marriage from around the country.

The picture of the black woman facing deportation evokes a range of stories. She is the woman alone: stripped of male protection by the violences of colonial history. Available, vulnerable, belonging to no-one. Her image is titillating, in the way that only claimed-by-no-one dark girls can be. At once an object of horror, charity and lust.

The audience has to respond to these suggestions for the campaign literature to work. We have to partake in the ambiguous evocations of these girls' skins. Otherwise that important real world political message doesn't take hold.

Of course, there is more than one type of picture. You might go for local paper pathos, and show close-ups of the woman's sad face, perhaps with her children. Here you cut out everything else and focus on the all-alone vulnerability of the woman. Campaign leaflets can use this approach too, while providing another kind of written commentary: less tragedy of local woman, more black families fight back. But either way, the picture goes for the heartstrings.

You might go for the good politics of the group shot – shouting crowds, banners and slogans, healthy resistance – but that kind of picture might be about anything. To make sure that people get the idea, you make sure that the placards show the name of the person fighting their case, preferably using a picture. What you end up with is a lot of people holding blown-up versions of your leaflet. See above.

After much discussion, everyone might decide that cow-eyed pathos is not the most appropriate of political messages. So, you look at different kinds of head shots: perhaps an action take, speaking at a conference, engaged in family business, being normal, not victimized. But even when the picture looks all right, the words have to explain that something bad is happening.

Somehow or other, each option must evoke that story of vulnerability, whether the blame is placed upon histories of exploitation and the actions of a racist state or on the exigencies of fate. No sympathy, no campaign; so mobilize these familiar tropes however you can. You have to work with what people expect.

The story of pleasure

In the same land, another story was beginning, holding its audience spellbound in a darkened room.

A yellow taxi pulls over on a street of smoke and neon, sleaze soul in the background. In steps seventies sex-queen, brown sugar foxette, all satin shirt and dangerous platforms. Out-of-style white cab-driver leers approval in the driver's mirror, only to see sex queen whip out her electric razor and show herself as a "man". The closing credits tell us that this little story of confused identities and sexual excitement is designed to sell us trousers.

Clever old Levis ride the moment again. Smart as a whip, they keep on playing the double exoticism of British audiences: exciting kooky New York and those hypersexual black folk. Extra points for having the wit to stage a lascivious white male gaze – a ridiculous skin-crawling leer, overestimating his charms, under-valuing hers. Of course, we all recognize the city raunch-chick persona he is responding to; very much a response to skin. All our expectations are twisted around by the revelation that raunch-chick is a masquerade; we've all misread the signs.

The story of pleasure works differently from the story of politics here. Politics seeks to change how people live, but in this endeavour must employ formulaic stories, plots that everyone can understand. Pleasure has no higher agenda – here buying the trousers is enough – and so can afford to play. The story of pleasure begins with formulaic representations, but then changes the plot for fun. Politics is too stretched for time and resources to mess about like this; ambiguity is a luxury this tale cannot afford. So imagination gets left to those only concerned to sell trousers.

Which ends up saying that leaflets are compromised and formulaic while adverts are avant-garde and innovative. That campaigns build on existing mythologies of "race" and "gender" while attempts to sell trousers are radically unsettling.

Isn't there a problem if Levis seem like better politicos than community organizations? Is this what comes from having no exemplary texts and overemphasizing the power of representations?

Of course, what is at issue in these two stories is how we see; in particular how we see markers such as "race" and gender. Both stories suggest that we learn to see differently, but one employs established tropes to elicit interest and the other disrupts established tropes to grab our attention in another way.

To understand the choices, we must hear another story about looking.

The story of the one and the many eyes

Once there was a man who hungered for knowledge. He convinced himself that only truth could bring him happiness. "When I know the world, I will know myself", he declared, "and when I know myself I will know contentment in all things."

His friends were sceptical: "It is your search for absolute truth which makes you so unhappy in the first place. Only acceptance can bring happiness to our brief lives. You will never find the truth which can undo the tragedy of mortality. You don't even know what you are looking for."

The man took no notice. "I know I must look", he replied.

And that is what he proceeded to do.

The man began to spend his time collecting images and cataloguing them under headings as a guide to his experience. At first he looked with no particular pattern or order, but after a while he developed rules to arrange his vision. He continued to do a lot of looking, because the volume of information was an indication of how close to truth he had come.[10] He kept craning his neck to see as much as he could, near and far, high and low. He swivelled his head quickly, doing his best to keep his eye on the moving picture of the world. In his ever-expanding catalogue, the man saved the salient details of all this looking, a mammoth scrapbook of everything that had

---

10. For an introduction to the roots of this encyclopaedic addiction, see Hall & Gieben (1992). For an account of regimes of sight through the eighteenth century in Europe, which corresponds loosely to one section of our simplified fable about looking, see Stafford (1991).

happened. As the volumes piled up, the man started to feel pretty pleased with himself. His only misgiving was that his scrapbooks could not stick down the world in movement. He had saved a thousand frozen moments, but he could not record the messy endlessness of what he saw everyday.

"Oh, well", he thought, "that isn't what is important anyway. Still pictures let me focus on the things I need to know and to cut away all the meaningless parts. This will cut down my work in the end. Better to mark a boundary around the main points – all of that stuff beyond the frame just gets in the way."

So he went on happily with his work, cutting out carefully composed images and deciding his own frame of relevance. Although he realized this was not exactly an accurate representation of what he saw, he believed that he served the higher truths of clarity and salience. The power of his eyes let him choose his approach to truth, and this puffed the man up with a sense of self-importance. If he could choose his own attitude towards truth, surely he was master of his own destiny. The man still believed that he was looking to find his place in the world, but he no longer believed that this place was determined by a power greater than himself. Practising sight revealed a world which was vulnerable to his own particular reordering: his eyes led him to truth, not any higher destiny.

From on high and down below and next door and round about, all the gods of all times saw the shiny swelling of the man's ego and recognized that he was falling prey to that disease of possibility and pain, modernity. The gods knew the future and pitied the man for his unthinking optimism and suffering he could not yet see; but they also knew that this was his destiny.[11] Human beings were weak and they must all be slaves to their eyes for a time, dominated by this sense of sight which marked the modern era, setting it apart from its premodern predecessors and possibly its postmodern successor.[12] The gods knew, too, that he was not the only one to fall in love with this sense of his own power. Later we will hear the story of the man's close kin, the self-fashioning men. For now, our interest is with the man and his scrapbooks and the things which looking does not make him aware of. The gods knew that:

> Whereas sight encourages the hubris of a subject who can direct his or her gaze wherever he or she chooses, hearing entails a healthy receptivity to outside influences, in particular the voice of God, which cannot be blocked by shutting the ears in the way we can close our eyes. Hearing calls for a response to clarify the mystery of the interlocutor.[13]

Human beings were so susceptible to the romance of vision, bowled over by the opportunity to look at what they wanted. Once they had decided that this was the way to learn things, no other kind of lesson could be drummed into their stubborn heads. Like children taking their first steps, the sense of their own agency overwhelmed them, shutting out any suggestion that this new-found power was not absolute.

11. The most famous account of the tragedy of modernity is Adorno & Horkheimer (1979).
12. Jay (1993): 114.
13. Ibid., p. 103.

The gods did not resent people's love of looking. The eyes of the wisest did much good, saving frail humanity from some of its own excesses and protecting people against the larger world which they could not appreciate.[14] They only worried that their mortal offspring had forgotten other routes to understanding and that this left them more vulnerable than before. Looking was such a contained sensation – troubling complication could be cut out of the frame, the lookers could make believe that they controlled what they saw. The gods feared that too much looking was making people forget their own frailty, believing, instead, that they were no more than all-powerful eyes. Human beings were ignoring their reciprocal relationship with the rest of the world and the result was big trouble.[15]

But all this happens later, in the future visible only to the gods. Our man with the scrapbooks is still absorbed with his cutting and pasting, convinced that he is at the brink of a new age. His friends come around to tease him occasionally: "So, how is the quest for truth? Any revelations lately? Hope you find the answers before you run out of space. We heard that your catalogues already take up the house, that your wife is threatening to leave you and that your children never come home. If you aren't careful this search for knowledge will put you out in the street, and where will you store your pictures then?"

14. For a critical account of the benefits of modernity, which does not perhaps do justice to the achievements of modernity, see Gurnah & Scott (1992): 132–44.
15. For more on this impending eco-horror, see "The newsreader's tale".

The man smiled back patiently; because he knew that they could not see what he could. "Actually, I've already found my answer", the man said, enjoying the disbelief of his audience. "Looking is my place in the world: I am destined to collect images and document the world."

This answer troubled his friends still more. Although they spoke harshly, they cared for the collector and his family divided by picture albums. "What kind of answer is that? When will your collection be complete? Do you intend to waste your entire life on this fruitless task?"

The man was ready with his answer. "It is only fruitless to your unseeing eyes. You understand only what you can hold and eat and see no further than your next meal. By learning to use my eyes, I have seen the destiny of humankind. The truth of vision will let us own the world, understand and control its workings, claim its fruits for ourselves. Our destiny is to be the owners of the eye. Only proper looking can cement our identity and our centrality. You non-lookers belong to a lost time. Soon you will learn new ways or suffer for your backwardness," And the man turned his back to return to the infinite task of looking and cataloguing. Unsurprisingly, his friends fell away like dust, leaving him alone with his eyes.

But he did not feel alone. His faith in looking gave him an illusion of connection with the world. More than this, vision appeared to make him master of what he surveyed; the act of looking itself began to feel like possession. As the man met other obsessive lookers, he forgot any way of thinking that was not through pictures. In the pleasures of scopic ownership, he forgot the other sufferings which allowed his unhampered looking. The looking people did take possession of the world, but not through their eyes. Like all conquests, this took place through force. The eyes of the looking people only confirmed a domination which had been secured by other means.

Strangely, this addictive looking saw only certain things. The real process of conquest fell from view, leaving only frozen fragments for our collector's eyes. Instead of horror, the man and his new friends saw wondrous spectacles and specimens of scientific interest: the messy cruelty was left outside the frame. Although the poor people of the world who were conquered cursed the looker's dishonesty – how could their obvious sufferings be invisible to people with such big eyes? – the cataloguers truly saw only within their limited frames. Others did the dirty work and they documented victories which they wilfully misunderstood. Documenting through your eyes became a whole way of life. The apparently peaceful and harmless business of looking and cataloguing escalated with the violence the looking people spread across the world; it was not the looking which hurt, but, somehow, looking helped the hurters.

"Everything in the European dream of possession rests on witnessing, a witnessing understood as a form of significant and representative seeing. To see is to secure the truth of what might otherwise be deemed incredible."[16]

For the looking people, everything seemed to come back to the eyes. Although they took ownership of the world through deceit and violence, chance and bribery, ruthlessness and luck, they experienced

16. Greenblatt (1991): 122.

possession through the act of witnessing. The material comforts of conquest could not be felt as possession in this way; ownership rested on what could be seen and verified. Even if the material things are what counts about possession, the story of ownership must be told as a witnessing and, sure enough, the looking people rushed to tell this story.

This brings us back to our man and his albums. The looking people came to own the world, but there was too much for everyone to see. Some possessions were too far away, some too long ago. All understood the importance of vision, but some were not able to be witnesses. To take possession of the world as a people, the lookers found that they must nominate individuals to recount the experience of their eyes. The rest could see through their accounts.

"The discoverer sees only a fragment and then imagines the rest in the act of appropriation ... The person who witnesses becomes the point of contact, the mediator between 'ourselves' and what is out there beyond our sight."[17]

The professional eyes of the great age of looking extended the gaze of their people.[18] When they could see only a part, they filled in the rest and marked the imagined image with ownership. When they saw what others could not, they saw on others' behalf, becoming collective eyes which relayed the experience of possession back to those at home. Sometimes, they brought back some of what they saw, to display the affinity between capture and looking.

17. Ibid.
18. For the more developed exhibition culture of later empire, a follow-on from these earlier dreams of possessive witnessing, see Greenhalgh (1988).

"The native seized as a token and then displayed, sketched, painted, described, and embalmed is quite literally captured by and for European representation."[19]

This was the work given to the album man. As the looking people grew more powerful, they wished to document their empire more systematically. The man's many years of amateur curating made him an ideal candidate to arrange the jumbled proof of world domination. He was charged with the task of presenting the bits and pieces of other times and places in a way which gave all viewers access to the heady sensations of witnessing and possessing.

> In the late nineteenth and early twentieth centuries, the process of collecting, staging and displaying exotica archaicized the past and domesticated cultural otherness. . . . The logic of the museum was inscribed into the parlor, and the museum itself was inhabited and enjoyed as an enlarged public living room.[20]

The conquering traveller has brought back objects as proof of his far-from-home victories for as long as history has been shared. The job of the album man is both to continue this tradition and to domesticate it. In the time of their rule, the looking people began to value and fear for the particular arrangements of their homes. When the men of the looking people travelled the world in order to possess it, they locked their women in their homes for safe-keeping. Later we will hear the tale of the two daughters, which

19. Greenblatt (1991): 119. For more on this, see "The girl in the window", Chapter 3, p. 127.
20. Seremetakis (1994): 224.

tells of this time. For now it is enough to understand that the regime of looking and collecting demands that the unfamiliar is tamed and brought into the constrained logic of the home. The album man laid out the debris from a thousand expeditions and arranged each selection in glass cabinets. When the non-travelling looking people came to see, they found that the experience of witnessing had entered a version of their own homes. Possession had never felt so comfortable.

> The parlor–museum encapsulates western modernity's petrification and consumption of ethnological and historical difference. In parlor sites, items of older periods and other cultures which had their particular aromatic, tactile, and auditory realities were desensualized and permitted a purely visual existence. In this process, vision itself was desensualized and subsequently metaphorized as and reduced to a transparent double of the mind unmediated by any material, spatial and temporal interference.[21]

The album man was pleased with his work. He felt he had no greater gift to share than his method of looking – to do this for the glory of his people was an honour indeed. When he thought back to the warnings of his old friends, he felt no bitterness, only sorrow for their self-punishing backwardness. If only they could see as he could, free from the distractions of sensory contamination and open to the absolutely rational eye which could not help but show you the truth. It was this effect he sought to reproduce

21. Ibid.

in his work, so that others might learn the power of their eyes. Humanity had always been in thrall to its body, pulled this way and that by the calls of hunger and sex, made vulnerable by the pleasures and pains of sensation. Living in our bodies had left us unable to think. The world was a mysterious set of forces which did things to us, kindly or cruelly, without warning or hope of protection. What people knew extended no further than what they felt. Humanity bowed to larger forces called fate or god and never learned how to make any progress themselves. It was this frailty which the album man hoped to overcome. If others could rise above their demanding bodies to see for a moment with the eye of reason, then surely the world would become a better place. Learning this lesson of seeing with new eyes would let human beings take up their destiny at the centre of the world. The album man arranged his displays with this thought in mind. He took the bits and pieces he had been given and made each into a demonstration of this lesson. Later the place of this demonstration was named the museum, and there various treasures, the crabs and the cups, the pictures and the leaves, the jewels of other worlds, were transformed into lessons in empowered looking.

> The museum had transformed the crab [or the cup or the picture or the leaf or the jewel] – had heightened, by isolating, these aspects, had encouraged one to look at it in this way. The museum had made it an object of visual interest.[22]

The man was careful with his work; he never assumed that people knew how to look. Also, he knew

22. Alpers (1991): 25.

that the unpredictable impulses of the body were never far away and that even looking could fall victim to this irrational sensuality. He removed distraction from his display, demanded silence from viewers, regulated the temperature to lull bodies into docility. He made sure that there was nothing left to do but look. After that, viewers had to make the leap to rationality themselves; but, how, he asked himself, could they not see what was before their very eyes?

All this time, the gods had watched silently; unable to change what had been written, despite their misgivings. This new belief in display was an indication of difficult times between gods and people, of a change of faith among mortals. Now the easy and immediate truths of the eye held sway, cutting people off from other sources of information in favour of the stabilizing fictions of rationality through imaging.

The distinction, rooted in Enlightenment struggles against authoritative religious doctrines, makes religious truth a matter of subjective belief, while the truths belonging to museums, universities, or courts of law claim to be self-evident to reason, rooted in experience, and empirically verifiable.[23]

The gods saw with sorrow that people preferred a system of belief which required no thought. Once learned, the new habits of looking let people decide what was at first glance. The totalized vision was all; the process of negotiation and adaptation of less certain methods of understanding were forgotten. Who wanted to live in that humiliating imperfection when sight offered total control of a world which revolved around your eye?

23. Duncan (1991): 90.

So only the gods mourned for a loss which humanity was too preoccupied to feel. Looking felt like such a close and immediate way of dealing with the world that no-one thought about the costs of disconnection. But the gods knew. Good sense was thoughtful *and* sensual, well-informed by feeling; the new ways of looking lost all this. People might feel more powerful, but their connection to each other and the rest of the world suffered.

"The moment of erotic projection in vision . . . was lost, as the bodies of the painter and viewer were forgotten in the name of an allegedly disincarnated, absolute eye."[24]

However big and powerful the regime of the eye made people feel, the gods knew that there was a cost to forgetting the body. The cruelty of the looking people's conquests already proved this. With their divine eyes, the gods could see that the looking people would come to feel the cost of this neglect of the body; but, for us, this story is to come. For now, the album man carried on happily with his business, engrossed in the good he was doing. Wasn't he recording the world, after all?

From around the edges of the picture the murmurs of the rest of the world gathered force. Not a shout, but the breeze of a million voices whispering. "What about us?", they begged for the album man's attention. "Can't you hear us?"

But, of course, he couldn't. He was too stuck in the misapprehensions of sight. If he thought of the rest of the world at all, he saw only their shiny surface.

The next story is about the consequences of this habit.

24.   Jay (1993): 117.

The story of the skin

Once there was a woman who wore a skin so beautiful that wherever she went people stopped to stare. Although quite ordinary in other respects, the surface of her body had a lustre like polished stone, a colour as deep as still water, a texture of satin silk. This one feature was so beautiful that people renamed her the skin-woman, in honour of this attribute.

The woman accepted this easily. She saw little reward in her own name; a troubled reminder of a half-known and translated history. Her life showed no promise of future notoriety. If only her skin was remarkable, then let the skin name her. Soon, the name "skin-woman" was so widely used that even she forgot her other, family, from-birth name. Her conspicuous skin over-rode that past.

Time went on and, with it, life. The word of the woman's exceptional skin travelled, bringing new witnesses to its strange beauty. Great thinkers of the region debated the woman's status: was it possible to be a beauty without a beautiful form? Was skin a covering or a feature? If she was a creature of skin, what kind of being did that make her?

For a long time this debate raged to itself, touching the life of the skin-woman not at all. The business of living was not disturbed by the mystery of her outer layer, the wonderment of her skin's pilgrims did not concern her. Her flesh remained hungry and mortal, and the call of the body was stronger than the picture of the surface. How could she be a creature of skin when the pull of her belly took up so much time?

"People like to look at my surface", the woman thought, "and they are welcome to do so – but my flesh is still solid. That weight is what I am."

And she continued to work and eat, living her life of local fame without reward.

But the longer things went on, the more trouble came to the skin-woman's life.

People asked her, "How do you live as just a skin? Aren't things difficult for you?"

At first the skin-woman just laughed. "That's just your peculiar belief. Look more closely, I'm far more than skin. As solid as you and just as capable." And she carried on with her business, too intent on her everyday chores to waste more time discussing her conspicuous hide. She couldn't feel the questions sapping her strength away.

"Even if you are more than a skin, surely your skin is your most important part. That is how you are known. Isn't it hard to have all your worldly achievements sucked up by your skin?"

Still the skin-woman kept her temper. "My life is full and useful, despite my skin. It is you who are mesmerized by my surface, I feel the depth of my life," and she hoped that people would see the foolishness of their talk.

But, of course, people never grow tired of foolishness. Instead the questions took on a life of their own.

"How do you live as just a skin, when skin takes over everything you can be? However hard you work, whatever else you do, your name is in your covering, not your actions. While others live in the world as social beings, you are reduced to two dimensions, no more than a picture of yourself. At least we take our names from what we do; you are no more than what others see."

The skin-woman just sighed and stopped trying to explain. Her life was more than what they saw, so let them think what they wanted. Then one day, as she went about her business, the skin-woman noticed a change. She had always been strong and capable, lifting the same weight as her brothers with her resilient limbs. Her body was well-adapted to her harsh life, and she moved through her work swiftly. But today something stuck. Instead of her usual solid strength, the skin-woman felt insubstantial before her tasks. Her body seemed to be losing weight, draining her strength away. Now when she went to do her work, she fell back exhausted immediately.

At first, she rested; certain that soon she would feel herself again. But time passed with no improvement. The skin-woman's body was fading away from some mystery illness. Her skin, on the other hand, was glowing. The more weak she became, the more lustrous its shine. It seemed as if the hundreds of undermining questions had wheedled their way into her immune system, quibbling away her body's defences, and now her skin was really taking over. While the woman became listless, her skin became incandescent, a thing quite apart from its owner. The skin-woman became so tired that she forgot her lost life of activity. Her days blurred into each other, nourished only by the small tributes donated by admirers of her skin. It retained its lustre, despite her condition. People were so mesmerized by it that they couldn't see her. In time she lost consciousness. Days later, still surrounded by people, she died.

When finally the audiences to her skin realized that the skin-woman had passed away, there was a great commotion. What would happen to this wondrous skin without the power-supply of a living organism? Would it be burned with its spent body, denying future generations access to this national treasure? The wise men of the day debated the issue at great length. Many learned papers were written, each purporting to uncover the essence of the skin's magical properties. The king consulted the court, and the court confirmed that all bounty of the kingdom belonged, by right, to the king.

In the end, the skin-woman was flayed of her beautiful hide. It remains on display, while people forget its owner.

". . . But [the looking people protested] the skin is always exhibition, exposition, and the minutest look is a touching that brushes against it and exposes it once more."[25]

Afterthought

Long ago some people might have called this "reification" or a process related to it. This would explain how the woman's skin came to take the status of a thing apart from her and suggest that people's fixation with her skin-thing was an indication of their alienated inability to relate to her.

The story is that the processes of capitalism place commodity fetishism at the heart of social relations, whether we like it or not. We all lose sense of our humanity as we relate to each other as things, through things: a sadness which we will see in many of the stories to come. Reification is the aspect of this process which elevates products or aspects of human life to the status of independent things-in-themselves. This is most obvious in economic relations – so that our social life is mediated through the representation of

25. Nancy (1994): 30.

labour-power, the commodity – but potentially invades all spheres of life. Out-of-favour Lukacs asks this question: to what extent does commodity fetishism construct all our inner and outer lives in capitalist society?

> The transformation of the commodity relation into a thing of "ghostly objectivity" cannot therefore content itself with the reduction of all objects for the gratification of human needs to commodities. It stamps its imprint upon the whole consciousness of man; his qualities and abilities are no longer an organic part of his personality, they are things which he can "own" or "dispose of" like the various objects of the external world.[26]

However out-of-date and fashion these questions seem, don't they touch upon the sad fate of the skin-woman, whatever the denials of her intrusive questioners? Isn't the mysterious process by which a physical characteristic takes on a status greater than and separate from the whole body/person who wears it something like "reification"? When skin becomes a thing in itself and subsumes its owner and her more varied being, aren't we in the reified world of things, not well-rounded, multifaceted, touchy-feely, flesh and spirit *people*?

Of course, the question is: how does this form of something like reification spring from commodity fetishism? Isn't this form of alienated living subject to its own history – a psychic terror of difference and capacity for violence unrelated to economic

26. Lukacs (1971): 100.

imperatives – a history not exhausted by the development of capitalist society? This story doesn't deny that; the suggestion is only that the mechanism enabling this ugliness may be connected to wider mechanisms of social ugliness, in, admittedly, mysterious and half-explained ways.

The lesson is not to look for answers from skin – because the question is: how did skin get so conspicuous? The stories to come tell of the failure of sight to appreciate the depth of the body, and the unhappy consequences which follow. In the stories to come, the mesmeric properties of the surface distract from the sensory needs of the flesh, as if the two are in competition.

> What is a body if not a certain detachment of the skin, of bark, of surface, if not a carrying off and setting aside of a limit that is exposed and exposes itself? The gesture of the limit, the gesture at the limit, is touch – or rather: touching is the thought of the limit.[27]

Hungry for touch, these are tales of the fraught struggle between skin and meat.

Visible and invisible labour

The stories about skin and eyes, ears, nose and tongue gave us new ways to think about ourselves. But some things didn't add up.

The stories about the commodity talked about the hidden inputs of labour. Work made all the wealth,

27.   Nancy (1994): 30.

but when it came to the exchange which revealed value, only the commodity could be seen. Labour's destiny was to be forever invisible.

The stories showed us all this without a doubt. We understood and believed what we were told, because the logic fitted what we saw. We recognized the tricks of the commodity form which seemed to make value appear from nowhere.

But our work seemed different. If we were not seen, there for a thousand gawping eyes, the work was not done. Our visibility was part of the labour we sold. That was an essential component of the work, our wage paid us to be objects of all gazes. Being invisible is one of the privileges we forgo because we are paid to let anyone have a look.

Instead of transforming our labour into a solidified repository of labour power outside of ourselves, we worked on ourselves. Our labour power was directed towards the creation of particular displays of our own bodies. The effect of the display was what we sold. That was the peculiar value which we exchanged.

Thinking about our own work after hearing these stories, it was difficult to see where the value was. Our labour did yield tangible transformations. Through work we became exquisite clothes-horses, pinnacles of speed and agility, voices of authority, spectacles of edification and distraction. Whatever the mistaken beliefs of our different audiences, none of this came naturally. These were the achievements of intensive effort. Our wages were recompense for this diligence.

But what was the exchange which revealed our work? What took the shape of our lost surplus value? It looked like we were the objects transformed by our labours – and what kind of work was that?

Instead of getting respect from comrades by being seen as transformative labour, the source of all value, we became commodities ourselves.

Of course, we understood that this was the consequence of any wage. What you sell is a part of you. For the moment of the bargain, when you have no choice but to sell, you are no more than a value-making thing. That's the lesson: the pursuit of profit can never respect labour. Even though there is no profit without labour, profit can only be squeezed out of labour disrespectfully. Until humanity turns some new corner, this is the bargain we all live under. We had heard this story and believed it.

But, still, there was something different again about our work.

Looking for answers, we heard another story, another tale about the West's rise to power.

The legend of work

Once, long ago, all people worked for themselves. Then, as now, work provided the necessities of life, but, unlike now, people laboured to provide themselves with what they needed. Their work was no more and no less than the getting of food, clothes and shelter for themselves and their loved ones. With no idea of exchange, all must learn to fetch and make these essential items.

Later, as the world grows older, people learn to share essential tasks. Some fetch food, while others build shelter. This system increases everyone's comfort. There is more of everything, and barter can get you anything you need. This is progress.

Later still, people grow tired of the limits of the barter system. Sometimes what you have cannot be traded for what you want. If the meatman has enough shirts, even the most beautiful garment will not buy dinner. The meatman may recognize the worth of your offer, but it is not of value to him. Again, progress steps in, and people design an abstract mark of value.[28] This thing can be exchanged for whatever you want, because everyone knows that it is a promise to exchange. It is just as good as meat or clothes, because in it people see the possibility of obtaining meat or clothes or whatever else they need from the market. People still share out tasks, but now they can swap what they make more easily for what they want. The gift of the gods which makes this possible is the thing called money, a chance to think about value as separate from things.

But, like all gifts of the gods, money has its dangers. If money is an abstract expression of value, the one thing which can be exchanged for all other things, why bother to make anything but money? The magical properties of money made people forget that what they really needed was the things money could stand in for; they forgot that money was only a promise of more useful things. Some people, thinking they were smart, gave up making useful things altogether. Instead they concentrated on making more money. The promise of value started to look more attractive than

28. For a critique of the model of progress, see Humphrey & Hugh-Jones (1992): 2. "[Barter] . . . has been misconstrued largely because of the persistence of the creation-myth in classical and neo-classical economics that in barter lie the origins of money and hence of modern capitalism. In this perspective money originates as a solution to the problems of barter."

the everyday value of useful things. People still wanted meat and clothes, but they preferred to be paid in cash.

The money form gives us an easy and portable marker of value: a year of effort can be carried in your back pocket. Now it is possible to work for someone else and be paid in this abstract marker. Everyone recognizes money, so it isn't necessary to have your own goods to barter with. Instead, you are your own goods, to barter for money, the only thing which can be exchanged for life's necessities. With the advent of money it becomes possible to make rational calculations about everyday life, because now value can be counted and quantified; some called this the rationalization of modern society:

> Money is concerned only with what is common to all: it asks for the exchange of value, it reduces all quality and individuality to the question: how much? All intimate emotional relations between persons are founded in their individuality, whereas in rational relations man is reckoned with like a number, like an element which is in itself indifferent. Only the objective measurable achievement is of interest.[29]

Others argued that money gives a basis for abstract systems of thought, because now we value the material world through this abstract marker.[30] Either way, it seems that money changes how people experience the world and themselves.

29. Simmell (1950): 411.
30. See Frankel (1977).

The idea of money, that empty mark of equivalence and exchange, suffuses our whole existence and signifies our experience in all manner of ways. Money is the moment when everything becomes portable, in imagination at least. From now on the different parts and roles of our lives need not live in the same place or time, need not come together as a whole for anyone but ourselves (and only then through the hard business of identity, subjectivity, positioning). Any last hope we held in the dream of organic community, those mythical people who knew us as we knew ourselves, slipped away now.

In the era of money, which for us is all time, all human life is marked by the logic of exchange. Even stories, the archetypal free gift, get twisted into this new shape. Now when we tell our chosen tales, there is no guarantee of audience understanding. The people who listen do not know us as we know ourselves, cannot smell the detail of the place we come from, cannot read the many contexts which come together in our speech. All they get is the bare nugget of the tale, the indefinable something which can be exchanged and taken away. We make that illusory value in the moment of exchange, the pact of attention between writer and reader, teller and told. There is no way of checking if others make the right use of what was once yours, no way of knowing if they make any use at all.

Our tales are no longer those of hearth and home, the understood-before-you-speak stories of close kin, whatever we may wish. Once told, all tales spin away from the teller, becoming something else somewhere else. Stories are no more certain than pictures, they just require a different attention.

In this world where people work for wages, all the products of human labour take on the mystical status of commodities. When people swap money for things to get what they need, the common unit of value is the amount of labour each thing conceals. Suddenly, all labour becomes equivalent.[31] That's the logic.

But of course, things never quite work out that way. In all sorts of ways, different kinds of labour never become equivalent to each other, and this is what our story is about. For now, it is enough to keep in mind different ideas about what kinds of work can be seen.

One of the great hidden/follow-on stories of *Capital* is the one about the reproduction of labour power. Employers buy this coveted item from the unhappy workers, paying them just enough to get them back at work the next day and stealing the rest of their product as profit. Wages must be enough to allow the reproduction of labour power, because you need your workers to keep going. However, the detail of how the workforce keep body and soul together is up to them. Capital doesn't pay extra for domestic labour, but there is no rule that women must perform these tasks for nothing. That economic arrangement is determined by another set of prerogatives, not only that of the profit motive. Which is not to say that capital in its tricky way could not turn this arrangement to its benefit.

"The idea that women should be able to stay at home – the better to mother their children – justified hard work, long hours, and economic exploitation for male workers."[32]

31. See Marx (1983): vol. 1; 66.
32. Kessler-Harris (1982): 51.

Good women stay at home; to raise their children, do their washing, hide their sexuality. The wage rewards public, beyond-the-home, activity. It is paid as recompense for the labour-power you expend, as a pay-off for severing your connection from the fruits of your labour. The visible relation between worker and product becomes invisible through the wage; you are paid to go home and relinquish your claim.

Domestic work – the work of good women – is hidden from the outset. The mother of all service work, work at home is endlessly without tangible product. First, nothing gets made; yes, there are beds and meals, the consumed-immediately products of everyday life, but there is nothing extra, nothing to show, nothing more to swap for the value of exchange. Second, this is all done in private, away from the public eye, for the secret love of home comfort. To be done properly, it has to remain hidden. Anne McClintock argues that this veiling of work in the home is necessary for the fictions of public and private spheres to work. The angel of the house is born in the moment of industrial/imperial capital and in that moment respectable femininity comes to mean the appearance of idleness: "Domestic work had to be accompanied by the historically unprecedented labor of rendering invisible every sign of that work."[33]

The work of the home was confirmed to be woman's legacy, but now the legacy included the demand that this work was done in secret, as if done by no-one or not done at all. By association, visible work done by women became a question to their femininity.

We sisters represent that questionable femininity through the particular mythologies of our skins. Each

33. McClintock (1995): 161–2.

of us works through a version of display: part of what we sell is the opportunity for others to abstract our image for their own fantasy. Even in a world where women are known to undertake untold waged and unwaged labour, this show-off work has implications for the kinds of women we can be. The following stories show that the belief that we are improperly gendered, both more and less than women, runs deep in the imaginations of the looking people. Each of us has a story which explains what this means.

In this second section, we come to understand the tangled tales of looking and owning, making and buying, seeing and being seen. Of course, in the manner of all second episodes, things become more confused and the ending seems further away than ever. We learn that we are hemmed in by both the ways of work and the ways of sight; and that we are accorded no value by either of these interlocking regimes. Unfortunately, and despite our devil-daring deeds, escape seems impossible. Refusing to be seen also accords us no value and refusing to work or working elsewhere or differently does not undo our strange status.

In the next section we begin to think about negotiating these tricksy arrangements and hear more about the difficult dilemma of being either too seen or not seen enough.

Further reading

For more on various ways of seeing and not seeing "race", see *White*, by Richard Dyer.

To recap the strange story of the commodity, go straight to *Capital,* vol. 1.

For more on the horrors of British immigration law, see *Women's movement*, by Jacqueline Bhabha and Sue Shutter.

For more discussion of the extra-special role of vision in Western cultures of modernity, see *Vision and visuality*, by Hal Foster.

To spend more time with the story of our reified lives, see *History and class consciousness*, by Georg Lukacs.

To think more about the status of women's work in the home, see *Imperial leather*, by Anne McClintock.

CHAPTER 3

The model's tale

". . . the stereotyped is not a false representation, but rather, an arrested representation of a changing reality."[1]

After all these stories of display and narrative, it is time to return to the four women waiting patiently before the king. This, the first woman's tale, is also a story of showing and telling. Here, we learn of changing ideas of beauty and ideal femininity. We hear that even as dark flesh begins to gain value on the catwalk, the trappings of this high-glamour femininity are made by the undervalued and unseen labours of other dark sisters. The history which determines these ways of working turns out to be the same past which casts dark women everywhere as victims and beasts, beautiful only as objects of these particular fantasies.

As we have told you, we have tried to make sense of our lives using the tools of great men. My story is no different in this respect.

I am a model, regarded as the epitome of femininity in our time. Young girls cut my picture out of magazines and dream of growing up to be like me. Young men name me as their most desirable date – the woman they most want to be close to.

When I was young, there was little chance that I would grow up to be like the women in the magazines. They were nothing like me, their skin made them something else altogether. However long my legs, I would never be a child-like blonde with wide infant eyes. We were different types of women.

1. Chew & Minh-ha in Taylor (1994): 441.

As a child not being blonde did not seem like a disadvantage. I did not yet believe that yellow, pink and blue were prettier than shades of brown and black.[2] Didn't everyone say how pretty I was? And clever, with my runaway mouth and grown-up turn of phrase? When my mother tied the bow on my party frock, I did not believe that I had a rival in the world.

But as I grew, I felt less sure. My world was full of pictures of pretty women – on television, at the cinema, on billboards, in magazines, in every shared public fantasy – but none of them were anything like me. Perhaps the world at large did not see me as pretty? Occasionally I glimpsed some vague shadow of myself, but these images were frightening or homely; never the prettiness I craved.[3] I began to doubt myself; and doubt makes it hard to fluff up your party dress.

Of course, I survived this disappointment. Like others, I learned to disregard these publicized criteria of value and developed other ways to love myself. Each time I swung down my local streets, the eyes and tongues let me know that I was beautiful. Too bad if the picture-makers couldn't see that – too bad for them. With an audience, I could feel my beauty. I felt affirmed. But somehow, on my own, the doubt returned. Looking in the mirror alone, I saw nothing I liked. The face in my head named "pretty" – the one from all the pictures – bore no resemblance to the one in the glass. However much I puckered and plucked, concealed and highlighted, I came no closer. Neither artifice nor training could make me into the

2. For a less confident version of this story, see Morrison (1979).
3. See Young (1996).

blonde child-woman from the poster. I was stuck with looking either kind but plain, or attractive but dangerous. Pretty never came into it.

But one day the choices all changed. I had already noticed something in the air. Now I got street attention all over town, not just in my own neighbourhood. In the bars and clubs of the city, people started to pay me attention. I knew something was up when I noticed blonde child-women wearing my clothes, shoes, hairstyle. Suddenly how good they looked depended on how much they looked like me.[4]

And that's how I became a model.

Now I wear clothes for a living and the world tells me loudly that I am beautiful. No longer kinky, mumsy, a special taste; now my look is the look of catwalk glamour. My head span from the new possibilities. How had this happened? Was this a brand-new world? Or the old one in disguise? How could I understand my situation?

I used the recommended methods of the great men and started to look hard for clues. I looked all around, to be certain that nothing was missed.

My new job seemed to make a new sense of my body. Instead of being seen as some variation of servant or prostitute – the fate of my foremothers in many locations – I was considered so pretty it made me rich. The world tried to persuade me that this was a sign of great change. The world was new and packed with new possibilities for my sisters. My success was an indication of this new climate. If somebody like me could become wealthy by wearing expensive dresses, surely doors were also opening for

4. For an account of the complex interchanges in urban culture, see Back (1996).

others like me. The skin which once marked my distance from prettiness now seemed like an asset. In the magazines it seemed as if all the dark-skinned women would now become princesses with lives like glossy fashion-page spreads.

The thing I had become was the picture which showed that all this was possible; seeing me made it true. I was a credit and inspiration to my people.

For a while I revelled in this role-model fantasy. I was having fun and being useful. Everyone loved me and the world was becoming a better place. In the creative world of fashion we not only sensed the future more acutely, we set next year's trends. And the trend was to affirm the beauty of dark skin.

But the women who bought the stitched-in-gold arm-and-a-leg frocks off my back still looked nothing like me. True, few were picture-book blonde child-women, but they wore another kind of value. Even my new-found wealth could not match their unshakable assurance.

I began to wonder if it was me or the clothes which people loved and affirmed. Did they look at my body or the hang of the cloth? A pretty face or a clever detail? Which was the star and did it matter? Did our ideas of beauty make any difference to the rest of our lives?

"But", I thought, "how can the world be changing unless it is true that my skin has new values and meanings?" I scratched my head and looked around.

Look behind

This is the glance backwards, to the time which has passed out of sight.

Yesterday this was not a body to look at; scrutinized, but not for pleasure. Instructive, freakish, monstrous; but sure as hell not beautiful.

Straightforward legacies here. The West is uncomfortable with its body, wishes to look but not be seen. But only looking can confirm wholeness, identity. Better look, just to be sure, just a quick peek. Pretty soon they are looking all the time, addicted to the peculiar fix of the gaze.

Look around

These are the sights closest to home, what the eye sees daily.

The glossy picture-books have changed pattern. Much less about the angles of the North, all pastel pale don't-touch snootiness. Now catwalk goddesses come in a range of shades. There is plenty to say about this; lots of talk about these picture-book women.

Some people say that a certain version of ethnic diversity can be good business at a certain moment; but that doesn't necessarily mean that things get better for black people.[5]

That story – the one which says, very sensibly, that changing the pictures doesn't necessarily mean anything about wider conditions – is a sticking-point for representation wallahs. Which for now might be all of us. We all know that representations are not easily linked to material conditions, that superstructure is not a simple echo of base, that what you say and what you do might be a million miles apart. . . .

5. See Back & Quaade (1993).

We just don't know what to do with that knowledge.
Looks like we are stuck with analyzing pictures.

Look ahead

This is another kind of sight, stretching beyond the limitations of the eye.

Bodies are becoming obsolete, apparently.[6] Physical display is one of those sad anachronisms, an out-dated ritual played out by those relatively new to the name "human".

We are nostalgic for the power of flesh. And this articulates with a racist fantasy which makes blackness no more than body, meat, physicality. We will hear this tale at the end of our story, when my sister speaks.

For now, I found that looking hard positioned me in a story which I still could not understand, a dilemma illustrated by my tale.

The song of the shirt

All the things you can't tell by looking; the most dangerous shapes of the world.

Once a king in a great land bought a shirt. Although it was very beautiful, this was not an unusual shirt. "I'm tired", said the king, "of being so special. How can I understand my people unless I live as they live, eat as they eat, wear the clothes that they wear?"

His courtiers clucked their agreement. Secretly they knew how hopeless this quest for authentic knowledge

6. For more on this and related issues, see Gray (1995).

was, that this wish to walk in the shoes of the down-trodden was itself a trick the powerful played on themselves. They had seen all this before, written the scholarly tracts themselves, pondered the relation between power and knowledge a thousand different ways.[7] But now they clucked their agreement. No point forgetting the first lesson of power – that it hears what it wants and pays your wage, so who are you to say any different?

"Good – that's agreed then", said the king, and the royal party prepared themselves for a shopping trip.

At the bazaar, the king took his time. There was plenty to look at: many garments from all over the world, varying textures, colours, styles. The king puffed up with paternalistic pride; what riches his subjects enjoyed, such choice, such variety. Surely this was the best of worlds.

Finally he made his choice and wore his new purchase out of the shop, ready to experience the world of the ordinary people. But, of course, nothing changed. No curtain fell, no flash of light, no sudden and life-altering insight. Just crunchy cotton against his skin and a coterie of the eager to please.

"Where is the knowledge I crave?" The king scanned the court accusingly. After all, it was their job to meet his needs, to keep him informed, to facilitate the business of kingship. "Who can unravel the secrets of this shirt?"[8]

Of course, he was a king, so a queue formed. All offering the risky temptation of enlightenment.

7. Most famously, see Foucault (1977) and, for accessibility, Foucault (1980).
8. For an indication of the reach and role of cotton in a long-standing global economy, see *Capital*, vol. 3, pp. 124–35.

The mystery of the commodity

A woman came forward to offer her story; she brought with her a sack full of books and pamphlets. Before speaking she rifled through her collection, selecting key works and marking pages. Although her face was tired, drawn, lined, she seemed quite sure of herself. She cleared her throat noisily and addressed the court as if there was a stadium full of people.

"Oh king", she began. "For many years I have contemplated the mystery which you seek to unravel. In my youth I worried about the inequalities of our evil society. It pained me that work was a source of suffering not joy.

As a girl I was apprenticed to the local seamstress, as was the custom in my family. I learned my trade well, diligently practising different stitches and finishes, mastering the trademark details of our region. I came to take pride in my skill and local people rewarded my work by the particular value they gave to shirts stitched by me. It pleased me to meet one of my shirts on a neighbour's back, to see my work perform its everyday purpose. People saw the value of what I did.

But as time passed, we found that just selling shirts to our neighbours would not keep us alive. There were rumours that in the big town women had learned how to sew many shirts in one day. We heard that every one of these many shirts could be sold in the big town, so that seamstresses were guaranteed to make money. Neediness made me pack my bags and I left my little village to find work in the big town.

Of course, when I got there, things were not so sweet. I quickly found work in a place where many women stitched many shirts, with great speed it was true. But I received far less than before for each shirt. Instead of riches, I made just enough to get by. After a while I lost hope of ever returning to the village.

Worse still, my shirts were no longer my own. The end-of-day bundles went to markets where no-one knew me. The people who wore my shirts knew nothing of my life. My hard-learned skills became invisible. Somehow, in the journey from my lap to the marketplace, the traces of my efforts disappeared. This burnt me with such a sadness that I had to go and see, unravel the mystery of disappearing labours for myself.

At market, I looked hard for the traces of my effort in the articles on display. Surely, some piece of me could be seen, some smudge of sweat or particular pattern of my fancy. I found my favourite shirt and scrutinized it hard for a sense of my own life and the circumstances of its creation – but it showed no sign that it knew me or that we had been such close acquaintances, companions through long nights.

It caused me much pain to lose my handiwork so totally. I had endeavoured to love my work. What was drudgery to others was artistry to me. Each shirt took on its own character in my hands, stretching into its own particular shape, growing into the expression of its pattern. I vowed to remain pledged to craft – no reason why the demands of living should steal away the achievement of my work.

But, that day at market, the evidence of my eyes told me that my things were no longer my own. Much later I read a book which explained my loss, which described the way my much-loved thing flew away from me into the new world of commerce, the way that 'as it steps forth as a commodity, it is changed into something transcendent'.[9]

The owner of the book spent many nights explaining this to me. When I looked at the book myself, I did not recognize my own story there – but through his mouth I came to understand that they were talking about me and others like me.

I talked endlessly about my work, my skill, the pressure to make more, make to order, make the same. I spoke of being a very small girl first learning to sew – of the achievement of my first shirt – of the difficulty of finding and keeping a job.[10]

My new-found teacher listened carefully, more intently than I had been listened to before, nodding recognition as I spoke. At intervals he pulled out his books, reading out passages and explaining quickly. He taught me that I live in a world where social relations were hidden behind the queer transcendence of certain things; this was why I could not see what was going on.

This is the reason why the products of labour become commodities, social things whose qualities are at the same time perceptible and imperceptible by the senses. In the same way the light from an object is perceived by us not as the subjective excitation of our optic nerve, but as the objective form of something outside the eye itself. But in the act of seeing, there is at all events, an actual passage of light from one thing to another, from the external object to the eye.

9. *Capital*, vol. 1, p. 76.
10. For working-class autobiographies from the phase of accelerated industrialization, see Burnett (1974); Vincent (1981).

There is a physical relation between physical things. But it is different with commodities.[11]

Out at market, my shirts forgot me altogether. There they were named in relation to the other things on display. The hard business of their origin was forgotten. My effort, the knowledges accumulated by generations of seamstresses in my family, the pains and pleasures of my working day – all that was lost. My name, my life, my employer, my wage-packet – none of that gave meaning to my shirt. The only name it carried was a tag indicating what other things it could buy. However hard I stared at that written number, it made no connection with my life and the people I knew.

It was in this state of confusion that I met my teacher. He told me why the product of my labour seemed so distant, belonging to another way of being. 'There it is a definite social relation between men, that assumes, in their eyes, the fantastic form of a relation between things.'[12]

Since learning this lesson from books, I have made it my business to understand the tragedies of work. I have studied the writing of many learned scribes, devoting long hours to mastering the intricacies of revolutionary thought. I have corresponded with the progressive thinkers of many continents, collecting pamphlets and letters in readiness for this moment. I abandoned the world of work now that I knew that it was the destiny of honest labour to be erased, rendered invisible by the forms of its proudest achievements. I learned well the lesson which I have come

11. *Capital*, vol. 1, p. 77.
12. Ibid.

to share with you; buying shirts will never bring you closer to their makers or even to their previous owners. At market shirts abandon their roots in human endeavour and become no more than an expression of barter, equivalent but never present.

> The name of a thing is something distinct from the qualities of that thing. I know nothing of a man, by knowing that his name is Jacob. In the same way with regard to money, every trace of a value-relation disappears in the names pound, dollar, franc, ducat, &c.[13]

You see, king, your shirt can never mean more to you than its price."

Convinced of her own argument, the woman fell back, exhausted. "To know your people, you must look at more than a shirt, you must see the whole picture, the total system, the international order . . ."

The king frowned. "But where shall I begin? What first? How will I know what is significant?"

"You can't", the woman replied, "All or nothing – see it all or see nothing."

This story left the king frustrated: no wiser than before and with no way of moving forward. No eyes could see the whole world, after all.

Seven-league sleeves

The learned woman came forward and offered her story. "My tale begins long ago and far away", she began, "and shows how the tale of your sleeves spans seven leagues."

13. Ibid.: 103.

"Quickly, explain", hurried the king, for he was growing eager for the truth.

"What the shirt is can be seen from where it comes. Fruit are named from their parent plants, children take their character from their upbringing; in the same way, objects take their meaning from their place of birth.

Once we knew who had made a shirt from the cut and weave; we knew where and how they lived, their ancestry and their beliefs. The life of the maker travelled in the world in the form of the shirt. In the texture of the finished product, we smelled the life which made it. Find out where something is from and everything else becomes clear. We understand the social relations which allow this to happen. A place name lets us imagine the shape of the working day which leads to this product, the flavour of refreshment, the landscape around. All of this becomes the meaning of the shirt.

But your shirt has no smell of place, no flavour of home. When you shake out its colour, no story of origin becomes visible. Only I can tell you of the many homes of the shirt. But first I must tell you my own story . . .

For many years I have devoted myself to study. While my sisters married and raised children, devoting themselves to the business of family life, I committed my life to loftier pursuits. I travelled far from home to gather the learning of the wisest scholars of our age. While other young women flirted at temple and at market, chit-chatting their way to adulthood, I shut myself away with my books. No ardent young lover could lift the purdah of my serious love of learning.

My sisters pitied me, giggling and tutting at my dull existence. 'You can't learn everything from books', they taunted, 'to know about the world you must live in the world. Shake off that library dust and come out in the sunshine for a change'. Every day they teased and coaxed, hoping that I would relent and become like them. But, certain of my chosen path, I concentrated on my books. I knew that the truths I found there were the key to all freedom, and, hungry for justice, I devoured the pages avidly.

My books taught me certainty: I learned about the shape of the world, the route which had led us all to this present. I looked around at the details of the everyday and felt sure that I knew what all these things meant. When my sisters returned from market, I explained to them the significance of their new-bought treasures. 'Taste a sweetmeat, sister dear', they clucked, 'sugar will unlock those sour furrows in your brow.'

'Don't you know that your moment of sweetness means death for the children of the poor world?' I hadn't yet learned the difference between teaching and scolding. 'Every mouthful lines the pockets of those who kill for profit, who destroy other cultures, who lie and cheat and scheme to sell their goods to the weak and unsuspecting. Can't you taste the barbarism of exploitation underneath the sicky sweetness?'

I was always pleased with my insightful critique of the pleasures of consumption. Thanks to my studying I was no longer seduced by the aura of commodities. I could readily sense the story of their origins.

My sisters were not impressed. 'There's too much shit in the world to keep yourself clean, you know. Refusing sweeties is no route to righteousness.' Exasperated by my supposed unworldliness they returned to their work and entertainment, resigning themselves to the uncomfortable friction between knowledge and living.

For some years I lived happily in this manner; devoted to my studies, I felt each day brought me closer to a perfect existence. The random fragments of the world fell into place. I understood what was going on, what came first, where the connections were. And knowing all this allowed me to live a full and happy life. All my choices were informed.

But one day my certainty started to falter. Returning from market as usual, my sisters offered a new delicacy. 'Have a taste, there is no bitter edge here.' At first the sweetmeat seemed familiar, and I began my old refrain. 'Can't you see where this thing is from, what it represents . . . ?' But looking closer, I felt doubt for the first time in many months. I put a piece in my mouth. Confusion overtook me. All my explanatory stories were conjured up at once, jumbling into each other, crashing through the tidy ordering of my mind; to my horror I could make no analysis of this product. Worse still I grew increasingly distracted by the sweet flavour.

'See', laughed my sisters, 'the world is not so simple.'

I crammed more of the familiar yet unknown sweetmeat into my mouth, flipping it around my tongue, searching for its answers. That night I ate until I was sick, retiring exhausted and none the wiser. The morning came, and I found no energy for my books. A day passed and another, and I remained mesmerized by this limit to my education. I gave up looking for freedom in books.

Of course, my sisters rejoiced at my return to the world of the everyday. They sent me to market and to temple, primped up in the ribbons of girlhood – pushed me into the company of a hundred laughing girls and sweet-faced boys. By day I was back in the land of the living, devoted to the wholesome business of staying alive. But at night I still dreamed of the power of knowledge.

For many months I lived in this manner. People forgot that I had once been lost in study. My library card expired without remark.

Then one day I met a woman in the marketplace. Unlike the other traders, she had no goods to display. Instead she told fortunes, of a sort. The service she promised was to reveal the secret lives of commodities. All day long people brought strange objects to her – and all day long she told the crowd the twisting narratives of these speechless things.

Listening to her stories, I remembered the pleasure of knowing.

One man brought a shirt like yours to be read; the story she told will help you to understand. She said, 'This shirt spans many continents. The cut was once fashionable in one part of the world – now this adaptation springs up in another. The print is a computer copy of an African design, itself derived from a pattern exported to Africa by the cotton industry of nineteenth-century England. The cotton is grown in one place, spun in another, woven in another – all these places change, according to the price of labour. When the new fashions come out, the company relays the new pattern instantaneously to subcontractors a million miles or a few streets away – depending on their calculation at that time. The pieces of the pattern are sewn together in many locations – back rooms and front rooms, bedrooms and workshops. Wherever these rooms are, the shirt is always the same. So each shirt has no one home – it is a product of all these multiple and hidden homes. The true meaning of the shirt is found in this set of relations, the exploitative yet inescapable interdependence of our little globe.'

Hearing this, I felt a weight drop from me. Study was the answer after all. Since then I have devoted myself to charting these intricate relations, to explaining the connections between things and their stories. Look carefully, and the meaning of your shirt is also the meaning of the whole world."

The king stared sceptically at his sleeve.

The story of the underground seamstresses

Next two women arrived, one angry and one subdued. The quiet one bowed her head as the other shouted her demand: "Enough pretty stories; it is time for the truth to be heard." She glared accusingly at the crowded court while her friend silently lay down to rest. The first woman began her tale, if a tale it was.

"The truth of this shirt is this woman's exhaustion. Nothing else is as true as this, the true cost of the shirt.

This woman works long hours for pennies. At peak periods she works more than 60 hours a week.[14] She receives no holiday pay, no sick pay, no pension rights. Her employer deducts national insurance contributions from her wages and keeps the money for himself. Her employer provides no facilities for his workforce. She works from home so the extra costs of production – heat, light, refreshment facilities – are borne by the worker. Her employer bears no

14. On struggles around the length of the working day, see *Capital*, vol. 1, pp. 264–86.

responsibility for his workforce's health and safety.[15] Although she knows other women who work this job, none are in a union. The trade union movement pretends these workers do not exist. There is no limit to the hours which she must work, no end to the demands she must face, no protection against this life-sucking force. The world is now so small that it is only the cheap price and quick delivery of her skill which hold this work here, away from the even cheaper sewing-machines of other women in other parts of the world. Holding this job wrecks her body and destroys her life, leaving no energy for children's games or a lover's caress.[16]

Your shirt is the barbaric product of this particular culture. She pays the price for those pretty colours on your back. The uniform finish hides the suffering of the maker – but that is the true meaning of this shirt."

The king scratched nervously and prayed for a more cheerful story. "Why doesn't she speak?" he asked, nodding towards the silent woman.

She lifted her face to look at him in response to this attention. "I can speak, king – although my

15.   For an older account of health hazards in the textile and similar industries, see *Capital*, vol. 3, pp. 91–6.

16.   This experience of work echoes wider trends in Britain and elsewhere.

"There has been a great increase in part-time, casual, and sweated labor in construction, clothing, catering, retailing, tourism, cleaning, and even printing in London and in the United Kingdom generally . . . Homework and sweated work have also increased. The clearest case is apparel. To be able to use the cheapest workers, ethnic minorities and women, smaller textile and clothing firms now tend to be concentrated in London and other cities." Sassen (1991): 294–5.

stories sound louder in other people's voices. But, if you wish, I will tell you another story of your shirt.

For many years I have worked sewing shirts and other garments in my own home. I work alone and for many years I thought that I was the only one. Now I know many others who work as I do – at home, when they can, when there is time, when there is work. In the dangerously private worlds behind the front door, women are wrecking their health with dangerous work.

> A lot of people are embarrassed by it. That's because of the money rather than the work. A lot of women are doing it and their families don't know they are doing it, because they clear everything away by the time they come home. They think there's a social stigma attached to it.[17]

This isn't the waged work of fulfilment, something to get you out of the house and into that much-heralded public sphere. Done in your own home, this domestic work is paid, but only just. This kind of paid work is dirty and exhausting; hidden in the fiction of the comfort of your own home, there is no safeguard against physical mishap.

> I've had a trapped nerve twice in my neck and my shoulder. Last time I was really poorly, I couldn't move. But you see you don't get sickness benefit. Injuries are quite common among homeworkers – wrist injuries and arm injuries, but there again it depends on what work you're doing. A lot of employers, if you're working

17.   McKenna (1996).

with glue, they don't tell you what sort of sub-
stances there are in it.[18]

Although done for money, the evils of the home contaminate this work.[19] Even if it is not about love, the
confusions of respect, community, custom, distort the
contract. The explicit bargain of the wage doesn't
stop the do-us-a-favour, you-would-if-you-loved-
me, women's-work-is-never-done taking of advantage.
Working alone at home, even for money, makes us
as vulnerable as wives.

> We did not realise that he was draining the
> blood from us. We trusted him whole heartedly,
> we did so much for him. We never refused to
> work the hours he requested, we worked up
> until 8, 9 and 10 in the evening. We worked
> throughout the weekend without having any
> second thoughts about working weekend. What
> reward did he give us? Now what am I going to
> do with 33p [pension per week in accordance
> with national insurance contributions]? Well,
> somewhere he has to pay for it.[20]

18. Ibid.
19. "Regulation of homework, with the goal of abolishing it,
    began in the nineteenth century as a crusade against 'sweated
    labour' and its contaminated products. Reformers con-
    demned homework for undermining labour standards such
    as minimum wage, maximum hour, and health and safety,
    yet they further attacked it for 'commercializing' the home
    and for degrading motherhood, childhood, and family life.
    They also emphasized the demoralizing environment of the
    home factory in ways that suggested that the home should
    remain separate from the factory and women should stay
    within the home." Eileen Boris, "Homeworking in the past,
    its meaning for the future", in Christensen (1988): 21.
20. AEKTA (1995): 11.

But do wives ever get recognition of their worth? On the contrary, they must become invisible as part of their work. Discretion is a requirement of the job. Good wives suffer silently.

> I have no advantages by working from home except that I can look after my children. I am being paid very low piece-work rate and have never received work on a regular basis. My two children are suffering from asthma and I think it is because of my work. Our heating and lighting costs have more than doubled, due to my work. Once or twice I have asked my employer regarding regular work and a pay increase, he said, 'I am only going to give this, take it or leave it'. With no choice I have to carry on because I know that all employers are the same. The thing that really hurts me is that the employers treats us like slaves, not workers. I have never understood this.[21]

In the past women have complained about working for nothing. Waged work may be exploitative, but at least it is contractual. Women who didn't work for money hoped that cash would make their labour visible. Instead of performing hidden tasks which received no public recognition, the magic language of price would ensure that women's work was recognized as part of the social good. The exploitation of the wage relation might have its problems, but at least there was the chance of agency, organization, struggle. Unlike domestic work, which just left you tired and alone.

21. Ibid.: 19.

What everyone forgot was how central the erasure of work had become to our ideas of femininity. Women work, but their labour is veiled in special ways; and this can happen whether or not money changes hands. Evenly publicly waged women blur their status through the softeners of coffee and counselling, filling half their days with unquantified, unrecognized tasks outside the contract. The extra confusions of waged work carried out in the home have left women more not less vulnerable. Perhaps in the end it all comes down to being seen.

> The whole issue of homeworkers tends to come and go in the public eye. There was a lot of publicity when the report came out but then it went quiet. There ought to be something to tell you – a label on a skirt, or something like that – to say a homeworker has had a hand in what you buy because it's so widespread. Even the cars people buy, there'll be a homeworker in there in a component, or whatever. Everything you buy, even high-cost products like Hoovers and TVs.[22]

We have come to expect some benefits from employment: clear contracts, agreements over hours and outputs, the benefits of sick pay and pensions, attention to health and safety. Homework recognizes none of this. Instead it becomes part of the blurry world of the unofficial economy: wealth-producing, but not for workers, semi-documented and only sometimes on the books, in the figures, part of the surveys, the graphs, the statistics. Homeworkers don't get seen in

22. McKenna (1996).

the ways which offer protection. 'People say homeworkers, they're invisible, but I'm not invisible. you
can see me.'[23]

My friend is right: your shirt is a symbol of our
pain, the particular pains of women workers caught
in the net of global markets and domestic ties."

The story of the magical costume

The next storyteller was unlike her rivals. Before her
performance she held many people in her gaze, touching briefly, smiling into eyes. By the time she had
woven through the crowd to stand before the king,
her audience already wished her well, felt especially
connected and warmed by her attention. Although
older than the other speakers, the woman made herself a special space. Her clothes were soft and bright,
wrapped tight with sparkle, draped low with glitz.
The lines on her face seemed to frame the brightness
of her eyes, gather you in to the comfort of her presence. Unlike the others, she was in no hurry to begin.

She questioned the king, "What do you expect
from this knowledge?" and the court shivered at her
nerve.

The king replied, because he wished to be remembered as a good king, "I want to understand the
shirt so that I can understand my people. I wish to
know how they live and what they feel." Her smile
made him feel ridiculous; no wonder he could find
no answer. She began her story:

"Every shirt and every wearer will make their own
meaning. But only living can reveal the depth of this

23.   Ibid.

truth. My stories will make no sense to you until you come to truly see for yourself.

Once I wore a shirt like yours, petal soft against my then young skin. I imagined that the colours made me as beautiful as any princess – and because I believed this, others did too. Then my shirt meant carefree good-times, the dreamy space outside work.

Later I wore my shirt while nursing my children. The downy fabric welcomed baby faces to snuggle in close. Although the shirt had travelled many miles, for me at this time it meant the most intimate aspects of home.

Later still, my shirt grew too ragged to wear. Flicking through photograph albums, my now-grown children point out my image. 'Whatever happened to that shirt? It was always my favourite. I thought that when I was a grown-up lady I would wear beautiful shirts like that everyday.' Now my shirt means memory, the special and particular history which is not written in books.

But none of these stories can tell you the meaning of your shirt, king, because that is a story only you can tell."

And that was the inconclusive end of this set of stories, with both king and court looking as puzzled as ever. Of course, in the end the king knows more – but still not how to be a good king. At best, his shirt may reveal some states of the world as it is, when he is hungry for a story about change.

After all these stories, the shirt seemed further away than ever. "I can see that my shirt comes from many places and out of many histories; but is that what my people wear? These are all the hidden stories of the shirt, secrets to be revealed by those with special knowledge. The shirt itself cannot conjure up these pasts. What I am looking for is the on-the-surface plain-as-day hit-you-between-the-eyes meaning of my shirt, the one all my people see. Enough about what they buy, tell me what they see."

The king called an end to the tales about origins in far-off countries and stifling workrooms. Enough already. These stories told him how bad things were, are, had been, hereabouts, far away, all over. What he wanted was something about the pretty promises of new clothes: an idea of how people really lived despite the high cost of living.

Hearing this a new group of women came forward, each an echo of the other, yet somehow distinct. The first spoke: "Our stories are intertwined, close cousins of each other as we are chapters of one book. Alone, our tales will entertain and amaze. Together, we may unlock the enigma which troubles your heart."

And, of course, the king bid them speak.

The story of the beautiful ladies and their magnificent garments

"We are sisters, born of one mother. Yet our lives have led us down differing paths, reshaping our features until our shared parentage is barely discernible beneath the layers of our different cultures. Let each sister speak in turn and you will see how pliant nature truly is, how we are nothing more than the shirts we wear."

Harem fantasies

The first sister stepped forward and began her tale.

"When white men first travelled the world, beyond the narrow compass of their own domains, their encounters with the other people of the world were filled with fantasy and misunderstanding.[24]

Much of this misunderstanding gave rise to violence; in the white man's gaze the peoples of our lands became monsters, dangerous creatures to be destroyed. Or tamed. Or displayed.

In these stories, only the white men were people. We were something else, another species, no threat to the white man's rule of the world. We may have had our own ways of living, customs which invited endless scrutiny and note-taking, but we were no alternative to them. As long as we were not people.

As long as we were not people the white men looked freely and without shame. They could no more couple with us than a cow could mate with a horse; we had our different places in the natural order. The endless observation of our bodies, the obsessive scrutiny of our habits; this was in the interests of knowledge, not lust. Desire had no place in the equation.

But some day, somehow, the spell broke. Their violent lust started to show. Now they had to know if sex was possible.

I am the living embodiment of this half-way incarnation, desired and despised at once. My best features – exotic promise, burnished limbs – are also my worst failings, the mark of my degenerance. Although desired, I must remain confined and hidden. An object of fantasy, I can never be a respectable beauty. People pay money to get close to pale impersonations of me, but what I am is accorded no public value. This is my story."

24. For an introduction to early European travel-writing, see Pratt (1992).

The girl in the window

"Once, long ago, I lived my life happily with my family. I was young and innocent and occupied myself with the carefree pastimes of youth. But I knew from the whispers of others that our world was not all sweet. Already our life was not what it was. Some force from elsewhere invaded our homes and disrupted our customs. But to my girlish dreams, this meant little. I still believed that the whole world was waiting only for me.

Then one day, while I dressed my hair, a stranger caught sight of me through the open window. I noticed the rudeness of his stare, but who was he? He was not even a believer. I saw from his dress that he was one of the unclean and ungodly people and thought no more of his impudent looking. My life went on as normal.

Sadly, my unclean brother did not return to his routine.

Some days later, again I noticed him at my window. This time I let him see my displeasure. Was this civilized behaviour? To watch at other people's windows and pry in their business? I met his look and pulled my most ugly and frightening face. See how you like looking at that, dirty old man.

To my surprise, he returned my grimace with a gasp. Instead of being ashamed, his face lit up. Anyone would think I had offered him some gift, instead of an insult. Perhaps I should have ignored him after all. I drew the curtain and resolved to know better next time. But sadly, it was already much much too late. From that day my trouble really started.

The unclean people were already changing our home. Although we resisted, they wielded the machinery of power. Despite ourselves, we fell under their sway. They were not our rulers, but their presence shaped our lives.[25]

One day my mother and father called me to one side. 'We don't want to upset you, but that peeping tom is causing trouble. Today your uncle heard a story in the market, a story which the unclean men have been telling. This is what he heard.' "

The story of the beauty in chains

This is the story the white man told.

"For some time I have travelled in this strange place, the East, believing this to be the land of men alone. My work brings me close to many native men: they live in my quarters, perform my domestic work. My commerce in this land is with other men: goods and information are exchanged through them. For all its sensual promise and feminine reputation, for me the Orient is insistently masculine. There was no pliant landscape on which to live out my fantasy.

I longed for the East of my dreams, but my human contacts seemed intent on confounding my expectations. Then one day I caught a glimpse of the East of legend. Immediately my heart leaped in recognition. This was my destiny.

Through an open window I caught sight of a young woman so beautiful that I was momentarily stunned.

25. "... the French occupation of Maghreb, the British presence in India and Egypt and their use of Alexandria as a transfer station to India, and the ending of the Greco-Turkish conflicts in 1828 'stabilized' the sociopolitical situation in the Orient, providing the necessary security for the tourist industry." Behdad (1994): 36.

Hers was the timeless beauty of the Orient for which I had been searching. Her skin was creamy soft and sun-kissed, the warm tones of body unhampered by constraining civilization. Her limbs were lean and pliant, her hair deep black, as the books had promised. When she returned my look, I gazed into eyes which saw no time. To them the earth was forever in its infancy and life had not moved on from the ways of that time. As she looked at me I saw her jolt out of her dream; here was another possibility, a way out of this stuck-in-time life. In me she saw the hope of rescue.

The moment passed quickly. She remembered the strong chains of her captivity, the harsh vengeance of her honour-bound culture, and dropped her eyes.

After the window was shut, I waited there a long time, hoping that she would regain her spirit, but I saw her no more that night.

On my journey home I pondered the young girl's plight. I had often heard of the hidden existence of Eastern women, held captive by those entrusted with their care. Now I had seen it for myself. The sad-eyed beauty haunted my thoughts from that day on; what a waste of young life. I vowed that I would find a way to free her, so that at least one flower of the East would not perish in darkness.

The next night I returned to her window and held her gaze in silent communion. Now I understood more fully the sorry hand fate had dealt her. From birth she had been raised to serve and please. Her own father, unmoved by the laughter of her girlish play, had cared only for the maintenance of family honour. Instead of indulgence, her girlhood was ruled by a cruel discipline which saw the seeds of whorishness in the most innocent of childish smiles.

Trained to hide her pleasure, she grew up to believe that obedience was the greatest virtue for a woman. Consigned to the corrupting company of women, she learned the twisted ways of a captive life.

From the older women who brought her up to fulfil her ordained role, she learned that, for her, there was no useful work in the world. Feminine obedience demanded that she be constantly available to whichever man came to master her life. To achieve this, all her energies must be devoted to preparing herself for him. After that, she must only wait. Other activities might spoil the finish of her preparations, or distract her from this singular duty. She would never know the simple satisfactions of women's work, for her house could not be her home. How could it be when this was the place where her body was subjugated to her master's will? When this was the place where she learned that she did not even own her own flesh? Her only course was to learn that most Eastern of pastimes: sloth. As time passed, even her youthful vigour would cease to resist and give itself up to the half-aliveness of a woman's lot.

It was then that she would be most vulnerable to the degenerate influence of other women. She would learn their peculiar time-passing rituals. Forced to endlessly contemplate her own body, her vision of the world would come to extend no further than the limits of her own flesh. Little wonder that the secret ways of bodily pleasure would prove attractive; how else might the long days be endured?

Like others before her, she would become an afternoon tribad, enjoying the touch of another woman while she awaited her master's call. Perhaps the unnatural constraints upon her would pervert girlish tastes, transforming romantic daydreams into sadistic fantasy. I had heard of the irrational tempers of these Eastern women and I saw now that the hothouse of their isolation gave rise to strange predilections and the most frightening of vengeances. Their own lives convinced them that human life is cheap, and so they forgot their own dignity, seeking only quick pleasure, and had no pity for the suffering of others, expecting no more of life than pain.

Boredom made these women hungry for sensation. Alone together they engaged in depravities which would startle and disgust the most unscrupulous rake at home. The practice of confining them to ensure their chastity instead had the effect of enlarging the sexual appetite at the expense of all other attributes. Instead of the education of the West, which raises the intellect and fosters aspiration, they were schooled to think of themselves as no more than bodies. As a result, their aspirations reached no further than the next caress. They truly became creatures of the flesh.

In age, their form revealed the consequences of this life. The years of depravity caused their carcasses to decay from within, making the most comely maiden a hag before her time. Before my new love, these unsexed creatures were the only women of my Eastern acquaintance. They were allowed a public existence, now that they offered no temptation to anyone.

The thought that this fate awaited my window beauty disturbed my waking hours. What kind of man would I be if I allowed this to happen? I vowed that it would not. From that time I have visited my love each night, silently communicating this hope of escape. Each night the pact between us grows stronger and more certain. Soon we will be together and she will forget the dream existence of her captivity."[26]

26. For more on the various aspects of this story, see Kabbani (1994); Lewis (1996); Behdad (1994); Apter (1992).

"I was horrified when I heard this story. How could a man live with so many delusions and still escape the madhouse? But, I thought, his madness is of no consequence to me. I forced a smile to reassure my parents: 'Don't fret. People will see that the man is a lunatic and pay him no heed. He is no danger to us.'

But still my parents kept their grave expressions. 'If only it were so, daughter. But we have seen the ways of this world and we recognize dangers which your innocence cannot see. In his foolishness, this man has come to believe that you love him and that you wish for nothing more than to leave us and your home to be with him. Already his actions show his flimsy grasp of reality. Now he will stop at nothing to prove his fantasy true. Sadly, dear daughter, this is a great source of danger to you. This strange man wishes to abduct you, a man who spies upon you in the night and stalks you by day. A man who has concocted an elaborate fantasy to justify his actions. Daughter, we fear for your safety.'

I saw the worry in my parents' faces and understood the pain these untoward events had caused them. Who was this stranger to distress my family in this way? I longed for vengeance, but instead I agreed to my parents' wishes.

For a time I went into semi-hiding: keeping my curtains drawn, travelling with escorts, watching my step. I waited for the crazy man to go away and for the rumours to die down. Then, at last, one night my mother rushed up to my room to exclaim, 'He's gone – he has broken his vigil.'

From then I was free of my unwanted admirer and I went back to living as normal. But still, I kept hearing fragments of his story. I was no longer the girl, but the same elements remained. Whenever white men came to our town, they came to prove this story, because this tale served some need in them.

> The mystique of the forbidden harem stemmed from the vision of it as a segregated space, a polygamous realm, from which all men except the husband (generally conceptualized as the Sultan) and his eunuchs were barred.[27]

They kept the story alive because it allowed them to believe that masculinity could be invincible and endlessly serviced; they looked at us and leered with the titillation of this fantasy. Despite myself, I carry this story now. Whatever I wear, people imagine they see a veil."

Biological racism

The second sister stepped forward to begin her tale.
"Once the white men felt they owned the world. They drew a picture and split the sections up among themselves. Somehow we, the people underneath the coloured segments, never came into the bargain.

The white men came to our homes all ready to rule.

Like my sister, my body was subject to close scrutiny. In the course of their travels the white men had learned other ways of telling stories. Now as well as words they used tools and charts, weights and measures. More than our behaviour, they described the most intimate details of our bodies.[28]

As a girl, my life was filled with talk of the white men and the tremors their actions could send through

27. Lewis (1996): 111.
28. For more on this, see Stepan (1982); Kohn (1995); Gould (1981).

our lives. Like gods, they remained hidden but dict-
ated our destiny. This is what I grew up believing.
I never expected to meet these mythical creatures.

Then one day a group of white men visited our
town. I had heard the hushed talk of grown-ups,
about the new evils creeping up to our doorsteps.
Now here it was, it seemed.

Everyone warned about the dangers of white men.
Our visitors busied themselves with their unpacking,
setting up home in the town centre. We children
gawped openly, the bravest brushing up close to see
if the flaky red came off their skin. I looked along
with the rest, disregarding my parents' warnings.

The white men returned our stares with amused
good humour. They showed us the strange objects in
their bags, letting us touch these things from another
life. In our turn, we let them pet us, stroking our
scalps carefully and making pictures of our image.

Time went on in this manner, and after a while
even our parents stopped noticing the white men in
our midst. They remained absorbed in their recording, hardly touching our lives at all. Perhaps there
was no catastrophe to come.

As I grew, it became obvious that one of the white/
red men had a particular interest in me. He drew
many pictures of me, with pen and ink and with his
magical machine. My parents warned me to stay
away, but my youth was flattered by his attentions
and it gave me pleasure to see so many images of
myself. In truth, I was perturbed by some of the
pictures; these I never mentioned to my family. However much I implored him to draw my face, to make
me look pretty, he insisted on another focus. However much it hurt my pride, he thought me most

beautiful from behind. And this was the view he recorded in a thousand pictures.[29]

In my heart I knew this wasn't right and that my parents' prophecy was coming true. But their prophesies were coming true in many other ways. Life in our town had grown more uncertain.[30] The young people had drifted away to seek prosperity elsewhere. Our way of life seemed to be over. Perhaps the white men had cursed us after all. So when my white man suggested that I visit his home, I didn't hesitate. I knew by now that it was his peculiar science which drew him to me, but I also knew that he was not my future and if his strange fixation paid my way to another life, I had little choice but to go along with him. I cursed my pride and swallowed my fate; and began the journey to Europe.

In Europe I began a life which was truly new. I learned that my patron was not alone in his fixation. I travelled widely, appearing among the most wealthy and educated of the time, and everywhere I met the same intrusive scrutiny of my body. Although the women blushed and giggled with feigned embarrassment and the men talked long and hard about the development of science, they all edged closer when they thought no-one was looking. Not one among them that wasn't hungry for black tail.[31]

I didn't like it, but what could I do? I dreamed of finding work, building a home, escaping from this

29. This interest is discussed famously in Gilman (1986). Also see Levy (1991).
30. For an introduction to the changes brought by Europeans, see Curtin et al. (1995).
31. See Corbey (1995).

circus-freak life, but my patron held me tight in my debt to him. Soon soon, he promised, when your passage is repaid. But it seemed that my debt was infinitely elastic, stretching away into a future which never came.

In the meantime, I met my distorted image on magazine covers and billboards across the city. I tried to escape into anonymity, losing myself in the crowded streets, public places where no-one knew me. But everywhere I was hounded by monster versions of myself. I learned to see myself through the lens of a troubled white gaze and what I saw scared me as well. In this mirror I saw my body distend until it was little more than a set of gargantuan sexual organs. In this picture, nothing could hide this other nature, this physiognomy built to fuck. Here I was mesmeric and disgusting, a bestial beauty whose buttocks overtook her whole body and whose out-size labia hung down heavily between my legs. I was beyond modesty and whatever I did my sex-driven nature must show through. No wonder I felt exposed.

On my travels I learned that other people shared my fate of living spectacle.

'Living members of other societies were frequently included among the exhibits, as in the case of the Ainu brought over for the Japan-British exhibition at the White City in 1910, which was seen by eight million people.'[32]

In that strange intersection between education and titillation, we appeared in a variety of guises. Sometimes the instructive exhibits of popular anthropology, sometimes struggling to appear entertaining beside polar bears and jugglers. At this time, everyone

32. Street (1992): 122.

seemed convinced that all this variety of display must contribute to the greater good of science. Whenever a new bunch of from-far-off people arrived to tour their ethnic zoo 'the anthropologists took advantage of these touring groups to measure and examine them'.[33] Whether they viewed us in our natural habitats or as touring exhibitions, the white men kept right on with their recording, certain that they would learn something eventually. They believed in their own ways of looking.[34] We, of course, were not so certain. The announcements of our various patrons increased our doubts:

> First Introduction in England of the band of 7 Australian boomerang throwers consisting of male and female Queensland Black Trackers and ranting man eaters! The celebrated bushmen from the continent on the other side.
>   Veritable blood-thirsty beasts in distorted human form. With but a glimmering of reason and gift of speech. Worth journeying a 100 miles to see these specimens of the lowest order of man.[35]

We were displayed to provide a counterpoint to white self-definition. We were the distorted human form which they perused in order to feel more perfectly formed themselves. Who knows what they thought

33. Poignant (1992): 51.
34. See Haraway (1989) for more on the development of anthropological and anthropomorphic looking and the connections between primatology and race thinking.
35. From R.A. Cunningham's pamphlet (1884); Poignant (1992): 53.

they saw? To them our sad captivity signalled lack of reason and imperfect speech, barbarity, cannibalism. In their fevered fantasies they maintained that black women copulated with apes, proving that we were closer to these creatures than the white people who should be our kin.[36]

When our famously displayed sister, Saartjie Baartman, the Hottentot Venus, died of her broken heart at the age of 25, after 5 years of exhibition to the rich and famous of Europe, Cuvier himself performed an autopsy.

> She had a way of pouting her lips exactly like what we have observed in the orang-utan. Her movements had something abrupt and fantastical about them, reminding one of those of the ape. Her lips were monstrously large. Her ear was like that of many apes, being small, the tragus weak, and the external border almost obliterated behind. These are animal characters. I have never seen a human head more like an ape than that of this woman.[37]

After such a damning by a man of science, who would not believe that we were less than human, more akin to apes than people? The scholars of our bodies set about showing why this was so.

They scrutinized our private parts and declared that this was the source of the trouble. We were built differently from white women and, so, our anatomy disposed us to lascivious behaviour. Theirs,

36. See Gilman (1986): 231.
37. Quoted in Gould (1981): 86.

of course, disposed them to virginity and domesticity. To show this distinction between pure white
women and voracious black women, our bodies were
displayed, paraded, dissected, measured. All this to
show our animal nature, a biological make-up which
disallowed proper femininity.

Again and again, they maintained that desire
had nothing to do with it, but still, they remained
obsessed with our private parts. Even in the most horrific of circumstances, our genitals were the focus of
activity. They purported to learn from their access to
this source of all human knowledge, the feature which
revealed the biological destinies of each link in the
rigid hierarchy of humanity. But their actions belied
the pretence of learning – we saw that our genitals
represented a lesser and masterable physicality for
them. Their excitement stemmed from the mix of
disgust and aggression which our bodies allowed.

'I also heard of numerous instances in which men
had cut out the private parts of females and stretched
them over the saddle-bows, and wore them over their
hats while riding in the ranks.'[38]

Yet, for all the violence, the stories about our sexual
hungers felt like lust. Why catalogue our immense
capacities, draw pictures of our made-for-sex bodies,
unless they wanted to believe this? I began to see
that, in me, white people saw a cruel mockery of
their own sexual distress.

I am an echo of my sister. Everywhere the stuff of
pornographic fantasy, I am no-one's romantic dream.
Whatever I wear, people imagine they can see my
sexual organs."

38. Excerpt from witness report from massacre at Sand Creek,
Colorado, quoted in Stannard (1992): 133.

Our daughters and our daughters' daughters carry these histories of white scrutiny with their bodies. Whatever they wear, their flesh keeps calling up this past. To hear why you must listen to this next story.

The story of fashion

Once clothing protected your body, denoted your faith or region or status, was chosen by tradition.

It is only later, when some people begin to believe that they are who they choose to be, that clothes take on new meanings. For these people, what you wear and how you wear it become increasingly important. These are the visual clues which let the world know who you are. Of course, care is important.

For a long time, even among the people of the first industrial nations, there was little choice in the clothes worn. People knew your work and your station by your dress, whatever you might choose to convey. The miracle of industrialization did not yield sufficient prosperity for ordinary people to present themselves as they wished. To friends and to strangers, the circumstances of their lives were clear – material constraints allowed them no choice.

Only much later, through some new twist of production, could more people in this part of the world participate in the self-authoring fiction of fashion.[39] This twist happens just at the last anxious, excessive blast of empire. Mass consumerism happens when the first industrial nations feel most certain that they own the world and most anxious about losing it. At

39.   For an account of the advent of mass-produced clothing, see Ewing (1974).

this time they told a story about the health of the nation.

Once there was a land of great power; the influence of this land extended over vast distances. The people of this great land revelled in their empire and saw themselves reflected in its mirror.

Then one day the world faltered. The land of the great found that it could not produce enough soldiers. And what was greatness if not military power?

> The early military setbacks of the British in the Boer War in South Africa in 1899–1900 raised the spectre of a physically degenerating British people, and increased concern that the imperial mission of Britain would be harmed unless the population could be unified and made more fit.[40]

War had become a way of life already; how else could power be maintained? But this was the first time the nation doubted its fighting capacity. Empire had been a confirmation of superiority; who dared to dream that the national stock might prove too weak? But this time, that was the charge. The nation wanted to enter a new war, carve up a fresh territory, and the men of the nation were not up to the job.

Inevitably, the women were to blame. Who else was in charge of the health of the nation? All this talk about women's rights was detracting from the family, so people said.

"Many periodical writers of a medico-scientific bent were busy depicting New Women as the mothers of a degenerate 'race', as the breeders of 'monsters'."[41]

40. Stepan (1982): 118.
41. Ledger (1995): 30.

If the national physique had become too puny then the cause must lie in the nation's homes. Rebuilding must start from there.

The women of the land bore the accusation with shame. Perhaps it was true, perhaps they could do better. Although they were mired in poverty, now it seemed that science could make things better. Obediently, the wives and mothers of the nation set about learning how to improve the race.[42]

They learned about nutrition and tried to incorporate food supplements into their family meals. Not once did they remind their accusers that lack of money, not lack of knowledge, had ruined their tables in the first place. They learned to be proud of their superior race and prized fertility as a gift to the nation. Most importantly, they learned that the human body benefited from care and exercise and that these things were the proper concerns of women. After all, the health of the race depended upon the care of the body and who better to provide this care than the nation's mothers?

The women of the land wanted the world to remain theirs, so they set about their tasks diligently. They formed societies for support. The Women's League of Health and Beauty promoted body care as a route to race improvement and world peace. On the banners of their march through Hyde Park in May 1935, the slogans stated "Women's League of Health and Beauty – Aim, Racial Health".[43] If only

---

42. "Many of its [the interdepartmental committee on physical deterioration] recommendations focused on the conditions of childbearing and rearing, giving pride of place to proposed reforms for the domestic education of mothers." Rowan (1985): 226.

43. Picture in Wilson & Taylor (1989): 75.

women would keep young and beautiful, everything else would fall into place. If the nation floundered, its women were to blame.

This cautionary tale about feminine beauty and feminine duty was repeated in many forms. The degeneration of the race was always due to woman's waywardness. If she had looked after her man, her family, herself, it would never have come to this.

Staying attractive became the duty of patriotic women. Being young and beautiful made you a credit to the race; so beauty becomes a certain sort of racial identity. In this story, exercise is a way of developing the physique of your stock. Keeping pretty and dressing nicely is a way of promoting reproduction and propagating the race. Working hard to be the best kind of sexual object you could be was a way that women could ward off racial degeneration. There was no place for sluts in the land of the great.

Fashion – the practice of mass consumption which becomes possible for some regions in the twentieth century – promotes a regime of self-care which coincides with the project of nation-building. This remains true until the advent of "youth" and its attendant cultures of dissent.[44] High fashion remained a technique of whiteness.

Until now.

Contemporary exotica

The model resumed her tale:

I grew up with this white-girl version of glamour. I saw the models who wore fashion, and they were

44. See, famously, S. Hall & T. Jefferson, *Resistance through rituals* (1976).

nothing like me. Instead they were the archetypal signs of a very particular gendered technology of the self. This was how we learned what white girls should be.

> Modelling came to epitomise dominant charac-
> teristics of western femininity: the importance
> of appearance; fetishisation of the body; mani-
> pulation and moulding of the body; the discip-
> line and labour associated with "beauty" and
> body maintenance; the equation of youth with
> femininity; and feminine lifestyles.[45]

To acquire these skills through consumption and discipline was to aspire to a version of femininity in the
service of the nations of the West. Of course, the
iconic role-models of this process reflected this desire
to remake the West, beautifully. It was only after the
disturbance of youth culture that I could represent
an alluring image of fashionable femininity. After
the explosions of youth, even made-for-profit fashion pretended to be underground, disobedient, off-
limits. My dark skin, with its echo of harem and
animal, was a handy shorthand for all these suggestions. For more wholesome looks, there was still an
abundance of child-faced blondes. The big markets
continued to belong to them.

   ". . . most of the successful models have conformed
to western stereotypes of beauty because 'in every
country, blond hair and blue eyes sell'."[46] But now,
there was space for those strange creatures of ultra-
femininity, models, to be more diverse. My skin gave

45.   Craik (1994): 70.
46.   Ibid.: 87.

me my own niche market; less lucrative, but still employed. So I worked, but still did not know the answers to my questions. I was left scrutinizing my own look. Perfecting my own specialism and obsessed with the connotations of my own body.

I thought that my whole life had come to take meaning from how I looked. The uncertain knowledges of vision made me what I was: encountering the pitfalls already described, hiding a whole world of messy social relations behind the quick fix of an image. But after all the stories, I began to think that maybe something else was going on. Everything showed how limited the insights of vision could be, told me that believing in the easy lessons of a clear picture would distort my understanding of the world. But if my job was not about looking, what was it about? I came across another account of my job:

"Successful models made it because of the way they wore the clothes, not because of their looks. Their bodies were traded as commodities, separated from their sense of self."[47]

This confirmed my suspicions; they were never looking at me, I was never the pretty one in my own right. What mattered was my ability as a sales vehicle; the interaction between my flesh and the cloth and what this might persuade the customer to do, the money they might part with. It was looking which decided the success of this venture, but not my look.

After hearing so many stories about what could and could not be seen, I found that understanding the images I formed did not unlock the secret of my world. I longed for a more solid understanding. If the looking world reduced us to surface, then the

47. Ibid.: 79.

stories of the commodity equally could not register any depth to our work. These jobs of display and service could be assigned an implied value; but, as always, the implications were vague. The stories of *Capital* promised to uncover the values of labour hidden in the commodity; but without some marker of this process of commodification, some quantifiable entity which changed hands, the magical equations which extracted the value of labour could not be formulated. We were left performing work which, although it was excessively visible, could not be registered as valuable. For all our pretty surfaces, our business lacked weight and depth. What I needed was a story to link the processes of looking with the experiences of flesh, because everyone knew that "fashion models epitomise the objectification of the body – being 'used as a piece of flesh'".[48]

To hear the meat of this argument you must listen to my sister's tale.

So ends our third set of tales. In these tales we sense a narrative beyond the easy stories of first sight. We hear of the hidden labours which constitute our social world and the blurred boundaries between home and work which aid exploitation. We also hear of the dangerous fantasies of sight which knock into all our real lives. Desperate to resist these abstractions, we yearn to reveal the delicacy of flesh. This is where our next tale begins.

48. Ibid.: 76.

Further reading

For more on the damage of white beauty myths, see *The bluest eye*, by Toni Morrison.

For more on Western fascination with the harem, see *Imperial fictions*, by Rana Kabbani.

For more on biological racism and black women's bodies, see "Black bodies, white bodies" by Sander Gilman, in *Race, culture and difference*, by J. Donald and A. Rattansi.

To read more about the West's deep need to display, see *Ephemeral vistas*, by Paul Greenhalgh, and *Anthropology and photography 1860–1920*, by Elizabeth Edwards.

For more on the particular place of fashion in Western modernity, see *Adorned in dreams*, by Elizabeth Wilson.

CHAPTER 4

The sportswoman's tale

If sight obscures so much, how can we reach the meanings of flesh?

In these tales we hear of the disrespected world of flesh. Unlike the immediately seen values of the visible, flesh conceals a range of attributes. We hear of the power of the trained body and the strange relations between sporting achievement and national glory. In some arenas, physical prowess is championed; yet the story of white male ascendancy called modernity constrains and conceals the body in the name of progress. In this story, bodies are the business of the other: other genitals, other skins, other places, other practices. Becoming human in this regime means giving up these unruly relations to flesh; these are the stories of how white men tried to impose their vision of physical order on us all.

The second woman came forward and began her tale.

I, too, have led a life of great variety. I grew up in a land where my people were viewed as perpetual outsiders. At times of patriotic celebration, we barred our windows against the excesses of patriotic fervour. The insults which our neighbours daubed on our walls told us to "go home"; their nation would never belong to us.[1]

I grew up through this sporadic terror, learning my lessons and discovering my talents. At prize-days, I collected the rewards of my achievements for myself, my family, my community of outsiders, but never for this nation which told me that I did not belong. When I trained for competition, I strived to

1. For more on the ways that "banal nationalism" is flagged in everyday life, see Billig (1995).

spite the expectations of king and country. At school my teachers encouraged my endeavours, but never suggested that my talent was any contribution to national achievement. However good I got, it seemed, I would never win the love of my hate-filled neighbours. When I won, it was only for myself and my own. The people of my family's adopted home never imagined that I belonged to their community.

Instead, the public face of the nation was suffused with longing for the past. Stories of national achievement dwelt on times before the arrival of new people. Public monuments recorded the great victories of times long gone. Empire and monarchy, industry and military – this was the stuff of national heritage. People believed that this past time of victory represented an easy idyll of mono-ethnicity. In hating us, they forgot the differences between themselves, and pictured grace as the happy moment just before the fall of our arrival.

The nation knew itself through stories which no-one had lived; no-one recognized their own life in these shared fictions of nationhood; none of this was about contemporary living. Instead, the nation constituted itself through a conveniently vague and portable plot-line of greatness, heroism and victory. Messy details of time and place could be inserted to suit the occasion, or left open to heighten the mythic resonance. The detail which remained across versions was that we were not present. Obviously, we were not the heroes and victors; but in these stories, neither were we the subjugated and civilized, or even the bystanders and observers. This myth of nation had to erase us totally. Otherwise the plot could not run and the feel could not be good. When I was a child, imperialism had become a distant and dirty word even to white people; so, of course, there had to be new names for national achievement.

We were taught that our histories of buffoonery and under-development were separate from their heritage of valour and innovation. Nowhere did they mention the "multiplier effects" of the slavery and colonialism on Europe's development. They did not say that "the benefits of foreign contacts extended to many areas of European life not directly connected with foreign trade, and the whole society was better equipped for its own internal development".[2]

In their account, it was only our good fortune which allowed us to bump into white people and escape into their hospitality. Now there was a chance that we would prosper under their care.

At school all my lessons reinforced this one story: that we were lucky to be here and must know our place. When I stumbled over the strange stories of white victory, this was taken as evidence of my backwardness.

"Don't worry", my teachers smiled, "not everyone has a head for books," and they pushed me out onto the sports field again. There I realized that many of the children of our community were devoting their energies to sporting achievement. None of us could mouth the celebrations of white victory successfully.

The kinder teachers tried to explain. *Physical recreation can provide both social involvement and relief from the pressures of living in a rundown environment.* "You need to let off steam. We know things are bad around here – nothing to do, nowhere to go. Sport is what you are good at, it gives you something to do with your time, something to work

2.   Rodney (1972): 108.

towards. Better than hanging around the streets getting into trouble." *To black young people, sports recreation can provide them with an incentive which provides real hope of escaping from that environment and achieving a new awareness and recognition in British society.* "This is your chance to really be somebody, to prove all those racists wrong. Maybe if you train hard you could represent England in competition – get rich – buy your mum nice things – be on television – get some respect. What other chances do you have? You won't get a job around here; you'll be serving a prison sentence before you're 20. At least if you work at your sport you won't end up wasting your life." *Sports development among young people from ethnic minorities has had a positive effect in their recreational patterns of behaviour.* "You know how heavy the police are around here; sport will keep you out of that."[3]

We listened politely; these were the kind teachers after all. We guessed that they were clutching at straws, could hear the edge of fear in their voices even though they liked us. As we grew older we listened more carefully to the news reports which spoke so indirectly about us.

With the growing public expenditure cuts and rising unemployment, many school leavers of ethnic minority origins will need to turn to an activity that is self-rewarding and through which they can seek status and self-confidence. We already understood that things were not getting better and the white people's capacity for victory seemed to be exhausted. Now we also understood that it was we who would bear the brunt of this. We were the ones being

3. Italics from Stephenson (1979) para 9, p. 59.

prepared for lives of disappointment and deprivation. Hearing the warning we worked harder to love our own strength, speed, bodies, selves. *Sports development will become an even more crucial factor among these groups of young people if they are not to turn through desperation and frustration to petty crime, violence and drug abuse.* No-one expected us to have any capacity for self-love. On the contrary, self-destruction was our destiny: beckoning at every corner, written in our family tree. Only sport could make us into something else; people with a sense of their own value. The value which the world around us denied. *Black minority groups may have a great deal of aggressive energy to burn up as a result of poor educational advancement and racism.* So it was the injustice we faced which enhanced our physical performance. Sport channelled our righteous anger into a prize for our tormenters. *There is evidence that participation in physical activity by ethnic minority groups within this country does not only contribute to their physical well-being but also to their psychological maturity.*[4]

For many years I pursued this route to respect. Over time my prowess increased: I won inter-school championships, played for the county, spent summer fortnights at training camps for talented youngsters. Unlike my troublesome peers, I was a credit to the nation. I accepted the back-handed compliments and the unsociable hours, and trained even harder. Maybe my trainers would come to see that we were capable of application after all.

Then, suddenly, one day my psychological maturity snapped and I gave up the youth championships,

4.   Ibid., para 9.4, p. 59.

the county finals, the school colours, gave up sport altogether. I wanted to understand how my people could be so despised and yet so celebrated. How could we be denied the benefits of citizenship, but represent the nation? Be inferior and superior at the same time?

When I won a competition, how could it become a white victory before my eyes? I asked everyone – old and young, far and wide. I heard many stories of hope and pain, but my question remained unanswered. Then, at last, in my search for understanding, I came across an old woman, her body contorted by the athletic excesses of her youth.

"Listen, young woman", she said, "I walked the path of your life many years ago, I know its turns and pitfalls. The story I tell will help you to understand."

This is the tale she told.

The story of the strong-bodied nation

"In a time of a great hardship a king began to doubt his own powers. He no longer felt powerful, sovereign, source of benevolence and fear. In the face of his people's troubles he felt only helpless. The time-honoured contract between ruler and ruled seemed to crumble away – leaving everyone lost and lonely.

The king was eaten up with fear. His nights were shaken up with dreams of falling, failing, drowning, wailing. In his dreams he fled endlessly from crushing boulders, devouring monsters. His bones broke and his flesh tore and he woke up whimpering, not yet free. By day the king twitched and shivered – still possessed. He ate little and trusted no-one. His advisers began to despair, of both king and country.

Then one day, after many months of inaction, the king ordered the court to assemble. When the chamber was full, the king commenced his address:

'Many of you have noticed a change in me – and it is true that I have neglected the duties of kingship. Now I have no choice but to make my fears public. I fear our nation is not what it was, that it has ceased to be a nation at all. My subjects seem to have broken their bonds to each other. Where once there was kinship, co-operation, community, I now see only violence and criminality. My people have turned against each other. More frighteningly still, they have turned against me. The crown calls no respect these days. Instead, I must protect myself against the many-pronged attacks by my people. Forever on the defensive, I try to make my power absolute, become despotic, tyrannical. I display my capacity for cruelty and am shocked at the spectacle.

None of this can go on if we are to survive. As king it is my duty to rule. But how can I rule subjects who have forgotten loyalty? No point making decrees without an audience. My subjects must remember their connection to each other, but my speeches cannot convince them of this forgotten fact. To remember they must first recover their lost allegiance to me. They must become subjects once more.

We will hold a tournament to elect a champion citizen. Only sweat and exertion can bring us back to healthy nationhood. As mighty ruler, chosen by god to rule over man, I challenge the citizenry to prove themselves. Trials will be held publicly, so the populace may judge the feats of the competitors. Send forth the proclamations – heats will begin in a week.'

The contest took place in a blur of celebration. As the king had planned, the nation was reinvigorated by this surge of physical exertion. People forgot the gloomy circumstances of their everyday lives and let themselves get swept away by the unfocused optimism of the spectacle. Instead of hating the privations of their lives and hating their rulers for allowing them, people bought flags and bunting and started to feel proud about nothing in particular all over again.

On the last day of the tournament, only the finest athletes remained. Each had their event of choice, the thing at which they excelled, but today the competition would be decided on the grounds of overall prowess. The winner today would represent the height of human physicality – strength with agility, speed with endurance – this would be a test of what the human body could achieve.

No-one was disappointed by the display of the contest. Each athlete amazed the audience with his or her bodily discipline. Each demanded respect for what he or she had endured. But at the final test, there was no dispute about the day's champion. The chestnut-coloured woman who stepped forward to claim her trophy had out-run, out-jumped, out-lifted all her opponents and each acknowledged that the prize was hers by right.

As the king decked the woman with the garlands of victory, he announced, 'I name this woman my most loyal and valued subject – her athletic prowess is a gift to the nation.' And, at this moment, the crowd believed him and rejoiced. But as the winner turned to begin her victory speech, a different feeling entered the stadium.

'Thank you, your majesty. I have trained for many years to reach this level of fitness and I am flattered that you regard my achievement as your own.

In this land my people suffer much persecution and violence and as a child I had no sense of belonging here. My family longed to return to their homeland and never called this country of yours home.

Even as a young athlete I found that I was denied training facilities in favour of my white peers. When I won tournaments, my trainers showed their disappointment at the failure of their white favourites and their faint praise cut my spirit. Later, when I achieved wider recognition in international competition, I found that no amount of media coverage would erase the colour of my skin. At the height of my fame, my family still lived in terror. No matter what I won, our windows kept shattering, our walls kept shouting abuse, our letterbox kept shitting into the hallway. Wherever I parked my car, I returned to swastikas scratched into its paintwork. However glamorous I appeared on TV and in magazines, I could still be tripped up by the places which would never allow me entry.[5]

Whatever I represented for the moment of competition did not extend to the rest of my life or the lives of my loved ones. When at last I saw this, I vowed to retire from competition. Why torture my body for this fiction of citizenship?

I have hidden myself away for a number of years now. Reporters have stopped bothering me and I have been free to follow my own training programme, a self-taught course of spiritual and physical development. It is this alternative training which has allowed me to win your tournament. My prize for this feat is the chance to share the story of my enlightenment and to explain the strange double status of dark flesh.'

5.   "Olympic athlete Michelle Griffith says she is proud to be black British after receiving racist hate mail saying she was not fit to represent Britain": entry for 2 August 1996 in Calendar of race and resistance, CARF no. 34, October/November 1996.

Although never allowed to be beautiful, black flesh has been accorded value, of a sort. In a time when white men and women learned new relations to their bodies, we became the mark of the physical to them. The re-ordering of their bodies led them to view ours with increasing anxiety and envy. These are the stories of those times.

The tale of the self-fashioning individual

When Scheherazade tells her stories we all know that storytelling is a strategy for the disempowered. The king has no need of a story to explain his actions – his presence is assured by his power as monarch; he doesn't have to talk himself into recognition.

Scheherazade, on the other hand, relies on her voice and her imagination for re-entry into the land of the living. Although she is the vizier's daughter, before the king her class status is reduced to that of subject. As a woman the vision of the king reduces Scheherazade to another example of female treachery and sexual excess – a status which the power of the king translates into deflowering and death. To survive in the world as a sexual being, to prolong her life beyond the dangerous awakening of sexual contact with men, Scheherazade has to talk herself into a different status. The performance of her storytelling has to make her seem something other than a threatening sexual hunger.

The ability to tell stories isn't about narrating the self here; Scheherazade does not tell tales which consolidate her own identity. She is as elusive on the thousand-and-first night as she is on the first. But the ability to tell stories, rather than the content of the stories themselves, is eventually what elevates

Scheherazade from the status of unruly cunt. And in the story her elevation is the elevation of all women. She stops the killing and reintroduces a gap between sex and violence in heterosexual relations.

Scheherazade does not tell stories about herself – but her narration alters what she can be. She tells that particular type of story which changes who you are in the world.[6]

Not all storytelling is like this. The histories of white men are packed full of stories, endless interlocking narratives, replaying the same themes again and again. This monotonous and seemingly unavoidable tale never seems to change, itself or anything else. Of course, when we look more closely, we can see that it isn't just one story; we ask ourselves:

"Can we legitimately speak of 'the European practice of representation'? There were profound differences among the national cultures and religious faiths of the various European voyagers, differences that decisively shaped both perceptions and representations."[7]

There are many different traditions hidden in this story of Europeans – if we forget this we are in danger of believing that there is really such a thing as white – but in the flood of information it can feel like the same story is being told again and again. However much attention we pay to the niceties of

6. Fedwa Malti-Douglas ((1991): 24) argues that Scheherazade proposes an alternative model of learning: "Schariyar's insistence that he must 'see' shows the force that is driving him. Again it is the fulfillment of this improper desire that sets in motion drastic narrative events . . . Shahrazad's path is clearly opposite. She narrates a text. Hers is the oral approach, in which the male becomes the auditor, the passive partner. Sight and hearing are cast in the frame of the *Nights* as alternative ways of acquiring knowledge".

7. Greenblatt (1980): 8.

cultural particularity, the stories of the powerful are always stories about themselves: even if they do not figure explicitly, the story is always about how right their privilege is.

"A class of people cannot produce themselves as a ruling class without setting themselves off against certain others. Their hegemony entails possession of the key cultural terms determining what are the right and wrong ways to be a human being."[8]

So you tell these stories to make sure that things stay as they are. This is that endlessly familiar story about reason, truth, justice and strength belonging to the already powerful, and the anarchic dangers of the weak body and wicked lies lying with the already dispossessed. This isn't about changing anything; the whole point is to keep everything the same. But hidden inside these stories which seem to keep everything the same is a never-completed set of transformations: the powerful never quite reach absolute and unquestionable power. In fact, the white men tell stories to cement a state of being which must be shaky, no matter what their stories say. The anxiety of never reaching the end goal of total mastery crops up in the stories again and again.

The white men tell their history as a process of perfecting these stories of being. They become modern as they realize that the stories matter and this growing into modernity is also about becoming white. Let's think about modernity in the broadest terms:

... that general period emerging from the sixteenth century in the historical formation of what only relatively recently has come to be called

8.   Armstrong & Tennenhouse (1989): 24.

"the West". This general self-understanding becomes self-conscious in the seventeenth century, reaching intellectual and material maturity in the Enlightenment, and solidifies as Western world hegemony the following century.[9]

You can learn all this by reading the books written by white men. Like all good secrets, it doesn't need to be hidden. Everyone admits that modernity means European ascendancy; the time when whiteness starts to mark the globe. The date of this new dawn is a point of contention: how can you pinpoint a change in consciousness, particularly one so uneven and ongoing? But across accounts certain themes recur. You could tell this as one story.

This is one of the stories it might be.

One day the white man woke up and decided to be something new.

"Things are not what they were", he said to himself. "I know now that I am the centre of my own destiny and I intend to let the rest of the world know too."

Previously the white man had cowered before nature, in fear of an all-powerful and irrational god. Now he remade himself in this image. He remade himself as an image.

"In the sixteenth century there appears to be an increased self-consciousness about the fashioning of human identity as a manipulable, artful process."[10]

Like all peoples, the white men had told stories before, but then the stories hid their own construction. Unlike Scheherazade, these people could not

9. Goldberg (1993): 3.
10. Greenblatt (1980): 2.

see the performance of storytelling as a valued skill or route to social elevation. They liked their stories to look like something else, divine truth or natural law, but not the suspect achievement of human innovation.

With the shift into the modern, white men begin to see their own stories, and even, after a while, to love them. The stories stop being a weakness and become a source of possibility. If telling stories made you who you were, then it was possible to be many things and to learn with practice to be more and varied. Instead of being deceitful, the art of self-fashioning becomes an aspiration of the most respectable of men. From way back then to right up until yesterday.

There are lots of famous versions of this story. We could say that with the Reformation it becomes possible to negotiate your own faith. Instead of being subject to the whims of a corrupt Church bureaucracy, now the thinking believer can consider the tenets of faith for himself. Or we could say that with the Copernican revolution the revelation that the Earth does not centre the universe raises Western man to the paradoxical power of investigating his own comparative insignificance – cue science and its attendant ambivalence.[11] We could say that the rise of mercantilism creates a new type of economic man; now trade feeds those nearly born entities, European nations, until no economic activity can be free of these larger concerns. Now even everyday business is

11. "The notion that man occupies an exalted place in the Universe, and the opposite idea that he is a small and powerless creature at the mercy of far stronger divine, natural, or historical forces, are not only contrary to each other but also complementary." Oskar (1979): 180.

conducted in service to a higher goal. We could say that the advent of improved techniques of navigation and map-making allow the famously European project of circumnavigation; rightly or wrongly, Europeans can now imagine themselves to be global subjects.[12] What links the chapters is the belief that European man can plot his own narrative upon the world; the ability to author becomes a whole new way of thinking about your self.

More recent chroniclers of this time of change acknowledge their affinity with these forebears. The idea that the ability to control self-representation gives you power over who you are and can be still has resonance today.

"It seemed to me the very hallmark of the Renaissance that middle-class and aristocratic males began to feel that they possessed such shaping power over their lives, and I saw this power and the freedom it implied as an important element in my own sense of self."[13]

We believe that the ongoing performance of our own particular story makes us what we are. The agency of self-shaping, whatever its constraints, is a key mark of being human for us. We believe in it. This is how we imagine ourselves, through the story of self we present. For us moderns, storytelling becomes a way of life.

However, the triumphant saga of self-fashioning is just one section of a larger cycle of overlapping stories.

12. Mary Louise Pratt explains circumnavigation as "a double deed that consists of sailing round the world then writing an account of it (the term 'circumnavigation' refers either to the voyage or the book)": (1992): 29.

13. Greenblatt (1980): 256.

All of this business remade the white man's body. Without even noticing, he began to feel quite different. Now when his cock twitched, he jumped back in alarm and looked around for someone to blame. After all, to be in control of your own destiny you have to be in control of yourself. It stands to reason.

In the land of self-fashioning white men, they told a story to show what this meant.

The story of the good woman and the bad woman

This was the story they told.

Once there were two sisters, perfect echoes of each other, except that one was good and one was bad. As was the custom, their father pledged them in marriage to a merchant of the city. At first the merchant resisted: "Why should I take your ill-natured daughter to be my wife? Better to marry the good daughter alone. Let some other fool take the other one."

The father replied, "It is true that my daughters are different in temperament. Yet in both I see that their mother lives, her spirit is in both their characters. I will make you a bargain. If you can pick out my good daughter from the pair, then you may marry her alone, the girl of your choice. But if you are not certain that you can identify virtue, then you must marry both and with them the whole range of female ways."

The merchant looked anxiously at the daughters, each of whom remained perfectly silent. He didn't want to take the bad daughter, but he could see no difference between the girls. What if he made the wrong choice? Better two wives than only one bad wife, and anyway, perhaps the good daughter would keep her sister in check? The merchant made his decision.

"You have me beaten. I will make a home for them both." The father was pleased with this, because he loved both his daughters and wished them both prosperity. The daughters were pleased because they loved each other more than any man and were not ready to forsake the companionship of sisterhood for the loneliness of wifedom. The merchant was pleased because he was sure of one good wife and, in his heart, he believed that he could tame any woman, however bad.

After the wedding the merchant and the sisters set up home on the edge of the city. They lived peaceably, but the merchant remained anxious. Each day he watched his wives carefully, trying to discern good from bad, but months later he was still not certain. Married life did reveal differences in his wives' temperaments, it is true, but the merchant could not be sure who was good and who was bad. He found that each wife brought him satisfaction and distress in equal measure.

In bed the merchant found that one wife pleased him greatly, while the other pleased him not at all. His first wife welcomed him to bed with boundless enthusiasm. Her appetite seemed endless, yet each encounter increased the merchant's satisfaction. With her he felt desirable – the object of her lust. Sex was not an imposition with this wife.

With the other wife it was a different story. In bed she lay quite still, gritting her teeth against his advances. Her anxiety wilted the merchant's desire, until he ceased to approach her altogether. As he crept back to the more welcoming arms of his other wife, the merchant worried about the peace of his home. Women being women, this would surely cause trouble. Even if she didn't want him, the one wife was bound to be jealous of the sexual monopoly of the other. Pleasures had their price, after all.

But, to his surprise, there was no jealousy between the sisters. If anything, they were jealous of each other's time and company. One wife was happy to couple with her husband daily, while the other was happy to be relieved of this duty by her sister; both remained happy as long as they had time together, away from their husband, and a place to share their giggled secrets. Although perplexed, the merchant was content with this arrangement. However, he could still not split good wife from bad.

Still, the merchant had reason to be glad that he had taken two wives, even if one was wife in name only. His bed-wife proved indifferent to the demands of keeping house. Her night-time energy turned to sloth by day and she lolled in bed until noon, waking only to perform her toilet and run out to the marketplace where she idled away her day with other young wastrels of the town. However thick the dust lay, the merchant could not persuade her of the benefits of housework. She laughed away his entreaties to be a proper wife by pulling him back into bed, a ploy which worked every time. Yet after each of these pleasures the merchant arose again with a sense of unease – surely a wife must have some sense of duty? At these times he thanked fortune for the blessing of his other wife.

His day-wife might have no taste for sex, but she kept house like an angel. Waking early in the morning, she cleaned with superhuman energy, cooked an array of delicacies to tempt her husband's attention away from moderation, attended to the business of their home as if this was the vocation for which she was born. Unlike her sister, she wasted no time flirting in the street and her modest appearance attracted no suspect attentions. When the merchant arrived home exhausted from his day's trade, the welcome she prepared in his home warmed his heart and he was filled with a grateful love for her dutiful nature.

Sometimes the merchant believed that this, his day-wife, was the good daughter. She was so accomplished, so modest, so unassuming. Surely this is what a woman should be? Yet no sooner had his night-wife returned from her day of dilly-dallying to throw herself into his arms than he was once again filled with doubt. The very sight of her licked his body with lust and the merchant thought: surely a truly dutiful wife must also perform the duties of the night? And once again he fell upon the body of his night-wife, certain that this was what a woman should be.

Time went on in this way. Each day and each night the merchant revised his opinion of what a woman should be – and still he could not tell the good daughter from the bad. The sisters remained close, despite their different temperaments. They shared secrets which the merchant could only guess at, shutting the door behind them to retreat into girlish ways. The merchant wondered at their lack of rivalry; they cared more for each other than for him, it seemed. What kinds of wives were these? Stuck in childhood, with no regard for the property rights of adult womanhood?

Still, puzzlement aside, the merchant was content with his life. His two wives served him well, tending to his body and his home. After a while, he stopped believing that he had been tricked at all. It didn't seem to matter which was the good daughter and which the bad; together they made a perfect wife. What husband could be happier?

One evening the merchant arrived back from work more eager than ever for the comforts of his home. Yet when he stepped in the door no wives rushed to meet him, with hot breast or hot tea. The house was quite still. When the merchant searched the kitchen, he found that the utensils which his day-wife made such clever use of had been packed up and taken away. In the bedroom, the merchant found that the pretty temptations of his night-wife's craft had also gone. The house had been cleared of the props of both day and night wives. The merchant never saw either wife again. The question of which was good and which was bad was never answered.

Much later, the merchant heard a story from a travelling trader. In a distant town two sisters kept house together, without the authorization of any man. One sister spent her days cooking, rare delicacies which she distributed to small children and passing strangers for no more than the pleasurable payment of their surprise. The other sister spent her days in the marketplace, talking and laughing with whoever passed and needed company. Each night she chose the most lonely among her companions to take home to bed and gave away sex for the sweetness of friendship. Both sisters saved their best love for each other and lived together very happily.

On hearing this story the blood of the merchant's uncared-for body froze with bitterness.

The self-fashioning white men exchanged this tale as a warning to each other. Of course, in every mouth the tale altered slightly. Some spoke at length of the importance of the marriage bed and heavily hinted at the badness of the day-wife. Others equated femininity with domesticity and accused the night-wife of dangerous impropriety. Sometimes the stories implied that women had no control over the temptations they represented and that the badness, such as it was, lay in men's weakness. More often, both wives were pilloried for their disobedience and deception and the poor merchant was held up as a sad example of what any man might become.

Whatever the version, the self-fashioning white men understood that this was a cautionary tale. However much energy they devoted to the narrative of their rational minds, women remained tied to the different demands of the body. And this embodiment of another set of possibilities was a constant distraction to the white men. The best efforts of self-fashioning could not completely escape this temptation. The call of the body might always disrupt the most carefully self-authored destiny.

The answer, as the men saw it, was to keep women in their place. As long as daughters kept to the kitchen and the bedroom, bodily business could be kept safe indoors. As long as this happened, the stories of self-fashioning could have free reign in public. And keeping women confined was a small price to pay for the progress of humanity.

Modernity splits respectable life into private and public sectors, and designates appropriately gendered behaviour for each sphere. While the white men discovered the pleasures of self-fashioning their public lives, women's tales remained no more than domestic tittle-tattle. Each had their proper sphere of experience. As we shall see, when the less-than-human break these rules, this becomes another proof of their less-than-humanness. No body, any body, ever gets over this distorting discipline at the centre of Western culture. We will hear later of the contortions the body undergoes in the rise to power of European people.

For now, let us return to the powers of different narratives. Despite the stories, not everyone became self-fashioning. Even in the eyes of the white men, some people were subject to a greater destiny, in thrall to an order beyond themselves. Of course, we were those people. Modernity does not free us into our own agency. Instead we become the limit of modern possibilities.

In many ways, this was still in the realm of looking. Our flesh was a source of disgusted delectation. Through us the white men relived the possibilities of the body, but felt none of the pain of its limit. We remained the object of someone else's narrating gaze.

Among ourselves we tell different stories about this time.

Some talk of the white man's interest in our bodies. Their stories are filled with depictions of us: of our deformity, our excesses, our downright difference from them. They could never stop looking at us, gripped by their own titillating fictions. They were amazed by both the similarity and difference of our bodies, could never decide whether they wanted to touch or destroy, longed for a return to the physical and thought we were it.

Others say that the white men cared nothing for our bodies, breaking them cruelly as proof of their carelessness. To prove their power, they tormented us. To increase their profit, they exploited us. To make themselves feel better, they tortured us. Our flesh took the shape of their unfeeling whims.

Others still believe both sets of stories. Under the power of the white man our bodies suffered beyond endurance. In the quest to extend their dominance our rulers forgot the limits of humanity. They could envisage no hardship too great, no task too mammoth. In us, they came to believe that human flesh is truly malleable; subject to no destiny but the march of human progress. However, this belief required that they should ignore our pain, discount our wounds, devalue our lives.

Even as we came to represent the immense capacities of human flesh, we were destined to be less than human. How else could our pain go unheeded?

Trade

When the white men began to view the globe as their domain, they marked its contours with the story of trade. Between 1445 and 1870 the bodies of untold millions of Africans were transformed into that tradable thing, a chattel. Their enslaved labour created the Europe of global ascendancy – although this labour was allotted no value, exchanged for no wage. Instead, these bodies assumed the dangerous status of free muscle-power, a fantasy of strength without needs or feelings. The secret stories of this time haunt our collective memory.

> he purchased John, for the express purpose, as he said, "to tame the d_d nigger." After the purchase, he took him to a blacksmith's shop, and had a ball and chain fastened to his leg, and then put him to driving a yoke of oxen, and kept him at hard labor, until the iron around

his leg was so worn into the flesh, that it was thought mortification would ensue. In addition to this, John told me that his master whipped him regularly three times a week for the first two months: – and all this to *"tame him"*.[14]

Between ourselves, we swapped these horror stories. It was important to remember each detail; otherwise, what they said was true, our sufferings were nothing at all. So among ourselves we memorized each stage of tortures inflicted on our long-gone kin. How else could we learn to read the white men's minds? But too often the fearsome stories raised more questions than they answered. What was it in us that the white man was trying to tame? Something so frightening that iron chains and dead weights could not hold it, that was still there when the flesh rotted on a living body. Something in us that threatened even when we laboured like animals, when we were beaten beyond endurance. Something that needed taming even when we were bought and sold as property. Nothing in the stories let us know what that imagined threat could be. What was it that the white people saw which made them act like that? What kind of fear could allow such cruelty?

We used the stories to anticipate what might happen. Perhaps the sight of our dark-skinned bodies triggered some hidden memory, so that they must forever try to tame us in order to tame something in themselves. Perhaps the strain of erasing their own bodies forced them to mutilate ours, taming the threat

14.   From the narrative life of William W. Brown in Katz (1968): 28–9.

of their own disowned physicality. Perhaps they secretly understood that no law could justify the buying and selling of other human beings, and what they tamed was their fear of punishment. Perhaps they were frightened of dying and managed mortality by slowly killing us. Whichever train of speculation we followed, the lesson remained the same. The self-proclaimed people of the mind feared flesh and this fear signalled danger for us, those designated as the people of the body.

When we told our warning stories, we reminded each other that there was no limit to the pain which might be inflicted. It seemed that only endless cruelty could prove that bodies didn't really matter.

> One day, before he went to his summer seat, he called a man to him, stripped and whipped him so that the blood ran from his body like water thrown upon him in cupfuls, and when the man stepped from the place where he had been tied, the blood ran out of his shoes. He said to the man, "You will remember me now, sir, as long as you live." The man answered, "Yes, master, I will."[15]

In their hands, our bodies cease to be sensate. There is no way for them to see our pain. Instead, bodies become things apart from humanity. Blood flows like water, but the whipper sees only his power, not his victim's pain. The important thing is to make the blood-dripping man remember him, the man with

15. From "My life in the south", Jacob Stroyer in Katz (1968): 29.

the whip. He, the man with the whip, cannot inflict enough suffering to make him sure of his own power. He still needs the confirmation of the whipped man's memory.

Try as we might, no twist of narrative could make us understand the logic of these tortures. A thousand actions told us that, in the white people's eyes, we were worth nothing, no more than lumps of flesh without the sense to suffer. Yet the white people feared for their position of power. They asked for our recognition, an acknowledgement that we were, indeed, subjugated. No amount of mindless violence can make them certain of this, so they must keep on inflicting more and greater wounds. Otherwise, who will recognize their control? Who will remember?

The stories we swapped warned of this double status, at once worthless piece of meat and essential witness to the exercise of power. Although less than human in white eyes, they gauged their humanity through us. Somehow our tribulations were important to their sense of self. We marked the limit and example of their most formative stories: the empire of the mind, the malleability of the flesh, the fear of sex and death – all these stories had their kinks and contradictions played out on our bodies.

If reason must be disembodied, our bodies were cut apart to prove this was so. Because, in their eyes, we were not reasonable, our bodies became worthless meat. Humanity was more than meat, so when we were butchered it showed that we were less than human. White violence reduced us to a collection of wounds and our flesh showed its frailty, craving pleasure, suffering pain. Forever beaten back into our bodies, we became the people of the body, unable to escape into the transcendent life of the mind. At the hands of white men, we became all the things which their self-narrations of grandeur placed outside the terrain of humanity.

> [the slaveholder] does not contemplate slaves as human beings, consequently does not *treat* them as such; and with entire indifference sees them suffer privations and writhe under blows, which, if inflicted upon whites, would fill him with horror and indignation. He regards that as good treatment of slaves.[16]

Not only did we fail to qualify as human; our treatment tested the boundary between humanity and others. We were a demonstration of what human beings could not bear, but we could bear it because we did not qualify as human. In the narratives of white men, these experiments did not even count as cruelty, because this was not the suffering of fellow human beings. Instead, we were this other species, creatures who not only deserved violence, but who benefited from it. Only torture could bring us closer to the white man.

Suffering white violence

The advent of dreams of self-authorship came about through a range of factors, a change in knowledge, consciousness and material possibility. But the initial burst of optimism soon stumbled against the difficulties of making stories true. Self-fashioning truly took shape

16. From T.D. Weld (1968): 110.

in a new era of European ascendancy: of discovery, trade and expansion, but also for us, of invasion, subjugation and violence.

The white men learned that the right actions could make their stories of self-authored destiny true. They kept on with their tales of choice and agency, only now they made sure that deceit and violence cemented their arrogance with material wealth and territorial possession. Soon it truly seemed that they were the centre of a world which bowed to their will. Their self-authorship was facilitated by our bodily subjugation – so that the people of the mind relied on the people of the body for their position in the world.

And all over this bowing, scraping world the peculiar logic of their version of humanity held sway. Sometimes they distinguished between us, consigning us to distinct genres of barbarity.[17] But everywhere the same boundary between the human and less-than-human prevailed. From Africa to the Americas, from Asia across the African Ocean to the Caribbean, telltale marks of suffering marked the peoples of the body, those who could not self-fashion their own destiny.

Everywhere the violence was bloody and meaningless. It lasted a long time, this era called modernity, and by the time people grew tired of its taste there was not a segment of the globe left untouched by its logic. The white eyes of European ascendency which saw the possibilities of human agency and profit maximization in every corner had seen it all; all humanity was implicated in this project which split us all into winners and losers, minds and bodies.

17. See Kohn (1995): ch. 1.

Every step of progress was inscribed upon our bodies – from mercantilism to industrialization, through colonization to imperialism to globalization and migrant labour and free trade zones and new world orders – for every benefit we paid a cost. Sometimes we paid costs for which there was no benefit. Mindless cruelty seemed to be part of the terror necessary to maintain white power. Our tormentors liked to heighten their victories through extra humiliation, the public violation of our most private places. No-one knew what was gained from these value-added abuses. Even the white eyes for whom the spectacle of suffering was displayed could make no sense of what they saw. The extra hurt of sexualizing violence served no discernible purpose.

> One night after a dance a poor rickshaw man took a soldier back to the barracks, and in the morning we saw him lying in his rickshaw, bleeding in a pool of blood. They'd cut off his private parts and put them in his mouth. We saw with our own eyes – all of us were going to work, and we saw it.[18]

The white women see the result of the white men's actions – it is displayed for all passers-by – but even they can give no account of the reasons for these attacks. They are reduced to the most basic of witnesses, able to record but not explain. They see, with those arbiters of truth, their "own eyes", but it is an unsatisfactory witnessing. Instead of reducing the rickshaw man to no more than a body, a creature who

18.   Gill (1995): 47.

did not deserve the privileges of modern mind-led humanity, the excessive punishment for no crime confuses even the white women.[19]

When we swapped our stories, our people tried to guess what it all meant. Perhaps this was a battle between men.[20] All this aggression towards other people's members. Perhaps the penis represented the threat which must be tamed. Except lack of a penis was no protection against violence. To them, we wore no distinctions of gender. For all their stories about the frailties and dangers of femininity, the woman they were describing was white. When they enslaved us, stealing our freedom and our labour, both men and women were measured on the same scale, as lumps of labour and quantities of flesh:

"The female in 'Middle Passage', as the apparently smaller physical mass, occupies 'less room' in a directly translatable money economy. But she is, nevertheless, quantifiable by the same rules as her male counterpart."[21]

That was our especial and warped destiny, to endure violences which, although sexualized, saw no gender. We, it seemed, wore our flesh differently. Our bodies did not fall into the respectable divisions of public and private; we could neither author our own destiny nor waver between the unachievable options of good womanhood. If modernity is the time when Western bodies learn to construct their social worlds according to the organizing principle of gender, then we escape this gendering because our

19. For more on the dynamics of racist castrations, in a North American context, see Harris (1984).
20. See Hoch (1979).
21. Spillers (1987): 72.

bodies are too broken and disrespected for this propriety. However much morbid desire our women-
folk elicited, they never became good or bad women.
Instead we all remained scarily vulnerable to the idea
that we were sexualized flesh, but not proper people.

Later, when the end of the slave trade gave way to
the rise of indentured labour, again we found that
our women were spared no suffering.[22] We were the
bitter strength coolies, who sold our souls for a wage
which was never enough to buy back our freedom.
Although we dreamed of returning home prosperous,
the bargains rarely paid off. Somehow, at the end of
our three, five, seven years, we owed the firm more
than before. We paid back our passage to this living
death from wages which never quite kept us, growing
debts which stole our lives and freedom.

With our freedom we lost all claim on proper
gender identities – for us the names of "man" and
"woman" would always be refracted through the
dehumanizing suffering of our people. Our tormentors focused on erasing and distorting the marks of
gender among us – castrating our menfolk to show
that they were at once more and less than men, rap-
ing women to deny them the privileges of femininity
and then torturing their bodies to prove that this
was no delicate feminine flesh. White people claimed
the proper constraints of gender for themselves alone,
confining their women and spoiling their men as if this
combination of social codes and collective neuroses

22. Hugh Tinker argues that after the end of the slave trade
     the plantations of the Caribbean and the Mascarenes de-
     manded "a new system of slavery". "Slavery produced both
     a system and an attitude of mind, in which the products
     determined everything, not the people." *A new system of
     slavery* (1974): 19.

was the one true mark of humanity. We, the improperly gendered, were relegated once again to the status of beasts.

Despite ourselves we became creatures constituted by different laws. Bondage reduced us to flesh which suffered sex but was not allowed the privilege of emotion. Subjugation distorted our experience of gender, denying us the pleasures of gendered affection. We reproduced, but could not parent as we wished. Instead, for us parental care demanded that we break our own line.[23] An entry from the diary of Dr Wiley on a ship carrying indentured labour from Calcutta to Port of Spain reminds us:

> November 4th 1872: Sommueh died at 8.30pm. She was in the beginning of the voyage suffering from chronic diarrhoea, got quite well and was discharged . . . when by accident or intention (I am inclined to think the latter) she suffocated her child, three years old . . . The other women frightened her by telling her she would be punished when she got to the colony . . . from the day of the loss of her child she gradually sank.[24]

Mother love demands that the child does not suffer the fate of the mother. If gender is a name given in relation to the logic of reproduction, then this name could not belong to us.[25] Or belonged to us differently,

23. See any number of stories, from Medea, who murders her children and feeds them to Jason, her colonizer and husband, to a more recent retelling, the story of *Beloved*, by Toni Morrison.
24. Tinker (1974): 160.
25. For more on the idea that the cultural forms of gender assume a biological imperative to be straight and reproduce, see Wittig (1992).

as those so fecund that mothering was over in the moment of birth, so bestial that the infant merited no care. The sanctioned weaknesses of femininity were not available to us. We killed our children to save them pain.

To our tormentors, the distortion of our affective bonds was proof that we were animals. Missionaries questioned whether we were "without natural affection" beyond "mere animal attachments"[26] or described "the horrors of savagedom" who "as a rule" smothered sick relatives.[27] In another bizarre twist, our supposed lack of human feeling makes us deserve treatment reserved for animals.

The cruelty of white people teaches us to view each other as undifferentiated flesh, linked by a common vulnerability to pain. Woman or man, child or adult – all are equally vulnerable. Whatever our different histories, that experience of undifferentiated cruelty haunts our gendering in later times. No wonder we sisters come to be such improper women, publicly exchanged without the dangerous protections of respectable femininity.

The journey from Asia to Africa and the Caribbean, like that from Africa to America, confirmed our vulnerability to becoming no more than woundable flesh, free of other names of socialization.

"December 13: While at dinner on deck one of the sailors struck a woman in the stomach with the grating of one of the boats, causing convulsive spasms and leaving a small tumour."[28]

26. Thomas Williams, missionary to Fiji in 1840, quoted in Stocking (1987): 89.
27. Francis Galton, from expedition to Africa in 1850, quoted in ibid., p. 93.
28. Dr Wiley in Tinker (1974): 161.

Instead of the dubious privilege of confinement, our reproductive capacities were destroyed and disrespected, forming the focus for violence which sought to prove that we were not *men* and *women*. Instead our flesh was stuck in a pre-social conception of boundless woundability. Our tormentors granted no reprieve to our children – they were just smaller lumps of meat. Instead of saving us from violence, the marks of our femaleness, our breasts and wombs and cunts drew the particular anger of our attackers. From the Americas, too, we heard that in the eyes of Europeans our flesh had no social meaning beyond its capacity to suffer. All our lives were equally unvalued.

> Numerous reports, from numerous reporters, tell of Indians being led to the mines in columns, chained together at the neck, and decapitated if they faltered. Of children trapped and burned alive in their houses, or stabbed to death because they walked too slowly. Of the routine cutting off women's breasts, and the tying of heavy gourds to their feet before tossing them to drown in lakes and lagoons. Of babies taken from their mothers' breasts, killed, and left as roadside markers. Of "stray" Indians dismembered and sent back to their villages with their chopped-off hands and noses strung around their necks.[29]

The varied history of our various family revealed this common trait: across the overlapping horrors of colonization and slavery, bond labour and genocide,

29. Stannard (1992): 82–3.

we found that our children were not spared and our flesh was not accorded the privilege of gender differentiation. Instead, we were just bodies.

We are the people of the body because history has made us feel our bodies so sharply.

We are the less-than-human because history has denied us the civilizing marks of gender and childhood. Our enemies retell this story of their own cruelty as a confusion about flesh.

The story of the people-eating people

Once, long ago, a man thought that by travelling west he could reach the east. In his time people imagined the world to be a great ball, so all directions would eventually lead back to their starting-point. In this time, the lands to the east held great wealth, many items to be coveted by the deprived and backward West. However, the journey east was fraught with hazards, of both natural and human form. Only some other, unexpected route could lead the people of the West to the treasures of the East. Hungry for easy profit, a fleet of three ships set out to find the back door to the eastern kingdoms.

In the stories told by great men this eventful and ill-planned journey changes the shape of the world. The journey west towards the East stumbles upon the new world, discovering that there are other worlds than that of the great men. The story of the West can never be the same again; from now on the West is in a different place altogether.

The discovery of human beings in the Americas, after all, posed a hard question to scholars who believed that the world had a seamless and coherent history: where did they come from? Neither the Greeks, the Romans, nor the Jews had known of their existence. How, then, could Greco-Roman and Hebrew texts be complete and authoritative?[30]

The coming of Europe to the Americas heralds both the beginning of the long era of European ascendancy and the whispering of its eventual demise. The great men are now central to a world edged on both sides by barbarity. What they have always believed now comes true.

But this is not the motive for our traveller's voyage. He does not recognize this new West when he stumbles upon it; to him this is still the East. But this is the far side of the East, more frightening than the worst traveller's tale. So, of course, our traveller is filled with trepidation. In his diaries, he talks about this fear: "The Admiral says further that in the islands which he had passed they were in great terror of Carib . . . and they must be a daring people, since they go through all the islands and eat the people they can take."[31]

Throughout his diaries our traveller remarks upon the beauty and gentleness of the people of these unknown lands. He is scared, but his fear is proved to be unfounded at every step. Instead of greeting this party of intruders with the hostility and violence which even they feel they deserve, the people of this place offer food and comfort to the travellers, give

30. Grafton (1992): 149.
31. *The journal of Christopher Columbus*, trans. C. Jane (1960), p. 147.

them presents, are entertained by their amusing difference. Unaware of the genocide to come, these people show their best face to these lost strangers. After all, why treat a handful of white men who don't even know where they are as any kind of threat? This could not be a colonizing force. These people cannot even feed themselves.

Knowing his own purpose, our traveller guiltily records these kindnesses. And although he encounters no such thing, he also records the rumour of dangerous cannibals.

The European imagination was already chockful of tales about people-eating people. This was the story which let you know you were somewhere else, away from the home and rules you knew.

"Europeans had always known that cannibals and other monstrous races inhabited the fringes of the known and *ipso facto* civilized world."[32]

Long before any of that dull talk about difference, stories about what people would eat were a widespread and popular marker between foreign and familiar. It was the attitude to human flesh which let you know that you had reached the edge of civilization. Europeans viewed the human body as helpfully vulnerable to the discipline of pain, and this frailty was used liberally in the name of god and king. Eating this same petrified flesh after the victim's death, however, was a sure sign of barbarism. And that was something other people did.

In fact there isn't much evidence to suggest that people from anywhere eat people. But there are a billion European stories about how this is what foreigners do, and that is what makes them foreign. Even

32.   Grafton (1992): 108.

our lost traveller, if you notice, hears the rumour about cannibals over the hill from another white man, who says he heard it from some locals. No-one ever knows who gets eaten.

This is a funny kind of a story, part of the strange genre of Euro-horror which depicts the rest of the world as savage and dangerous and then scares itself so much that it has to go out and kill that danger. Perhaps the people of this other place had a premonition of the sufferings to come and developed the rumour as a way of frightening these gullible white men away. Later subjugated peoples learn to masquerade as savage, clicking into the projections of their tormentors as a means of resistance.[33] But in this moment of initial contact the evil of white men is still unimaginable. These white men look like the circus coming to town – everyone wants a look and no-one suspects that there is any threat here. So either there really are cannibals up in those hills, or the people of that place really believe there are, or a familiar trope of the Euro-imaginary has been inserted into the story by the travellers themselves.

Isn't option three the most likely? Now that the stories of great men are crumbling? Don't we look back at old stories and see nothing so clearly as the fears of the tellers, disbelieving everything except this trace of their anxiety?

Our traveller finds a new name for this primal fear. He hears that the Caribs eat human flesh and from this rumour the word "cannibal" comes to denote this practice. It doesn't matter that the rumour comes from the Arawak, long-time enemies of their neighbours the Caribs. The rumour is convincing

33. For some exploration of this strategy, see Fusco, "Performance and the power of the popular", in Ugwu (1995).

because our traveller already knows this story; the name fits his expectations.

This is the story which the traveller brings.

Far, far away, across the sea, the world is peopled by a different shape of human being. These are the people beyond civilization, the people who offend against moral law. Our traveller knows that these are people without God, or without the one true God; but this is not what troubles him. Their misplaced belief is nothing without the particular behaviour which proves their savagery. Of course, the true extent of their savagery was shown in what they ate and what they fucked. Beyond civilization were people who had sex with members of their own family, who penetrated the forbidden zone of the anus and who celebrated and confirmed these practises with meals of human flesh. All these things went against the laws of man, God and nature. Nothing could ensure the safety of travellers in these strange lands. Any amount of violence was justified.

This is the story our traveller arrives with.

We already know from the stories of the self-fashioning white men and the tale of two daughters that the rise of reason means the excision of the body from respectable people's sense of themselves. The idea that you could be in control, speak yourself into existence, author your own destiny – all those ideas which say that (some) people are the main thing happening in the world – assume that the body can be subdued to fit in with this project. That's how you prove the sovereignty of the mind and the law of man, by controlling the body.

If power does not extend to the soul, it may be exercised upon the body; indeed secular power *is* essentially the ability to perform certain operations upon the body: to remove it from one place to another, to confine it, to cause it extreme pain, to reduce it to ashes. The conviction that the soul is entirely separate from the body licenses the exercise of such power, while the exercise of such power helps to produce the conviction that the soul is entirely separate from the body.[34]

The soul, the mind, the spirit, reason – all those names for the intangible essence of humanity, the thing we really are, aside from the shell of flesh which carries us – have a separate existence from the body. Its very vulnerability shows that the body is of a lesser order, because it is open to abuse in ways that the elusive soul/mind/spirit are not. Once you have bought these two propositions, it is a short step to seeing the powers of reason as augmented by the ability to torture the body. Fleshly torment does not impinge upon the authority of the mind, particularly if mind and body belong to different people. It is not even an offence against the gods, because their province is above and beyond such earthly pains. The body is not reasonable, it is greedy and demanding and unpredictable and weak. Much better for everyone if the laws of the self-fashioning mind also employ the extra defence of disciplining the body to keep it in its frail and mortal place.

Our traveller believes an early version of this story. He thinks that telling the right story in the right way makes you powerful in the world. When he arrives at this place which he cannot identify, he makes a point of staging a pantomime of speeches and flag-flying to claim this uncertain territory for his own

34. Greenblatt (1980): 80.

people. When he goes home he takes back witness accounts of this strange event, as proof that this land now belongs to them. For him, this is how you take ownership. "For Columbus taking possession is principally the performance of a set of linguistic acts: declaring, witnessing, recording."[35]

The talk isn't even a back-up or record of some more concrete occupation: no armies, no fences, no colonial settlements. At this first taking possession, the record is of a speech. They take back a piece of paper on which they have written "we said this is ours" and have no doubt that it is. As long as others have heard, the story is authorized as true.

And because our traveller believes in the secular exercise of power, he torments the bodies of the native people as part of this taking control. This is still no military occupation. The new land is not taken by force of numbers. There is never any question that all the people of the new land will be subjugated by the traveller's party. They are few and they are lost. They cannot take possession by might, because on this trip there is little to show their might. The technique of witnessing is all that they have got. But this technique still needs some augmentation by physical cruelty. The technologies of performative speech and written records need the back-up of brute force to operate successfully.

The Europeans who ventured to the New World in the first decades after Columbus's discovery shared a complex, well-developed, and, above all, mobile technology of power: Writing, navigational instruments, ships, war-horses, attack dogs,

35. Greenblatt (1991): 57.

effective armor, and highly lethal weapons, including gunpowder. Their culture was characterized by immense confidence in its own centrality,
by a political organization based on practices of
command and submission, by a willingness to use
coercive violence on both strangers and fellow
countrymen, and by a religious ideology centered
on the endlessly proliferated representation of a
tortured and murdered god of love.[36]

However much talk there is about the power of witnessing, these storytelling talents are always supple-
mented by a host of other factors. The ability to tell
the particular stories of these people at this moment
is facilitated by material histories of technical development and cultural constructions which at once legitimate and disguise violence. Of course, our traveller
mobilizes the entire machinery available to him in
his will to make his story true.

Arriving in a strange and unknown land, our traveller covers his own incompetence with a tale of
man-eating savagery and the just-in-time arrival of
Christianity and European civilization. Civilization
is signified by a new set of attitudes towards flesh,
human and animal. Columbus believes that introducing European livestock to the New World will
cement European domination. He suggests:

Payment for these things [livestock] could be
made ... in slaves from among these cannibals,
a people very savage and suitable for the purpose, and well made and of very good intelligence. We believe that they, having abandoned

36.   Ibid.: 9.

that inhumanity [of cannibalism], will be better than any other slaves, and their inhumanity they will immediately lose when they are out of their own land.[37]

Others have suggested that the introduction of European domestic animals brought a fresh source of protein to the Americas, thus alleviating the dietary necessity of cannibalism.[38] Into the twentieth century, the myth of savage man-eaters needs sustaining – as if cannibalism is a weakness of technical capacity and the introduction of European farming methods made possible the leap out of the primitive into the good Christian habits of raising your own meat.

Others still suggest that European invasion caused the destruction of Aztec protein plants, obliterating the indigenous source of vegetable protein. Arens writes of Montellano:[39] "he informs us that amaranth, which was a staple grain and major source of protein for the Aztecs, was banned as a cultivated crop by the Spaniards, since it was closely associated with the natives' traditional religious rituals."[40]

To the European eye, the people of the Americas had no source of protein-rich food except each other. Domesticated animal meat was a means of placating these protein-hungry people and diverting them from the horrors of human flesh.

Europe brings the economy of meat in its ugliest forms. Unable to see the sources of (dietary) value in the New World, our Euro-newcomers call up their

37. Phillips & Phillips (1992): 202.
38. Arens (1979): 72.
39. Montellano (1978).
40. Arens (1979): 74.

longstanding belief that people unlike themselves eat each other in order to legitimate all manner of violence and introduce new habits of flesh-eating. If the people of the New World must be made slaves in order to pay for the civilizing arrival of livestock, then this is how progress must proceed.

> The economic transaction as Columbus conceives it will be undertaken for the welfare of the souls of the enslaved: the Indians are exchanged for beasts in order to convert them into humans. This transformation will not enfranchise them; it will only make them into excellent slaves.[41]

In the economy of our traveller, flesh becomes human when it is subject to the witnessing and torment of his representative power. Until they are bought into slavery and Christianity, the people of the new land are equivalent to animals. Beast and person are interchangeable; this is the assumption which makes the transaction possible. The false equivalence suggests many things: that the sufferings of these almost-people are no more serious than those of animals, that the torment of their flesh is sanctioned because their pain never enters the representational systems of the witnessers and tormentors, that animals will do this place more good than its people.

All of these suggestions rest on the underlying assumption that these people eat human flesh and are thus in need of the most brutal of civilizing approaches.

"The operational definition of cannibalism in the sixteenth century was resistance to foreign invasion

41. Greenblatt (1991): 72.

followed by being sold into slavery, which was held to be a higher status than freedom under aboriginal conditions."[42]

When the world changes shape and falls victim to European domination, stories about meat and flesh are central to Europe's account of its rise. The new world is conquered by the old through many transactions of flesh, human and animal, in both directions. Meat – clean and unclean, proper and improper – haunts the imagination of ascendent Europeans.

Much later, the eye of a now faltering reason still fears the counter-logic of the flesh. The disintegrating amalgam of the West is still characterized as addicted to the word, endlessly witnessing and recording in a quest to overcome the mortal body. The regime of the West believes that the products of the mind are more enduring than those of the body, that mortality is inescapable but talk can live on.

". . . language and the body are locked in a struggle of attrition, in which the word is ultimately bound to triumph while the flesh is doomed to be undone."[43]

Flesh still gets a raw deal – is disrespected and tormented, blamed and ignored. But now, people start to point out that this distaste is central to Western culture and that the mastery of the physical is illusory. The story of the two sisters has less currency as women tell more stories of their own. The descendants of barbarians learn the techniques of performative speech and recording of the European conquerors. All the different people of the body tell of the sufferings they have undergone in the name of someone else's reason.

42.   Arens (1979): 51.
43.   Ellmann (1993): 27.

In the end, it looks like the Europeans and their descendants are the people-eaters after all.

> Just twenty-one years after Columbus's first landing in the Caribbean, the vastly populous island that the explorer had re-named Hispaniola was effectively desolate; nearly 8,000,000 – those Columbus chose to call Indians – had been killed by violence, disease, and despair.[44]

Who consumed more flesh than Europe? Sucking in the vitality of many nations and spitting it out as their own product?

Turned on their tellers, those old tales of secret feasts on human parts begin to make some sense. What is more convincing than the African belief that Europeans are bloodsuckers – "consumers of African vitality" (Arens, p. 13); where has the vitality of that continent gone if not into European bellies? Europe and her descendants have grown fat on our bodies; who are they to despise flesh?

Later, when Euro-culture is in some disarray, it becomes apparent that the privileged sight of European conquest is not unrelated to more fleshy urges to ingest, incorporate, own. By the time we get to the admission of ". . . the anthropophagous foundations of the drive to see",[45] sensible students of European subject formation know that there is more going on than just getting a good look. Getting big and strong is not only about knowing and mastering those threatening beings beyond yourself, but also about ingesting that threat until it is no longer scarily apart

44. Stannard (1992): x.
45. Ellmann (1993): 41.

from you and is instead comfortingly a part of you. But by the time Europeans begin to admit how scared and anxious they are – about themselves, their bodies, their place in the world – half the globe is already eaten.

Epidemic self-destruction

Long after Europe has overrun the rest of the world and begun to fall into decline, another version of the people-eating horror story emerges in Papua New Guinea.

"In 1957 kuru was a newly discovered fatal disease of the central nervous system that was occurring in epidemic proportions among the inhabitants of stone-age settlements in the central highlands of New Guinea."[46]

Kuru was, it seemed, a previously unknown disease which affected only an enclosed community of people. The people affected were those strange historical throwbacks, contemporary primitives. By the time these people had changed their lives to adopt the ways of peasant society with a cash economy, kuru had gone into decline and eventually stopped altogether. As a challenge to Western science, kuru represented a rare chance to really show off the benefits of modernity, to show that civilizing people out of their own culture was also of medical benefit. By 1957, kuru offered an opportunity which may never come again: ". . . the initial investigation of kuru was high adventure, taking place as it did among people

46. Farquhar & Gajdusek (1981): xv.

who had only recently begun to have contact with Europeans."[47]

This was old-style intrepid stuff, charting the unknown, bringing knowledge to primitives. Inevitably, kuru has taken on a mythic status in Western disease folklore. All those old fears about hidden places and unfamiliar practices re-emerged. The particular anxieties brought about by new epidemics of previously unknown kinds pre-empts the scary limits of medical science which return to haunt the later twentieth century. At this point the well-developed mythologies around incurable illness which shape our ideas of mortality hardly exist.[48] Instead our intrepid scientist–explorers fall back on older stories to explain this unexpected phenomenon: the alleged cannibalism of this enclosed population.

We were often asked when and how we first came upon the idea that cannibalism was involved in the spread of the disease. It is useless to speculate about the origin of this idea; I know of few Europeans who did not arrive at such a conjecture. All the missionaries, traders, miners, and government workers and their families in the Eastern Highlands knew that most of the indigenous peoples in that area had been cannibals – mostly endocannibals, eating their close relatives in mourning rites – prior to and at the time of first missionary and government contact. Missionaries and government workers had engaged in a vigorous campaign to discourage the practice, and the government often imprisoned

47. Ibid.: xv–xvi.
48. See Patton (1990).

people for continuing to eat their dead kin after administrative control had been established. Europeans thus often suggested that "cannibalism probably spread the disease".[49]

Although all Europeans seemed to agree that the consumption of human flesh caused the disease, as it caused all the ills of savage peoples, in this instance this was not a timeless practice awaiting the interruption of modernity (in the form of white people). Instead, here it seems that the practice of cannibalism appears with European contact, from around 1900.[50] Admittedly, in this telling Europeans reach the coast and cannibalism reaches the still-uncharted-by-white-people highlands, but they appear together. Isn't there an echo here of the operational definition of cannibalism in the sixteenth century? An allegation which legitimates any act on the part of Europeans? Whether or not any bodies were actually consumed, the idea of cannibalism – a particular sacred flesh-eating among mourning family – is central to the struggles around European intrusion, to everyone concerned. The rumour of this practice gives shape to the repressions and resistances that take place.

When kuru begins to die out, European investigators put this down to the benefits of their presence. The people of the kuru area have altered their way of life, largely as an accommodation to economic demands. Like people all over the world, the people of the region adapt to trade and a money economy, learn to accumulate wealth and to grow cash crops, negotiate with the effects of different people coming

49. Farquhar & Gajdusek (1981): xxiii–xxiv.
50. Ibid., appendix 4.

to their home. To European eyes, the people regain their health by learning civilization. The period 1950–57 is characterized by the following description:

> Gradual disappearance of many cultural practices: warfare, cannibalism, infanticide, suckling of piglets by women, institutionalized premarital sex with cross-cousins, nudity of male children and old men, use of *wati-mabi* (penis display) except in jest in *singsings*. Polygamy and child-marriage decline, due to official discouragement. Goats introduced by Seventh Day Adventist into some North Fore villages.[51]

The gamut of inappropriate behaviour displayed by savages is attributed to the people of the kuru region – until the coming of Europeans. Then, they give up eating human flesh and learn to raise livestock, they give up the unnatural cruelties of killing their own and coupling with more than one other and the unnatural affection of having sex with family or sharing breast milk with even domestic animals. They learn to cover their bodies, especially the dangerous sight of the black man's penis.

What is appropriate to eat is only one segment of this package of changed habits and consciousness. What is described is a complete reorganization of attitudes to the body and its maintenance – the adoption of Western propriety – and this is what cures this diseased people, we assume.

However, the root of kuru remains unknown – what if savagery is not to blame, despite all the imputations?

51. Ibid.: 294.

the phenomenon of cannibalism in many regions of New Guinea, including areas adjacent to the kuru region, seems to have been medically innocuous. The dreadful and decisive accident appears now to have been the rare intrusion of a Creutzfeldt-Jakob-type virus into a community practising this sort of cannibalism.[52]

Arens makes the tentative suggestion that the newly arrived Europeans may have unwittingly introduced the new factor which allows this virus to develop. Given the mortality rates displayed by other peoples suddenly subjected to European disease, this story has some attractions. While commentators have looked to rituals around cannibalism for explanations of kuru's transmission pattern, no-one suggests that this is where the virus springs from in the first place. The closest we come to plotting the disease's genealogy is to place it within a family of types.

With the first report – in 1963 – of the transmission of kuru to chimpanzees from cell-free suspensions of human brain, kuru became the first human disease proved to be a slow virus infection, thereby stimulating the search for such etiology in other chronic human diseases. By 1967 a worldwide form of presenile dementia, Creutzfeldt-Jakob disease (CJD), was proved to be caused by a similar virus which remains to this day indistinguishable from the virus of kuru except for unstable biological properties of host-range, incubation period, and virulence.[53]

52.   Ibid.: xxiv.
53.   Ibid.: xxi.

The close kinship between kuru and CJD anticipates a later tale about European attitudes to flesh. For now, we must remember that kuru, the disease of the savage people-eater which came from nowhere, resembles nothing so much as the group of illnesses which grow strong on the weaknesses of European culture at the turn of the next century.

Later we will hear more of the European hunger for flesh and the centrality of meat in the rise of the West. For now, we must make time to remember the consequences of this preoccupation. The fantasy of the people-eating people had other echoes. The people of the mind feared the excesses of their own cruelty, their own obsessive quest to find the limit of human endurance. The stories they told of other peoples translated this fear into an outside threat. If savages were endlessly cruel, it was justified to use violence against them.

Sometimes they took time to document a disregard for the body. This was, after all, a key mark of barbarity: indifference to the pain of others. Importantly for the story, these were abuses without reason. The scale of punishment revealed the inhumanity of the law. The thoughtless display of power revealed an inadequacy to rule. Attention to detail distorted the expectations of technical discipline, showing that even with science these people would never be civilized. Some stories told of strange and despotic rulers: infants on thrones who played out their whims on the hapless forms of their subjects. In this story, the most minor trespass – a wrong look, a stolen loaf – could lead to mutilation and loss of life. To them, we were always the wretchedly powerless populace of the *Arabian nights*, subject to absolute rulers beyond reason.

All proving, of course, that conquest by the self-fashioners of Europe was a blessing, not a curse, and that the new rulers were kinder and fairer than these native tyrants. What the kindness of this conquest entailed was a new regime of flesh and meat: confusions about the values of human and animal flesh, rumours about their interchangeability, tortuous reworkings of all kinds of meat . . .

The sportswoman sighed herself out of character: Once I had learnt all these stories of mind and body, flesh and spirit, I began to see how my destiny had been plotted. Through centuries my people had been consigned to the realm of the body and denied the privileges of the people of the mind.

After I had heard all these stories of burnt flesh and lost bodies it was difficult to taste the sweetness of my sporting victories. Now my own developed physical capacities seemed like another extension of the monstrous distortions which we had always been subjected to. Of course I could run and jump and throw, because my other capacities had been stunted. We had become the white people's monstrous machines – our destiny was to be no more than bodies, to them at least.

Of course, this wasn't the whole story. I could see from my sister's tale that my body could become mine once more. She had remade her history to review her own flesh as her own – that was what her time in the wilderness had taught her. Now I wondered what stories I needed to learn to reclaim my body as my own. What would it take to make my flesh sweet again? It seemed that what I needed to know was the narrative route to knowledge, the plots which led you to the special rewriting stories which transform all our experience into our dreams.

Whatever feats I performed, I remained no more than resilient meat. I had to learn to talk the talk which convinced others of my worth.

In this, the fourth set of our tales, we have heard the confusing story of the role of the body in the modern age. From this we understand that physical prowess is attributed no value in itself. To gain social recognition, bodily endeavour requires the services of an authoritative voice. This is the subject of our next set of tales.

Further reading

For a famous account of the white men and their attempts to self-fashion, see *Renaissance self-fashioning*, by Stephen Greenblatt.

To pursue the role of slavery in the ascendancy of the West, see *How Europe underdeveloped Africa*, by Walter Rodney.

For more on the histories of Indian indentured labour, see *India in the Caribbean*, by David Dabydeen and Brinsley Samaroo.

To understand more about the special place of cannibalism in the Western imagination, see *The man-eating myth*, by W. Arens.

For an insight into the will to circumnavigate the globe, see *The worlds of Christopher Columbus*, by William D. Phillips and Carla Rahn Phillips.

CHAPTER 5

The newsreader's tale

In these tales we hear of the ways in which the world has been divided – into people of the mind and people of the body. This, we hear, is the history we inherit. The thinking people are built to rule, while the bodily people are built to toil.

Now, however, history is changing, moving on, taking that logic further. The next stories we hear are about the demise of the people of the mind, their downfall accelerated by the complaints of their uncared-for bodies.

In this fresh moment, we hear of the changing shape of the whole world and the ongoing challenge to remake ourselves as human.

This is a story about brains and bodies, the connections between intellectual and physical prowess and the differing values accorded to people.

My story too spans great distances and many ages. Like my sister the sportswoman, I grew up in a land where my people were persecuted. In school I was taught that learning would never belong to me. No matter how hard I studied, the lessons I learned debarred me from the source of knowledge. When I practised diligence, my teachers whipped me with faint praise – I was careful, tidy, but no independent thinker. When I took risks to dazzle them into respect, they scolded me for my lack of discipline and called my imagination childish. Although relieved to encounter my attentive obedience, my teachers could not help letting me know that they thought their efforts were wasted on me. However well I repeated what they told me, they did not believe that they could teach me to think for myself.

I loved my books, in spite of all this. Once I had learned how to read, my body no longer felt like a trap. Access to all those printed words let me fly beyond the fear of everyday violence which stalked my child-life.[1] Literacy showed me a world where no matter what size, shape, colour, I was, I could choose not to be a victim. Books told me that there were other ways to live and that they could belong to me. The stories I read told me that teachers were bound to misrecognize talent, and I took some solace from this.[2] Perhaps the things they said were not true after all.

But my books also told me that the world of knowledge did not belong to people like me. However much I studied, I never met my echo in the tales of discovery and scholarship which I devoured. My people were recipients of rationality; despite its benefits, it remained foreign to us. Diligence would never allow me to speak with the voice of reason, because, try as I might, that authority belonged to someone else.

Burdened by this bitter lesson, still I worked hard to gather the education which was allowed to me. Defying my teachers' expectations, I passed examinations and enrolled at a college in a distant town. There my loneliness pushed me closer into the embrace of my books, substituting their company for more human comforts.[3] While even at college my teachers regarded me as a safe student rather than a star, here I found that diligence began to pay off. Although I still lived without praise, my marks matched those of more favoured classmates. Leaving college, my

1. See Commission for Racial Equality (1988).
2. You could take this whole volume as an exercise in learning from fairytales that the truth is always hidden and magical and unexpected and that wrongdoers always have their bad behaviour returned to them.
3. For more on this lonely educational experience, see Williams (1991).

education appeared illustrious, even if people doubted my personal attributes. I learned the limited sense in which my qualifications were the same as anyone else's.

Sadly, looking for work I was reminded again that people like me spoke with no authority. Stressing the value of my education only seemed to anger prospective employers. In the end, I stopped looking for work to match what I knew and resigned myself to taking directions from others. My talents went unrecognized, but at least I worked.

Then, one day, things started to change. I took orders, but now I was asked to present this information in public. I was commended for my voice and my manner, not my mind, but I was commended. When I spoke in this context, people found me convincing. They liked the way I looked and sounded; when I spoke they felt they understood. In my mouth, things which were difficult or frightening became agreeably everyday. As news of my talent spread, I was offered other, more challenging jobs. Soon the public listened for my voice when they wanted to hear the truth.

That's how I became a newsreader.

Now I make my living by telling people what is important and true in the world. Although this truth is not seen to emanate from me, without my mediation no-one knows it as truth. It is my voice which is associated with authority and discernment; even if I do not choose, I speak for those who do. Suddenly people take what I say seriously. They listen out for what I have to tell them, without any thought that I might be outside the limits of rationality. In the new world what it is rational to believe is determined by what I say.

My new job brought me many pleasures. Although I still encountered resistance in places, largely I commanded a respect which made me glow and grin. Although I was hired for my voice, not my mind, I found that no-one was immune from the new authority of my speech. Now when I made suggestions, people were trained to believe what I said by the tone of my voice. At last I felt that my work was beginning to belong to me.

However, I was still confused by this change in fortune. Why was the world listening to me now, after telling me for so long that it was not my place to speak? What did it mean when my voice became the indication of accuracy and relevance?

I, too, started to look around for clues. I waited at this crossroads of history, when knowledge belonged to no-one, and asked the travellers I met what the answer might be.

After some time I met a woman who promised to answer my questions. She was also dark-skinned, displaced, on her way between places. This seemed to be a theme.

As questioner, I asked her, as I had asked many others, "Stranger, tell me about the world and what it means; my body brings me trouble in ways I can't understand. Yet I feel the world changing and nothing stays the same."

"I heard that you hungered for knowledge", replied the new traveller, "so I have come to share what I have learned. For many years I have studied the plight of our peoples, examining the many meanings given to skin and flesh, tracing the role of the body in all our destinies. I have encountered many strange beliefs and have witnessed human cruelty so great that life lost all its sweetness. I will share all of this with you – from the entertaining to the scary – but first you must listen to my story.

When I was young my teachers scolded me for paying little attention to my books. 'See', they shouted, 'you are just like all the others. Why do we waste our time trying to teach you half-wits? Your minds are not made for school-books – better to tell you about contraception, that's what you lot really need to know.'

It was true that I didn't take to school. I didn't believe what I read in the books there; it seemed so different from what I learned at home or from the lending library. Like other children, I wanted to learn about this valuable thing, knowledge. But the stories I was told at school said that it belonged to others, our palers and betters – only they had the capacity to gather and appreciate knowledge. This was the only lesson I learned from school: that my capacity to learn was limited.

For a time I walked away from schooling in disgust. I wanted to know, but no-one would tell. So I looked elsewhere – the books they never told us about in school, the hidden histories of my all-too-visible people. From this, I began to understand that the best stories were not always the most easily available. Knowing that helped me to return to schooling.

Now I looked at my school-books with fresh eyes. Suddenly I saw the addiction to looking which passed for learning, the jump-up-and-hit-you obviousness of how facts were made. Now when I went looking for my own truths, I wanted to disprove what my teachers had said. I was suspicious of the knowledge ladled out at school. My experiences there made me certain that this was not the place to further my knowledge about my own peoples. I had already seen the disrespect with big words which passed for scholarship about our homelands. This was not what I meant by knowing.

But too many roads led back to the academy. In the end it seemed better to see what these people had to say; maybe those big books did hold some clues after all.

In the university libraries which I frequented, I did find books which hinted at some history of my body. The stories I found there made me cry, but I persevered with my studies, certain that I would eventually uncover the secrets I longed to know. But so much of what I found described only what learned men saw. Like my beautiful sister, I found that stories about looking filled up space and obscured some of what I found important. Even the books which promised to explain why the world was this shape, why people lived as they did, seemed to look too much to understand.

I learned that Europe had developed an understanding of the natural world based around verification: if facts could not be seen, they could at least be made appreciable. What was knowledge if not this sensory grasping of how the world was?

Later, when the social world began to seem a thing apart from nature, Europeans again relied on their eyes to understand their condition. After the heroic and truimphant witnessing which had brought the whole world into line, of course, our rulers believed that their well-trained vision could illuminate the source of social unrest at home.

In Britain, early industrializer and workshop of the world, the sudden concentration of the working urban poor raised new spectres of fear for the respectable. Becoming proletarian in this extended changeover of 'the industrial revolution' also entailed disrupting diet, courting disease, living in crowded and insanitary conditions. Becoming ready wage labour also meant losing habits of family structure, and previous fictions of a God-given hierarchy in society. In the long shift into modern experience, the sight of your eyes becomes the last certainty. Once the world is disrupted by the population shifts of urbanization, social relations must be constantly remade through our ability to interpret each other's identities. Looking is the privileged vehicle of this interpretation.

Equally, when our rulers first approached the social world to look for understanding, they were still in thrall to the scopic universe. Britain, particularly, developed a state machinery to survey, police and aid its population.[4] Knowledge was on the surface and available to interpretation; so the early sociology of the reports of government inspectors did not see social relations or, and especially, economics. Later writers taught me to know better than this effort to see secrets, because of

4. "The industrial–urban society coming into being between 1815 and 1851 was confronted with four principal social areas in which it would be obliged to act. First there was the care of an increasing number of social casualties, to be provided by means of the Poor Law. Secondly there was an altogether new problem, namely the need for state surveillance of the conditions of work, chiefly in the factories and mines. Thirdly, because of the new concentration of people and industries in the cities, the state could not avoid an involvement in the conditions of living, chiefly through measures to promote public health. Finally, there was the question of education: what should government do about the needs of society and the rights of individuals in this respect? These were the four basic social functions into which the state was to be drawn between 1815 and 1851 in order to ease and contain the pressures of industrialisation and to fit the working population for their tasks." Checkland (1983): 82.

... the precise manner in which they offer a notion of the poor grounded not in economic categories but in those features predicated on the existence of an essential self. Represented as an essence because it was something apparently enclosed within a body, this self was to be discovered under the skin, almost like perfume confined within a bottle until its stopper is loosened. The essential self, moreover, was not confined to simply any body, but to a body with a definitive gender, and one seemingly cut off from the social, economic, and historical world.[5]

The surveying state proposed that the shape of the world was given by nature and the job of the scholar was to identify visual clues to this underlying truth. Inevitably, what the scholar saw was the shape of her own social world. Society as it was justified by nature or essence. The sight of your eyes could only confirm your beliefs, not uncover new secrets at all.

Before, when I was told that mass production also altered consciousness, I had no sense of what this might mean. Now my retold stories flicked open fresh clues. So massive a change in our material lives must have consequences for our apprehension of material things. Perhaps reification was a word to express alienation as an increasingly visualized experience of the material world? Implying that industrial production mutes sensory perception, instead resurrecting a desensitized sight as people's understanding of their connection to the world. Perhaps this was the frame story for all my sisters' tales?

5. Levy (1991): 30.

In the end, my encounter with scholarship left me little the wiser: I understood the fears of white people more clearly, but not much else. I learned that people could be read like stories, interpreted into meaning – but all my instincts told me that the interpretations barely began to explain the shapes of the world. So much was still to be told. In the books I read, heritage still belonged to the privileged and our history was lost beneath our contact with Europe. Perhaps that was our history now, that process of being overwritten? I still wanted to get closer to my own past and I saw that these techniques of understanding which I had studied so diligently had been developed in our homelands. Now I wondered if assuming the eyes of the traveller would let me catch a glimpse of our lost past. After all, this was how the stories of our past had been written."

The tale of Sindbad the travel-writer

Once upon a time, long, long ago, a man dreamed of crossing oceans and travelling to the end of the world.

"Why can't you be content with your life?", asked his friends and neighbours. "Your life is sweet and full, filled with the comforts of the familiar. Travel will just make you sad."

The man smiled. He listened to these taunts every day. Sometimes his neighbours grew angry, verging on violence, trying to shake him into agreement. At others they tried to coax, expressing selfless concern. Either way they kept on pushing and prying, unable to leave it alone, so great was their fear of the unknown. The man kept on smiling. He knew that there was a whole world yet to be seen. Instead of fear, he felt anticipation. He sensed that seeing strange lands would make him more, not less, himself.

He had heard travellers' tales before. His childhood was filled with accounts of strange creatures and misshapen people across the ocean. As a child, these stories had made him shiver agreeably, safely tucked up in his own bed, away from the dangers of foreign lands. Now, as a man, he found distant lands tempting. The fears of his childhood had shrunk as his sense of self grew.

> To judge from what European travellers had to tell, a whole series of important cosmological changes occurred towards the end of the seventeenth century . . . all these changes led to a less dramatic, more peaceful view of the relationships of Christian Europe to rival agencies and civilisations and the outside world.[6]

Maybe a little earlier, maybe a little later – certainly not for everyone, but for enough to count – sometime "towards the end of the seventeenth century", the white men of Europe began to conceive of themselves in a new way. We have already heard one part of this in the story of the self-fashioning white men. This new possibility gave the class-privileged men of Europe the chance to think of the world as centred around them. The rest of the world became theirs to survey.

"A growing self-confidence increasingly reduced the threatening and frightening powers, which earlier on had set the stage for the pilgrims' and explorers'

6. Harbsmeier (1984): 73.

dramatic adventures out there, to more manageable proportions."[7]

Our travelling man, although of a more confused class location than the average self-fashioner, benefits from this change in perceptions. Distant lands may hold unknown dangers, but now there was no reason to believe that these were supernatural forces or monsters beyond human capacity. The wise men of Europe had learned a new consciousness and now the edge of civilization held no fears.

In fact, on the contrary, the edges of civilization now became places of heady attraction. With their new sense of potency, European travellers could now see the potential benefits of charting other domains. They owned the technologies of travel, warfare and recording; wherever they went, they could not fail to augment their own sense of self.

"By etymology as well as definition, 'barbarians' everywhere were considered unable to speak or write properly for themselves; neither did they master the right script nor have the right language, if they were considered to have any language at all."[8]

The ability to represent, by association, belonged to the civilized. And the story their travels told was that of their own ability in comparison with others' barbarity. This sense that the world is out there for you to see and that it exists to confirm your own sense of self is another theme of modernity, part of the West's coming to self-knowledge. This promise, as typified by travel-writing, marks the early modern period: the idea that you have a place of privilege in a wider world.

7. Ibid.: 73.
8. Ibid.: 72.

"Like the learned, those who lived in a vernacular world were both curious and alarmed about the lands at the extremes of the habitable world. They, too, had an ample literature to read and marvel at – a literature which often stimulated reflection of all sorts."[9]

From then on, the period of European ascendance which we call modernity maintains this sense of globality. Of course, this is the particular global experience of the Western (potential) traveller, carrier of civilization and human innovation to regions which lack these lucky qualities. It is centuries before there is any admission that there is any two-way traffic in this process. But the sense of the accessibility of other parts of the world runs through modern experience, nevertheless.

"This is the utopian moment of travel: when you realize that what seems most unattainaby marvelous, most desirable, is what you almost already have, what you could have – if you could only strip away the banality and corruption of the everyday – at home."[10]

From this point, we, the rest of the world, occupy a special place in the European imagination. From now on, their stories of self will always be peopled with some version of us. My concern was with the stories they told. Listen to a portmanteau version of a favourite tale.

The story of the people without brains

Once the world was a different shape from the one which we know. In that other time, some people not

---

9. Grafton referring to the writings of Marco Polo and John Mandeville (1992): 70.
10. Greenblatt (1991): 25.

only believed that they owned the world; they went out to mark it with their name. They carved their name on every surface they could reach, and then moved on to the homes, gardens, parks and fields of other people.

They prepared themselves against the scoldings this bad behaviour might bring: everyone else is doing it, we are doing them a favour, anyway, they don't know any better and in the end it will be better this way.

To prove the point the name-marking people told this story.

When the world was born, people came in many shapes. Each tribe at this dawn of time lived separately – and over time each took the shape and colour of their landscape, the flavour of their foodstuff, the temperature of their surroundings. Soon the family of man split into separate branches, each adapted to the needs of their lifestyle. This proved that some were born to think and others to labour.[11]

Others told another story, citing St Augustine to prove that all people stemmed from one root, that we were all descendants of Adam. Science had grown too big for its boots, thinking that it could overturn God's law and forget the kinship between all people.[12]

11. "Polygenists argued that the different races of man were so different from each other in their physical, mental and moral attributes as to form not mere varieties of one single species, but instead several distinct biological species of their own." Stepan (1982): 29. "To a large extent, the story of racial science in Britain between 1800 and 1850 is the story of desperate efforts to rebut polygenism, and the eventual acceptance of popular quasi-polygenist prejudices in the language of science." Ibid.: 30.

12. "In 1800, most British scientists . . . were monogenists, believing that all the varieties of humankind . . . were . . . members of a single human, biological 'species' and united in a single brotherhood by their common humanity." Ibid.: 1.

Whatever the disagreements between proponents of one root or many roots for humanity, all agreed that the dark-skinned world was lacking in intellectual capacity. Even if people were physiologically similar and the Bible said that everyone had an equal moral capacity, the great men of the West could see that the rest of the world was not ready for their progress. It didn't matter if the failing stemmed from biology or lack of contact with civilization; what mattered was that these people were too far behind to catch up now. Who really believed that these backward people of inferior intellect were equal to the achievements of European culture?

The story about the people with no brains was quite simple, obvious even. By now its main plot points are known to everyone.

(1) The world is split into lucky and unlucky people. Some people are rewarded by life and others are not.

Almost no-one disputes this point. Whatever disagreements arise later, only the most doggedly unworldly thinker believes that all lives are equally blessed. Which is a different thing from saying that they should be.

(2) The amount of luck you have is somehow earned or deserved through accomplishment. This is another way of saying that people make their own luck and hardship is something people bring upon themselves.

(3) To make point two more palatable, its adherents argue that people suffer not because they are less deserving, but because they are less talented. This is an unfortunate accident of nature which, although regrettable, is how the world is. It is not, therefore, something which can be argued into abeyance: right-

minded people should concentrate their intellectual energies on dealing with the consequences of this unavoidable situation instead of fruitlessly trying to talk it out of existence.

All of these statements belong to the point of view which says that social inequalities are rooted in nature, or in a version of culture which might as well be nature. So learning should be about managing these inevitable inequalities, rather than banging on about how all people are equal. This is a dispute we are all still having.

For a long time the scholarship of white men has sought to justify (white) privilege. Writing of the time between 1800 and 1850, Nancy Stepan remarks, "The standard textbooks in anthropology took the idea of a natural hierarchy of human organisation and function for granted. The only question remaining was the technique best suited for revealing the hierarchy."[13]

Whatever technique of understanding was employed, the important things were already decided. Different times used different words, but all agreed that the people of the rest of the world were not the same. And importantly, a "not the same" which was lesser. By the end of the nineteenth century few assumptions have changed.

"In turn-of-the-century evolutionary thinking, savagery, dark skin, and a small brain and incoherent mind were, for many, all part of the single evolutionary picture of 'primitive' man, who even yet walked the earth."[14]

For the hundred years which most surely cements Europe's global dominance, the story of the people

13. Ibid.: 18.
14. Stocking (1968): 132.

with no brains remained a favourite tale. Splitting the world into capable and incapable people, whatever the determinants of this split, transformed the story of the theft of the world's resources into a tale of moral imperative.

Of course, the people of the mind reasoned, the people without brains needed protection. They, sad souls, would never learn to write their name on the world. The name-marking people, on the other hand, met their own destiny only when they graffiti-ed the globe in their image. Who else but the owners of knowledge and reason could be fit to own the world? What they did they did for the good of these others who could not think for themselves.

For every instance of bad behaviour, the people of the mind had another version of this story ready. No-one believed it but themselves, but they didn't care. They had learned how to make their stories stick like truth, so what they said affected the shape of the world.[15]

Much later, when the world of European ascendance was crumbling around them, the story of the people with no brains jumped up once more, out of the anxious mouths of the dying descendants of Europe. Once again, *The bell curve* used scholarship to argue that people could not argue about their lot in life, because it was given by nature.

When Charles Murray and Richard Herrnstein resurrect the never-quite-buried debate about cognitive

15. "When asked if he believed missionary preachings, the son of Somosomo's [in Fiji] king responded: 'Everything that comes from the white man's country is true; muskets and gunpowder are true, and your religion must be true.'" Stocking (1987): 91.

capacity and class and race, they know they are touching a raw nerve. Their overarching argument – that intelligence is measurable and that the measurements indicate that intelligence is inherited, with black and poor people receiving lesser capacities from their forebears – was, it is true, out of fashion with the science establishment. However, the tale of the people without brains had retained a vibrant popular life, so the prettily presented tome of tables, diagrams and statements of the obvious found a ready audience with people who already believed in its conclusions.

The main points of the argument expressed in *The bell curve* are easy to anticipate. The authors state their own interests early on: they maintain that the twentieth century begins with a world order in which aristocratic power is finally being overtaken by the influence of business and enterprise:

> Our thesis is that the twentieth century has contained the transformation, so that the twenty-first will open on a world in which cognitive ability is the decisive dividing force. The shift is more subtle than the previous one but more momentous. Social class remains the vehicle of social life, but intelligence now pulls the train.[16]

Once again, the inequalities of social life are described as a good and inevitable thing: the most talented rise to the top of society and their talent is fed through generations of mutual reinforcement through inbreeding. Any efforts a society may make to try to overcome these inequalities – through welfare measures, affirmative action, changes in education – are bound

16. Herrnstein & Murray (1994): 25.

to fail, because inequality is enshrined in that unarguable entity, our genetic make-up. In fact, the authors argue that these ameliorative measures end up making things worse for everyone. Instead they suggest a change of approach.

> It is time for America once again to try living with inequality, as life is lived: understanding that each human being has strengths and weaknesses, qualities we admire and qualities we do not admire, competencies and incompetences, assets and debits; that the success of each human life is not measured externally but internally; that of all the rewards we can confer on each other, the most precious is a place as a valued fellow citizen.[17]

Of course, like the other attempts to sweeten domination into a moral project, this all means that people should know their place and not rock the boat. Instead of believing that people are born equal and that their potentials are stymied by the inadequacies of our social structure, Murray and Herrnstein suggest that we go back to believing in natural hierarchies. Accepting this order would cut out the frictions of contemporary society and allow the talented space to realize their potential to be rich, powerful and privileged. Everyone else has different potentials to develop and must be content with assets which yield little reward, other than the status of an inferior but respected fellow citizen. A commentator summarizes the case:

17. Ibid.: 551.

> People are pretty much where they should be – members of the so-called "cognitive elite" are ensconced in the wealthiest communities, while the poor (dubbed the "dull" or "very dull") languish, and deservedly so, in run-down, crime-ridden neighbourhoods because they are unable to do any better for themselves.[18]

For all the triumphant talk about the rule of the intellectually gifted, Murray and Herrnstein are retelling another popular story about how scary the world has become. Despite its talent, the elite is under siege from a less cognitively gifted mass; the fear is that the world of the inbred underclass will overrun the world of the inbred elite. As another commentator identifies, "Herrnstein and Murray are part of the fin-de-siecle gloom movement."[19]

They describe a world in which education has altered the life aspirations of class-privileged women to such an extent that the cognitively gifted privileged class is not being reproduced, let alone expanded. Instead, it is the black and white poor who are having children young, while underperforming on every index of social value which Herrnstein and Murray recognize. The logic of *The bell curve* may argue that the cognitive elite deserve their privilege, but it also warns that this privilege is under threat from the ever-expanding mass of the cognitively challenged underclass. Their dead weight prevents the elite from leading society towards its true potential. The mind people keep being held back by their responsibility to the people with no brains.

18.   Jacqueline Jones in Fraser (1995): 80.
19.   Hacking (1995).

Even now, when the Euro-peoples were frightened about their future and hardly believed in their own superiority or ability to progress, the desperate still fell back on old dreams of intellectual superiority. Of course, with this old story another old story was also resurrected.

Instead of brains, the stories of the name-marking people said that the unthinking races owned excessively developed genitalia. Simple measurement made this apparent: skull capacity, brain weight, g-factor – all the numbers led to the conclusion that the name-marking were brain-full and intellect-heavy. Another set of figures and diagrams showed without a doubt that the least intellectually gifted were compensated by their biologically determined sexual capacities. Think back to our sisters on display. "Sarah Bartmann's sexual parts, her genitalia and her buttocks, serve as the central image for the black female throughout the nineteenth century."[20]

As we approached the twenty-first century, the suggestion had not died. Some people had no brains, but they had something else. "Even if you take something like athletic ability or sexuality – not to reinforce stereotypes or some such thing – but, you know, it's a trade-off: more brain or more penis. You can't have everything."[21]

Nature evened out her gifts, and although the name-markers were envious of the other package of bodily pleasure, overall they were pleased with their destiny. And there was nothing to stop them looking at what they did not have, after all.

20. Gilman (1986): 235.
21. A. Miller quoting J.P. Rushton in "Professors of hate", *Rolling Stone*, 20 October 1994.

In exchange for lending the services of their superior brains, the name-markers embarked upon an obsessive adventure of anatomical voyeurism. They had brought so much good and so many benefits to these no-brained people, they reasoned (reason being their forte), that the harmless pleasure of the gaze was the least they were owed. And anyway, it was in the interests of science that these facts be gathered and documented. How would humanity progress without more and better knowledge?

The name-markers relished their role as documentors; it was a task which agreeably confirmed and demonstrated their own capacities, while highlighting the lesser attributes of others. Science congratulated man on his clever anticipation of the natural order. The name-markers' instinctive knowledge of their own superiority was itself an indication of what scientific method went on to prove. Of course, it was those who could conceive of an order to the world who were most equipped to investigate it.

But in the midst of all this self-congratulation, doubts remained. Would brains always necessarily beat genitals in the play-off of human progress? Perhaps it was dangerous that the least thinking should be the most fecund?

Brains were no good unless their owners continued to rule. The name-markers envied the easy reproduction of their less gifted kinfolk, but they also feared it. They began to devote their attention to ensuring that the brain-heavy minority was not overrun by the genital-heavy masses. This is the story hidden within my next tale, "The tale of the West's descent".

The newsreader continued her tale:
These were the stories familiar to me from my childhood and from these I learned that I was one of

the descendants of the people without brains, that I was destined to be destroyed by my own fertility, that education was wasted on me. Despite my best efforts, the legacies of these stories infiltrated my life, keeping me from any belated inheritance of reason. This was what the world believed; who was I to think differently?

But in my new job I began to hear fresh versions of these old damaging tales – here, at last, was the new instalment we had all been waiting for.

It seemed that the home of the thinking conquering people was in decline. That strange and mystical thing, the West, was losing its power. Now all those old tricks which had fooled us for so long just didn't work any more. I knew this was happening because the people of the West told me so. In my new position as speaker of truth, I heard a new episode in our mythology.

The story had several sections.

After so many years of believing in perpetual progress, now the people of the West believed that their world was getting worse. To them this seemed as unstoppable as it was frightening. For as long as anyone could remember, people in the West had expected that their lives would be easier, more affluent and comfortable than those of their parents. This was their birthright, as the children of progress.

But suddenly, all that had stopped. Things were not getting better. For many, even in the blessed West, things were getting worse. The old eradicated diseases of the poor returned as children grew up in the conditions of past superseded generations.[22]

22. See "TB will kill 30m in next 10 years", *Guardian*, 22 March 1996: 3; "Europe hit by return of diseases", *Guardian*, 8 March 1996: 3.

The people of the West were looking for someone to blame.

High on the list came us, the rest of the world. Before we had been strange but full of promise. Our homes had provided the unmarked territories of Western discovery. When they could sell no more things to each other, they shipped their surplus out to us and kept making money. As long as we were there, where they expected us to be, progress could keep happening. The people of the West relied on us to be there, to keep them in cheap raw materials, to buy up their leftovers, to keep them wealthy over the odds. When the free lunches stopped, they blamed us.

The West was changing shape, irretrievably, irreversibly. No longer workshop of the world, it was proving impossible to make more and more things. Of course, some factories went on, some products were manufactured: but not enough to keep everyone in work, let alone getting wealthier. Things changed so much that the industrial nations started to talk of deindustrialization, a word to explain the unexpected sufferings of their people.

All of this, of course, was the fault of the rest of the world. We had become wayward, wanting to follow our own paths of development. Worse still, we had run out: there were no more untapped markets waiting for the entertainment and enlightenment of Western capital. Without these free rides, the economies of the West stagnated and declined. Without economic growth, standards of living could not be sustained, let alone improved. The people of the West felt the pinch, and blamed us.

Before, we represented unknown lands of adventure and possibility. We needed the guidance of the West to channel our potentials, but we were still full of potential. Now the rest of the world stared back at the West looking like their worst nightmares. All the hidden threats were now out of the closet; everything the West had feared seemed to be coming true. No longer did they look at us and see the seeds of future wealth and achievement. Now they saw flesh-eating phantoms coming to eat what little they had left. In the new world of the dying West, everything was directed towards destroying this threat.

Before they had welcomed the cheapness of our labour. Now they feared that only we would work and that they would catch poverty just from being near us. Stay where you are, they said, that is where you belong.

Before, they had believed in their own superiority. No-one could shape the world in their own image as they did. Industry belonged to them. Now they feared the efficiencies of the East, promising that it couldn't happen here and that those ways work only with the less-than-human anyway.

Before they were the warriors, fighting righteous wars on other people's land. They loved themselves for this showy valour, the particular virtues of always being ready for a fight. It was true that, even then, much of their fighting was done by us. Since then other changes had happened. Now they made and sold the business of war and we bought it up hungrily. In the ensuing fights among ourselves, the people of the West somehow lost their nerve. Now they feared our aggression and irresponsibility.

Since I had learned to speak the truth the people of the West thought that I was one of them. They spoke freely before me, swapping a thousand tales of fear and rumour. One story I noticed again and again, cropping up in various mouths, in different segments, all with one conclusion: that things would never be the same again. To the best of my memory, these are the key points.

A compressed history of the world: the quest for total knowledge in the 1990s

The people of the West believed that industrialization belonged to them alone. It was their invention, after all, and only they could handle its danger-filled benefits. The course of history seemed to bear out this belief. The rest of the world seemed unable to follow the example set by the West; unlike them, they never grew into the name "industrial nations". No matter what happened later, somehow that name always belonged to the West. No-one else seemed able to manage the difficult process of industrialization. Some places got somewhere with guidance, but never really made it work.[23] Others kicked against the necessary disciplines, and gave up access to its benefits.

It was these wayward people who really troubled the West. Unlike those who failed under guidance, these people were no fools. The people of the West suspected that they had capacities equal to their own. They, too, could easily become part of the chosen and dwell in the beauty of the developed world. Only their contrary natures held them back; so thought the people of the West.

The leaders of the contrary people knew this and persuaded their people that this was proof that they were right. Why did the people of the West care so much to meddle in other people's business? Surely

23.   For more on this point see Chatterjee (1993b).

this was a sign of their greedy grasping natures; they could leave nothing alone. In all the stories they told, the people of the West were the enemy. They warned each other of the feigned concern of these devious people and saw each intrusive gesture from the West as a prelude to a larger-scale attack.

In their turn, the people of the West concocted stories to explain this inexplicable contrariness. They viewed the contrary people as their eccentric cousins, somehow held under the sway of dangerous despots who could manipulate their vulnerable minds. In all the stories they told they decried this brainwashed society and mourned the lost freedoms of their mis-led kinfolk, viewing each resistance to the progress of Westernization as the foolishness of an addled mind.

Both sides viewed the other as sad cases under the power of evil despots hell-bent on world domination. Both sides told endless stories about the plight of their led-astray cousins. In the end the family rift grew so huge that it dissected the globe. We all lived in the shadow of this quarrel.[24]

Then one day, miraculously, it seemed that the fight was over. The contrary had finally seen reason and proved the people of the West right after all: 1989 was a sea-change year, and now it seemed that history was restarting on the West's terms.[25]

After the contrary people had come around to the West's way of thinking, it seemed that the last obstacles to progress had been removed. Now freedom was available to all – apart from those too barbaric to appreciate it, of course.

24. See Paterson & McMahon (1991); Boyle (1993).
25. For more on this, see Boyle (1993).

Many people rushed to take advantage of their new-found freedoms. The names of the past were challenged at every corner. As everyone demanded the right to choose their own names, blood was spilt freely. Crowds of unnamed people ran quickly to freedom, from persecution, from, to, around self-determination, running towards something familiar or towards something new, running because those around them ran. Everyone knew that the world was shifting. But, as usual, we were shocked to see how bad progress could look.

For the barbaric people beyond progress things changed differently. The contrary people had sheltered some of the barbaric for many years, intent on distracting them from the influence of the West. In another uneven relation which echoed the uneven exchanges engaged in by the West, the contrary people swapped goods and technology with their own dependants.[26] When the contrary changed their minds, their dependants were left without protectors. The new climate of freedom affected these vulnerable people in particular ways. With new freedoms, new horrors appeared.

The story of the poor world in the new world order

> If there are certain broad features that post-colonial nations may be said to have in common as a result of their shared experience of colonialism these lie in the following: the central role of the state; inequalities in social structures; the

26. See Allison (1988); Katz (1990).

contrary pulls of nationalism and regionalism (or centralization and federalization); and the conflicts between "tradition" and "modernity". The particular consequences of this history as they impinge upon gendered issues are remarkably similar.[27]

In a popular story about travel, a young white man enters an unmarked establishment somewhere in Asia. He is anxious and alone, visibly shaken by the quiet threats of the foreignness which surrounds him. When he spots the proprietor, an elderly Asian gentleman of legend, with daughter, the young man takes out his money and resorts to the universal language of signs. He forgets speech and decides to go with the more portable communication code of the visual.

What the young man does is to draw a curvy shape with both his hands in the air. Unsurprisingly, given all our histories, the elderly gentleman reads this as typically inappropriate behaviour from a white boy and the daughter edges behind her father, away from this nasty request for a woman.

The white boy laughs when he recognizes the parody he has been taken for, and assures them, "No, no – Coca Cola." Hearing this new universal language, father and daughter laugh back with regained good humour: "Ah – Coca Cola", before the father explains, "Sorry, this is a hardware store."

The white men have always coveted our women. In the uncertain era named "postcolonial", we expect cocky tourists to try to relive the easy access of former times. The substitution of an iconic Western

27. Rajan (1993): 6.

consumer good for the woman signals a shift in the story, an indication of how these postcolonial times will be.

In the story to follow, our bodies seem insignificant. The sign for woman's body becomes a marker for other things, the products which may or may not herald a new era for the no-longer-colonized nation. Of course, changes in this story also affect the stories about our no-longer-colonized bodies. Remember, we have heard the story of how the Western world rethinks the body in modernity. Now let's move on to what the rest of the world thinks.

"The search for a postcolonial modernity has been tied, from its very birth, with its struggle against modernity."[28]

Inevitably, modernity as a synonym for European ascendance has been hard for the rest of the world to stomach. After all, their modernity required our subjugation, whether or not they admit it. To become self-fashioning in our turn, to tell our own stories again, we must kick against this thing, modernity. Even, and most especially, when we want it badly.

"History, it would seem, has decreed that we in the postcolonial world shall only be perpetual consumers of modernity."[29]

What choice do we have but to find some other route to self-authorship? Who is surprised if this alternative route lacks much of the promised sweetness of progress?

Let's think about another kind of story, about another kind of dark girl and our fantasies about her.

28. Chatterjee (1993a): 75.
29. Ibid.: 5.

Mother India is one of the old-time stories about ancient belonging and nurturing homeland. We could talk all day about why she is "mother"; but let's just say for now that some people deserve a forgiving love and hope that home will offer it.

Instead of dwelling too long on all that nation-as-woman stuff, let's talk about marking territory. No-one thinks that land is like flesh. Land is hard and dusty, wet and swampy, what life lives off, not life itself. Flesh is feel-good feel-bad dangerous mortality. Flesh makes people, and land makes . . . territory?

That mysterious thing called culture organizes our understanding of the material. However real and immediate flesh and land feel, what they mean depends on what story they are in. To know what is going on you have to get a handle on the stories.

Coca Cola in and out of India

If the world has changed shape, as the stories in so many mouths suggest, what indications do we have of this shape-changing?

We have been constructed in the shadow of the West as the shadow of the West, living our lives in shadow, away from the light of enlightenment. That is the world we know. We have learned to think as our masters and mistresses think, to see through their eyes and to believe in what we see. Even as we feel the earth tremble beneath our feet in the shift to a new order, we seek verification for a change which cannot be seen.

Now we too are addicted to looking. We look for our place in the new world.

Living in Britain

The South Asian diaspora looks to the sub-continent as an anchor for identity formation, however myth- ical and uncomfortable. India, Pakistan, Bangladesh, Sri Lanka – these names must be fixed "national origins" if the particularity of the South Asian diaspora is to be maintained. A certain amount of belief in a distant national fiction seems necessary and reassuring to dispersed communities trying to name themselves in difficult circumstances. Unlike the classic diaspora, which sees homeland as a goal to be reached in the future, here the story of travel says that the homeland is safe and whole and can be returned to sometime. We are not rootless, because our roots are there, waiting for our return.

So when I tell stories about India they are much more indicative of second-generation nostalgias than anything else. For my purposes "India" is the name of authentic homeland, the pristine nation whose integrity is threatened by an intrusive world. When I choose this India as my topic of talk, I claim this clean realness for my own compromised identity. History may make me a ragbag of cultural forms and partial knowledges, but the appeal to my lost nation lets me speak with authority. No matter that I am foreign there, that I have always lived here, that I live India through the out-of-date memories of my displaced family. In the West the diaspora Indian stands in easily for all India. This is the representa- tional system people are used to, and if I accept this deal I am ensured a certain amount of respect. Not the respect accorded to the we-speak-truth white men, but not the ridicule that studying Milton or British government incurs. So the nostalgic take on India is also a longing for a different name for myself, a name which is entitled to speak.

This is a story about diaspora children looking for the authentic names given to them by lost homelands. Inevitably, the story is constructed using the cast-off tools of Western knowledge production. How else can we think, when we have been here so long? In the story, the sad-eyed children of the diaspora turn their heads back to see where they have come from and with an effort of faith try to see the authentic India beneath the sediment of unhappy histories. Far from home, our children fear that Mother India is again under threat, that her real self may be eaten up by international forces before we ever get back home safe to her bosom.

In this particular story, this born-abroad fiction is echoed and disrupted by a born-again Hindutva which aims to "Hinduize politics and militarize Hinduism" in the name of a true India whose identity is under threat.

Coca Cola is the name of international consumer culture in this story: kind of sexy but kind of dangerous.

The story is about the trials and tribulations of these characters, seen from afar through the magical periscope of living in the West.

In 1977 the then Janata Government of India made the unprecedented move of forcing Coca Cola out of operation in India. There are a number of accounts of this event, but some of the rationales include the idea that national industry and culture must be safeguarded and promoted, and that for this to be possible the state must protect homegrown industry against "foreign" multinationals. This is an echo of a longstanding Gandhian line which says that industrialism is the cause of India's poverty, against the more Nehruvian approach which sees prosperity in the development of a centrally controlled industrialization. In relation to this debate about where the real danger lies, the dangers of neo-colonialism have also been invoked. Everyone agrees that the independent nation must stave off this nebulous but dangerous threat; but whether this is best done through the self-sufficiency of small-scale production or by accelerated industrialization with a view to international competition is to be decided. Coke could be shown the door either in an effort to resist Western consumer culture or in an attempt to make space for Indian manufacturers of soft drinks to find their own way. However we interpret this event, what seems clear is that at a certain point it was expedient for a national government to exclude a very powerful international company. An attempt was made to stem the seemingly inevitable move towards the global in the name of state-sponsored national integrity.

After Coke's departure, several "Indian" companies became successful in the Indian soft-drink market. However, these drinks continued to be marketed with thinly disguised reference to "international" products such as Coca Cola.

Now, after the demise of the Soviet Union and the rapid economic expansions in South-East Asia, economic policies in India are being reformed. India now wishes to embrace the global economy and global culture. As part of this, Coke has returned to India, it seems triumphantly.

I've been very interested in this story: it mobilizes some of the main fun buzz-terms of my professional life, it links ethnic flavour with international glitz, it lets me play authentic identity and pomo rootlessness, all in the same breath. All round there seemed to be a lot of mileage in it.

But it's only as I try to re-tell the story that I realize how difficult it is to tell. So most of this is an exercise in getting things straight in my head.

As newsreader my job is to narrate the world, while knowing the limits of narrative. I'm used to using stories to try to understand the world; but, like many others, I'm getting bored of endlessly discussing representation, signification, metaphor, metonymy, powerful symbols and resistant readings. Even though I should know better I'm still lustful for the evasive real world, for mastery of that more concretely satisfying arena. I'm nostalgic for a journalism which believes it can reveal the truth.

I hoped this story would provide a route into this world of fact and certainty. It was a story I wanted to cover, the kind of special interest case that I was allowed to investigate myself. This tale about the changing shape of the world echoed my own mysteriously changing status. It was important to me that I made this story my own. I knew how the editors worked, so when I first outlined my interests I pretended to know what I was looking for. I laid out my objectives . . .

To document the interplay between global and national cultures through a case-study of Coca Cola's activities and profile in India.

The aim is to develop a framework which can illuminate the new versions of nation which are articulated through these global interventions into the local space, and to offer a more detailed account of the factors involved in the integration of an international product into a particular national space.

There is a vague pretence of specificity here, but it barely hides my embarrassing yearning for a general truth. This is a story of mythic proportions and what

I am looking for is a metaphysical showdown. Which narrative will claim the sacred territory of Bharat? What do the outcomes of these battles mean for the future of humanity? I wanted this to be a transferable story, something to help me deal with being frightened and mortal, some guide to being good . . .

I like this story because it is such a rich moral fable, and because I have gone back to thinking that learning is about salvation.

Whether or not we choose to admit it, all of that diligent knowledge-gathering, the memos and the overheads and the handouts, the exclusives and the in-depths and the on-the-spots, all that frenzied activity is based around the assumption that knowing is better, the preferable option.

I think for us being good is still very much about gathering knowledge. It's hard not to think that a more "accurate" description of the world is not a better thing. I take research and reporting to be the name we give to this spiritual struggle, a way of sharing more lonely battles.

For this to happen I need to explain why my chosen allegory might help us all.

In the extended debates around the processes of globalization, little attention has been paid to resistances to this process at the level of the state. Local culture has tended to mean immediate community and it has been these locations which have been scrutinized for their reactions and resistances to global trends.

This piece of research seeks to question the assumption that national and global cultures counteract each other, and instead examines the ways in which international commodities become integrated into particular settings as part of a dialogue between the local and the global. The suggestion is that, rather than the idea of the nation falling out of this equation altogether, in fact some processes of globalization include both a resurgence of nationalist rhetoric and, more surprisingly, the emergence of a more resilient version of the nation-state.

I set up the answerable riddle to reassure myself. Are things more globalized or more localized these days, I wonder? More interconnected or more fragmented?

Of course, the answer is both.

These are old and familiar stories. The world is getting smaller, tighter, more the same. You can buy the same things everywhere. We are all increasingly interdependent parts of a ghost whole which pulls our strings but lives nowhere.

Yet at the same time the world is increasingly fragmented, filled with violent localisms and incompatible particularities.

And – surprise, surprise – the nation-state, obsolete form of another era, springs back revamped through these windows of aggression and confusion.

But I'm jumping ahead.

Let's start with a handy and perhaps apocryphal soundbite. Another journalist tells me that in a global survey of teenagers 82 per cent recognize the symbol for Coca Cola, compared to 40 per cent who can read the sign for the United Nations. This almost-fact makes my next suggestions seem true without any argument.

Coca Cola is the essence of America – the dream America of permanent boomtime where everyone is young and firm and fun-loving. These iconic products give us our most tangible take on the reach of Western capital in its flighty and flexible disorganized forms. These are the marks of conversion-cum-domination, an indication of people's dreams.

Everyone understands Coca colonization: it makes sense in ways that other kinds of argument (flexible accumulation?) don't. It hits that commonsense spot. Which is why it is the stuff of contemporary mythology, perhaps? The frighteningly unrepresentable social relations of the global economy become conceivable when we imagine the reach of familiar brands as a new map of the world. The reassuring misapprehensions of the cartographic imagination allow us to believe that the important things in the world can be visualized; imagine the right colours on the map and you get the picture.

Recently I have been describing the good journalism of popular cultural studies as a statement of the blindingly obvious – a slogan learned from a student – and keeping faith with my job involves keeping faith with this, the promise that the things worth knowing are readily available if only you know how and where to look, that we are all wise beyond recognition and dulled only by the wickedness of the world.

This is part of being good: the belief that we all know what we need to know, if only we could see it. So what I wanted was a story to give me that particular rush that you get off everyday revelation: right under your nose, romance on your doorstep, being home all along. Suddenly knowing how we got here and sensing what might be possible.

So when I got my big investigative break, I saw a chance: to pay attention to some of those big old-fashioned stories, so familiar that we forget that we know them. The multinational corporation, the erosion of local cultures, the embarrassment of Western-style consumerism amid widespread poverty. Nothing we haven't heard before. The world is chained together

by a series of unequal economic relations; less powerful places are in thrall to more powerful places even
without the back-up of an occupying armed force.
This whole razor-wire net cuts into the flesh of the
locationally unlucky through the mysteries of international trade agreements, global fordism, debt, the
seemingly endless disposability of certain forms of
labour. *And*, importantly for our purposes, you can
see this incomprehensible hodge-podge of exploitation
in the spread of international consumer products in
places where there isn't enough income for shopping
really to be leisure. Get the picture?

I had long realized that if I used diatribes against
Coke and McDonalds I could make the most over-
general sweeps of cultural theory come true. Resisting the iconography of certain products and their
attendant labour formations makes "culture" – pictures, stories, fantasies – the terrain of struggle. Iconic
talismans make the devil of globalized capital into
an enemy which can be seen and fought. Or so we
hope, thankful for the distractions of an exorcism.

My first reporting strategy was to mobilize the
key terms of the rational West in my pursuit of the
truth – Capital, History, reason, knowability – mix
them up together and out pops an authentic depiction of reality. This is the big hard real world.

In the aftermath of the collapse of the Soviet Union
India has lost her favoured position as "non-aligned"
gateway to Asia. As in so much of the "Third World",
disarray in Moscow has repercussions all over.
With no Eastern Bloc for back-up and even old
rival China playing liberalized economy alongside
the scary discipline of police-state repression, India
needs to revamp her international profile. Whatever
the human costs, the five "Tigers" are making the

running in the Asian economic miracle. Still-hungry India can't show much to recommend the years of protectionism and planning. Time to play dice with the big boys.

Since 1991 the Rao administration had instigated a number of economic reforms. There have been PR visits to the West, a loosening-up on the transfer of goods and currency and capital, incentives to foreign companies. Of course, the plan was to win the 1996 elections, to resist the threat of balkanization; to safeguard national government and the nation-state in fact.[30]

But national integrity is a tricksy story to tell; particularly if you are relying on foreign cash.

Back to the main plot.

The elusive search for truth: what did happen back there in 1977?

In 1977 the newly elected Janata government excluded Coca Cola from India, or Coke decided to leave rather than bow down to the demands of any national government.

It's a funny story, peopled with the archetypes of all good neo-colonial mythology. The monstrous multinational eats the children of the village until the bravely reconstituted national government sees it off. Or the too-rigid doctrines of the planned economy wallahs steal the democratic joys of consumerism from the villagers until the market freedoms of a new global order sweep into town. Various familiar

---

30. In fact, the BJP was the largest single party after the 1996 elections, but could not form a government because of the non-co-operation of other parties. A coalition of left and regional parties formed a government, with the support of the defeated Congress Party.

faces of evil appear: the foreign company which destroys local cultures wherever it goes, the bureaucratic state which cannot meet the aspirations of the population, the gullible consumer who has no sense of what is good for him or her. The good guy can be made up later once you decide whom you hate the most.

In my family I had heard the story as a good joke on the too-big-for-its-boots American company. In this version Coca Cola couldn't believe that any national government, least of all hungry-for-Americana India, would ban its product. The family story, agreeing with Mark Pendergrast, puts the famous Coke formula at the centre of the plot; here knowledge is wealth. A Promethean story which places learning at the heart of power and morality.[31]

Fortune magazine (10 January 1994) tells me that Coke was forced out because it refused the government's demand to cut its stake in its wholly owned subsidiary to 40 per cent. Here power is wealth. India wins, Coke loses. Here the stake is honour: humble postcolonial nation sees off the insults of boorish multinational cash and regains a sense of its own value and identity.

According to the *Financial Times* (17 April 1991): "[Coke] . . . walked away from [India] in 1977 following an Indian requirement that most foreign companies reduce their equity holdings in subsidiaries to 40 per cent. Both Coke and IBM immediately pulled out of India." Here wealth is wealth. Coke wins, India loses. Here the story is one of gambler's bravado. India attempts to call Coke's bluff, to negotiate with no cards but a lot of front. Coke walk away to more

31. See Pendergrast (1993).

profitable fields and bigger adversaries, more able to bear the loss of the Indian market than India is able to bear the loss of foreign campanies. The rich folk win again, the little guy never stood a chance.

In 1977, after an extended state of emergency during which both right-wingers and trade unionists were persecuted, the public was forcibly sterilized, and all kinds of information was withheld, the Congress Party was dislodged from government for the first time in post-Independence history. The Janata Dal Party – an opportunistic alliance formed in response to the dog's dinner of Congress administration – dented the Nehru dynasty, first family of independent India, by resurrecting some alternative narratives of Indianness.

Under the leadership of Jayaprakash Narayan, a former ally of Nehru, a mass campaign was mobilized in favour of lower prices and the rooting-out of corruption. Narayan adopted a version of Gandhianism in which only a return to the village as the central unit of political and economic life would take India forward. This imaginative leap hit the spot for many people, particularly when Narayan formed an alliance with the Jan Sangh, organization of the people, later becoming the Bharatya Janata Party (BJP). This is the core of the alliance which ousted Congress in 1977.

Since 1947 India has had a strange relation with the West, and has certainly displayed changeable behaviour in relation to the role of international business. The 1977 election result was supposed to put the country back on track: time to regain that vision of what free India could be, put some pride back in the postcolonial nation. And that meant showing the multinationals who was boss. No more foreign-controlled business interests shaping Indian life; Indian-based businesses must have majority Indian ownership. If the country must be wracked by poverty and exploitation at least let this come though a system of production within the hard-fought-for nation. Another old lesson: successful independence for the postcolonial nation requires the emergence of a native bourgeoisie. That's what becoming a nation means in this story.[32]

So why the different configurations of national ruling class?

Since 1991 lots of energy has been devoted to persuading everyone that the national ruling class in India is powerful as a link to international capital. No-one believes in capitalism in one nation these days. Power is teamwork and communication.

Resistance to this internationalizing process has become the terrain of the true defendants of the Hindu nation, the blood-and-honour brigade; so the options seem to be multinational consumer capitalism or violently excluding religious racism. Being good becomes increasingly mysterious.

My second reporting strategy embraced my dubious status as representative of the South Asian diaspora and challenged the ability of the Western audience to ever understand my people. This was the titillating discomfort which my employers longed for and expected.

"Who are you to always be looking at us. Will you never learn any better?"

"If you want to hear I can tell you a story about natives or a story about yourselves. But don't count on learning anything . . ."

The occidental gaze is a funny thing. Even when we are taught to distrust its will to mastery, to unlearn the logics which place that look as the hidden

32. See Spivak (1988).

origin of all stories, or of all stories worth telling or hearing, it's hard to refuse. Shut your eyes and you're still in it, despite yourself. Strain to hear the voice of the other, be still and humble. Practise passivity. Relinquish goals. Work hard at giving it all away. And somehow the control freak of the Western subject still creeps back in. As if we can't help but try to get the picture.

> The instituted knowledge of society, as it exists in recorded history, is the knowledge obtained by the dominant classes in their exercise of power. The dominated, by virtue of their very powerlessness, have no means of recording their knowledge within those instituted processes, except as an object of the exercise of power.[33]

Our will to knowledge reveals our own longing to partake in the power of the dominant. Ordering information in a way which makes it plain that mastery is not a reasonable expectation is hard hard hard. If I tell you a story about human frailty how can any of us appreciate the paradox of its lesson? How can we learn about just how difficult it is to learn things?

Sometimes it is hard to identify evil. You can smell its presence, trace the tracks of broken bodies, but the creature itself is never there. It might be a fantasy but the wounds seem so real. Something somewhere must be responsible. Even when destruction falls from the sky it is a sign of some cosmic confrontation or the forgotten sins of a previous lifetime. If there is suffering there must be a perpetrator, a secret to be

33. Chatterjee (1993a): 161–2.

uncovered, a guilt to be exposed. There must be something which has led to this. Some image to give character to these events.

In my story Coke is the object of choice: the stand-in for all other objects, the talisman, the fetish, the archetypal commodity, the most thingy of things. If I show you a Coke bottle we all understand what objectification means. Remember, reification is a feature of everyday commonsense for us. Even if we can't spell it, we know how it works; the concept is blindingly obvious. I don't have to explain. Coke can stand in for a whole range of unfigurable processes.

Coke itself helpfully spells things out for us. The former chairman declared in 1923 that Coca Cola should always be "within an arms reach of desire"; if there is a commonsense theory of globalization, Coke is it.

The company champions "think global, act local" as its nineties strategy: international company, local bottling plants, local personnel, commercials and sales strategies varying according to location. All of those insights from the bulky theory books are echoed in the company bumpf.

In India Coke has bought up Parle, maker of Indian brand cola Thums Up, for $40 million and is working on becoming part of the Indian landscape. Instead of homogenizing, here international products interact with local surroundings to take on new location-specific meanings; textbook stuff, life is complicated, unpredictable things happen, what has gone before will always affect what follows. Coke benefits from Parle's familiarity with local markets and, crucially, hitches onto Parle's network of bottling and distribution outlets. Parle owns two bottling plants in Bombay and Delhi and has 60 franchized bottling plants across India. The deal promises to continue marketing the brands of both companies – but Indian manufacturer Parle no longer exists. Instead Coke has bought up Parle's 60 per cent share of the Indian soft drink market and become market leader overnight.

Some Indian business sees the threat in this. Rahul Bajaj of Bajaj Auto, largest scooter manufacturer in the world and an Indian firm, says, "There's no level playing field between Indian companies and foreigners. In one stroke, Parle as a company has disappeared. If this happens to several other companies, will it be good for India?" (*Financial Times*, 9 November 1993: 6).

With Coke the other big foreign companies to enter India in 1993 included Peugeot the car manufacturer, GE Capital and Morgan Stanley finance companies, Nippon Denro steel company, whisky maker Seagram and the spirits arm of Guinness. The cars, cash and drinks are all aimed at India's 200 million middle class. Evil here is the suggestion that there can be a consumer revolution in the midst of widespread and desperate poverty. Coke represents the immoral and inappropriate incursion of these alien cultural practises. For some, this product embodies all that is evil about the living arrangements of developed capitalism. Exorcism is the only route to salvation.

For others, of course, evil wears a different face.

Fear

Isn't fundamentalism the most frightening nightmare of your time? The hidden and unquantifiable threat behind every unknown situation? Belief beyond reason, anachronistic movements of faith, violent clingings to certainty in an uncertain world? Without doubt the name of the enemy for enlightenment project girl in the newsroom of the West; no space for the niceties of equal opps and soft feminist gains here, no flirty arguments or teasingly obedient quests for rational knowledges for Daddy. Fundamentalism marks out all those scary places where that baby-doll cutesiness just won't wash. Where hard men chant old truths and waste no breath on doubt or discussion.

In recent years India has had its share of these events. The destruction of the mosque at Ayodhya and the ensuing violence are an indication of more general trends.[34]

The stories about the pristine nation have a certain tasty nostalgia about them, perhaps particularly tasty to hungry-for-authenticity diasporic eyes? These stories promised to reshape the nation so that it looked like pretty pictures of its past, untouched by nasty alien forces which distorted its best features and made it something else altogether, not the thing we named home. No wonder people wanted to hear. Even shiny happy Coca Cola had a hard run for its money in comparison to this story of the best times of a long-lost childhood, the most familiar which we had not seen for far too long. The story of the clean nation demands that we conjure up an imaginary picture of the land. A metaphor of visibility which could be felt and sensed, but somehow never quite grasped through

34. In December 1992 Hindu activists associated with the BJP and sister organizations destroyed the sixteenth-century Babri Mosque in Ayodhya, because they believe it to lie on the site which marks the birthplace of Lord Ram. Reports suggest that police did nothing to stop them. In the violence which followed, many lives were lost, more than a thousand in Bombay, the vast majority Muslim.

the eyes. Again, like Coke, we are talking about marking the map with the symbols of a certain culture. If you can spread your iconic images far enough, the whole territory can become yours.

Coke has been doing its best to do this. Shopfronts wear the trademark signs, even when they do not stock the product. Adverts which picture no more than the Coke bottle itself are displayed in all kinds of semi-affluent streets. We can see that Coke has arrived here. The other story masqueraded as a resurrection of the essence of India submerged beneath this come-lately covering.

The other story

The Rashtriya Swayamsevak Sangh (RSS), an organization committed to reforming the Hindu self and creating a Hindu identity aware of its cultural heritage, has resisted liberalization and particularly Pepsi and Coke as "the most visible symbols of the multinational invasion of this country". Echoes of Gandhian boycotts and the noble India of the independence movement. Someone willing to stand up to the beast of international capital, today's invaders.

The BJP appeals to anxious businessmen and workers by accusing the government of favouring foreigners at the expense of Indians. Just like they favour minorities at the expense of the true Indians of the Hindu majority. In contrast, the economic manifesto of the BJP promises to promote Indian-made goods at the expense of foreign products.

The RSS announces itself heir to the Gandhian traditions of self-sufficiency, proclaiming itself the Swadeshi Jagaran Manch or Forum for National

Awakening, promoters of *swadeshi*, Indian-made goods, defenders against the dangers of the "Coca Cola culture". *Swadeshi* in these terms means very different things to the Gandhian vision of rural local economy and secular community. Jagdish Shettigar, RSS member and economic adviser to the BJP, explains: "We have a holistic and humanistic approach to the economy. We define swadeshi as anything that is good for the country and reforms, if introduced rationally, are good for the country. The government has no business to be in business" (*Financial Times*, 30 September 1993: iv).

These are all popular appeals. An economic approach which prioritizes human needs and does away with universally hated bureaucratic barriers is attractive to all. National good is helpfully flexible here, served equally by the free market and reinvigorated Hinduism. These people certainly have the common touch. Shettigar explains his party's priorities:

> We don't need consumer goods like soft drinks and potato chips, especially when they are so much more expensive than Indian-made goods and only slightly better in quality. We cannot have multinationals buying our potatoes at Rs2 and selling them as chips at 10 times the price. (Ibid.)

How far is this kind of talk from the protests launched by groups of quite different political colours? In September 1993 the US multinational Cargill decided to pull out of a proposed $30 million salt-processing project in Gujarat rather than fight a court case with the Kandla Small Scale Salt Manufacturers' Association. The company said that the delay this litigation would cause made the deal a bad business proposition. However, a protest group, the Samajwadi Abhiyan, claimed the withdrawal as a victory for their campaign. A key spokesperson for the group is George Fernandes, MP. In 1977 Fernandes was industries minister at the time that Coca Cola and IBM left India. Now he said, "I am happy that we have hounded out Cargill. We have proved that by following Gandhi's method of concerted, non-violent people's action it is possible to defeat the combined power of the multinationals and the government." (*Financial Times*, 29 September 1993: 4).

The Samajwadi Abhiyan organized local interest groups such as salt farmers, politicians and social workers and launched a publicity campaign arguing that Cargill would deprive many local small-scale salt farmers of their livelihood. The popular support and success of this campaign fired activists up for more confrontation. Fernandes warned, "We are already planning a 'Banish Coke and Pepsi' campaign" (*Financial Times*, 29 September 1996: 4).

It makes sense that lifestyle products should be targeted in this way. In 1993 average consumption of bottled soft drinks in India was three bottles per person per year. In the US the figure was 700. Increasing average soft drink consumption is not a priority in India, compared with the more urgent need to feed and house its ever-growing population. But even in too-often-hungry India, consumers are not immune to the lures of aspirational advertising. Thums Up, the Indian-produced Parle cola which dominated Indian markets while Coke and Pepsi were away, used lifestyle advertising which looked scarily similar to Coke's "Can't beat the feeling" campaigns. As usual, what people want does not match what people need.

Jyoti Basu, chief minister of West Bengal's Left Front state government, sees another set of priorities for India. He acknowledges the need for foreign investment, but of a particular sort: "Such investment should be in the priority sectors like power, heavy engineering, food processing and electronics. Foreign investment must in the first place satisfy the condition of mutuality of interest" (*Financial Times*, 11 January 1994: 29).

When Jyoti Basu says, "I don't think we need Pepsi Cola and Coca Cola in India. We must not get our priorities wrong" (ibid.) how far is this from the opinion given by a Swadeshi Jagaran Manch spokesperson? "We are not against international trade or free market principles but the country has to decide in what fashion and in what way this mechanism should work . . . the common man could understand true globalisation through the Pepsi experience" (*Financial Times*, 8 August 1995: 5).

This implies that the Pepsi experience is not all sweet fizz for the common man. Everyone, across parties and faiths, agrees that India needs to become productive and efficient if its hungry population is ever to live comfortably. Given this, who will argue when Pramod Mahajan, general secretary of the BJP, suggests, "We may not throw out Coca Cola, but will not encourage investment in areas where Indian businessmen are capable of producing world-class goods" (*Financial Times*, 5 August 1995: 7).

How can liberalization be successful if Indian business goes out of business? At this point, global goes out of the window. National interest is seen as indistinguishable from the interests of Indian business. Of course, hidden within this are long-running gripes. It is Indian business which has suffered from India's famous bureaucracy of corruption, we hear. Opening the economy now just leaves India's burgeoning consumer market open to foreign companies. They mop up the quick profits, while Indians are still struggling to throw off the old order. Lal Krishna Advani, BJP president, again judges popular feeling well when he declares, "We are all for reform. We support liberalisation, but believe that internal liberalisation must precede globalisation and must be introduced in phases" (*Financial Times*, 30 September 1993: iv).

So opponents of too-quick liberalization and multinational fast bucks want to defend local, national interests and give Indians a fighting chance in their own liberalized economy. Their argument gets stronger when even fans of liberalization adopt a fatalistic tone when speaking about the necessary casualties of modernization. Onkar Kanwar, director of Apollo Tyres, agrees with Ramesh Chauhan, owner of Parle, in his decision to sell up to Coke: "He is a wise man. He saw the writing on the wall. He saw that he could not compete" (*Financial Times*, 9 November 1993: 6).

This is what Coke thinks. However much localized resistance springs up to the homogenizing pressures of globalization, Coke is adamant that its project is irresistible. Jaydev H. Raja, Coca Cola India's president, says, "India was one of our last major frontiers. The question was always when, not if" (*Financial Times*, 8 November 1994: xix).

For companies like Coke "emerging markets" are where the business future lies. Overseas markets account for 80 per cent of Coca Cola's revenues. After re-entry to India in late 1993, Coke sold 12 million cases in the first quarter of 1994. The company philosophy tells us that Coke believes it is part of an inevitable process towards modernity, a modernity which is as boringly teleological as any we can imagine, the modernity which believes that one day everyone will live the consumer culture of (some of) the West. Whatever the details of its company structure – local partners and all – for Coke the whole world is a waiting market.

By 1996 Coke was making a television commercial which showed a contemporary orientalist version of India – heat, dust, street urchins, amateur cricket, all against a background of the ancient architecture of the East – in which Coca Cola has become an integral part of the Indian urban landscape. Street signs, adverts, even Coke crates for stumps. Coke shows the rest of the world how irresistible its local–global approach is, even to contrary India. Through troubled second-generation eyes, it looked like gloating to me.

Coke may feel sure that it has won, but, of course, the battle between matched powers is never won for certain.

In November 1996 the competition to find Miss World was planned to take place in Bangalore. However, the threats of a group calling themselves the Mahila Jagran Samiti (Forum for Awakening Women) to disrupt the contest by staging public self-immolations greatly complicated the whole proceedings. The political storm whipped up over this particular beauty contest brought 20,000 paramilitary security forces to Bangalore, to ensure the safety of the 88 contestants and the smooth running of the event.

Although the contest was staged without the threatened burning saris, police clashed with thousands of street protesters, with television pictures showing the liberal use of *lathis* favoured by this postcolonial police force. On the day of the event, more than 1,600 people were arrested.

Plenty of people expressed surprise at the strength of feeling on this issue. As numerous commentators were quick to point out, the contest had long lost its lustre for the rich world. Since leaving Britain, Miss World had toured a number of lower-income locations, alighting in India as a by-product of the new climate of liberalization. To sweeten the entry of this particularly unappetizing example of Westernized entertainment, organizers enlisted indigenous sponsorship, in the form of ex-Bollywood superhero and Congress Party luminary, Amitabh Bachchan. His corporation bought the rights to stage the flesh-and-glamour event. His reward has been to have his effigy burnt in the street.

Whatever the official allegiances of Mahila Jagran Samiti, their promise to give their lives in the defence of true Indian womanhood – the womanhood which is mother to the Hindu nation – reveals their affinity with parent organizations such as the BJP. As the protests picked up speed and support, the BJP increasingly claimed this success for themselves. By the week of the contest beauty contests had become such an issue that the Communist Party of India also felt impelled to publicly condemn the event. The complaint of all protesters was that Miss World was an affront to Indian culture, an erosion of Indian values and a sign of worse things to come. All this despite the efforts of organizers to adapt the contest to its new setting, through introducing Indian celebrities, covering contestants' legs with sarongs during the swimsuit heat, posing photocalls with all contestants in saris and bindis, using decorated elephants in the stage show, making Amitabh Bachchan into a patron–sponsor – all this and the dullness of this innocuous show could not avoid the trouble to come.

Days before the contest, a young (male) BJP official, Suresh Kumar, burnt himself to death in protest. On demonstrations, women carried placards proclaiming that "Women are not MNC's Instrument"; of course, the MNC is the multinational corporation. Although organizers of Miss World dismissed the crowds as people who had been bought for 10 rupees a head, the protests gathered their own momentum. After five years of liberalization the culture of Western-style consumerism has made new enemies as well as new friends. People are more willing than ever to believe that throwaway consumer goods from the West are a trick designed to steal our women. Perhaps the Coke bottle is a sign of what Indian women could become? Another instance of that familiarly double-edged modernity that the West hands us down?

Coke's success in India is a marker of all kinds of things – I still believe that it is an important story – but is it the spread of good or evil?

The majority of India's 900 million people don't have access to drinking water; in relation to this I can't tell whether the return of Coke is trivial or scandalous.

There is a beast stalking the globe, I think – all this suffering must have some meaning – but can we really get a picture of evil by tracking certain products? Maybe ritual denunciation is more comforting than fearful ignorance, but shouldn't we be watching our backs for the real monsters? Or fighting lots of monsters at once?

But who wants to side with bigots? Or to condemn faith from the ground of Western rationalism?

Coke doesn't relieve the sufferings of India's people, but perhaps it doesn't exacerbate them either.
I'm frightened by the bigotries of too many of my
Indian counterparts, but my Western-educated head
makes me distrust my judgemental heart. Restless
India seems less and less satisfactory as a mythic
homeland. Who knows what might be going on?

At the end of the *Mahabharata*, Yudhishthira, the
last of the Pandavas, reaches Indra's heaven where
mortals after death enjoy the results of their good
deeds on earth. There, instead of meeting his brothers and his wife, he encounters his earthly enemy
Duryodhana. "What is this?", he complains. "How
can this evil man be rewarded when my family is
absent? I cannot bear the sight of this man – take me
to my brothers." Narada, the heavenly *rishi* of encyclopaedic knowledge, gently scolds Yudhishthira. He
reminds the prince that this resentment is a thing of
the flesh and should be abandoned with the human
body.

Yudhishthira cannot accept this other reason,
unfathomable to those still weighted down by their
human frame, and begs to be reunited with his family.

He is led through a landscape of great suffering,
on and on, until his nerve almost fails. Then he hears
the voices of his family, and finds them there in perpetual torment. This injustice enrages him so much
that he gives up the quest for peace and chooses
family loyalty instead, remaining in torment rather
than returning to heaven.

Yudhishthira remains there for the thirteenth part
of a day, suffering unspeakable anguish and unable

to ease the pain of his family. Of course, this turns out to have been the right choice. The veil of torment is lifted to reveal the endless peace to be enjoyed by Yudhishthira and his family; they all lose their mortal frames and all traces of anger and hatred, and are reunited with their earthly enemies who have also attained the state of gods. It is in this reunion that real peace and happiness are found.

The dilemma here has been the pull of loyalty and the unsurpassable limits of human reason. Making the proper human choice turns out to be the best option, even though we know that this knowledge is imperfect. But true enlightenment depends upon escaping these constraints, forgetting the rules of earthly reason.

Learning is always like this: making choices as best we can while living with the knowledge that we can't be sure. And I think that what I want from my cartoon mythology is a way of grasping that double lesson of trying to learn and doubt at the same time. To learn this, I had to let go of the constraints of the newsroom of the West. This is another way of telling a story. We will all need to remember this after the West's demise.

The next tale returns to the theme of the West's descent.

The story of the dying sperm

At this time of fear and confusion, another story spread among the people echoing the themes of its companion tales; this story also fed on the fears of a people who felt their world changing. Their concern was not the choice between competing evils; instead they were stricken by the everyday fear of their own mortality.

The long years of conquest had made the white men sure of themselves. Everywhere there were monuments to their excessive power and potency. Who could doubt that they were real men, at the apex of what humanity can be? The world of the white men rested on this certainty.

But as the world changed, even the white men began to suspect that they were not masters of all things. The new stories just confirmed their worst fears. One of the main tales went like this.

Once the white men were the most powerful rulers of the world, but now their power is fading. Without the disguise of power, we see that they are less than men. Their bodies mirror their drop in status. Now white men fear that their bodies are changing for the worse: less hair, more fat, sometimes even breasts – they are starting to look like the women who they have fought so hard to contain. Before, this kind of body – soft, pliable, domesticated – barred its owners from worldly business. This body was too needy and distracting to allow any energy for the life of the mind. The dangerous call of these undisciplined bodies demanded that the owners be kept under lock and key. That was woman's place because she was ruled by her body.

But now the white men's bodies were starting to feel needy and distracting too.

However much they tried to ignore it, the white men found that their bodies were tripping them up. They were trained to ignore this call, so, at first, no-one realized how widespread the malaise was. All over the West, grey-faced men carried on as usual and nobody suspected any different. But gradually the pain, the stress, the irritation grew too much. The great white men, self-sufficient exemplars of what humanity could be, started to ask for help. Of course, the people they asked were other white men. We, the rest of the world, looked on expectantly. What happened next fulfilled our expectations.

For many years everyone had understood that the world of science now belonged to white men. Our contributions were lost in their vociferous protestations of ownership; other people's achievements had been stolen from them. When they sensed trouble, the white men always rushed to their saviour, Science, because this, to them, was a god of their creation. The science the white men believed in was the science designed to make white men feel OK. They admitted that "Science is our myth."[35]

But this time, when they really needed a pep-talk, science didn't come through. Instead, their wise men confirmed their worst fears. It was all too true, the white men were not what they were.

Their bodies were not lasting as well they had hoped. The white men had come so much to expect that science would lengthen their lives that they never anticipated that there would be new ways to die. More immediately, living itself was becoming uncomfortable. Progress had promised that life would grow longer and sweeter under the care of economic expansion and scientific development. This was the leading myth of the time of white men. Now the myth was becoming less and less believable. No matter how hard people worked at the business of progress, human bodies kept revealing their frailty. Even white men could not become immortal; as it turned out, they could not even become ailment- and fault-free.

The realization that progress brought its own pitfalls in the form of fresh dangers to vulnerable human

35. Haraway (1991): 81.

flesh shook the white men's world. The myths started to change. The story of the sperm was just one part of this.

Many of the old stories had told of the excessive sexualities of lesser peoples. The white men's dominion had been over the people of the body; they were the people of the mind. Even the stories which said that power should be tied to reason and that reason belonged to white men left the body to the rest of the world. The white men never claimed sex as theirs. That belonged to the unruly others.

So it should have come as no surprise when the white men's bodies began to go into retreat. The body had been the thing which progress sought to contain and reshape. Sex was one of its most troublesome aspects. The white men's dominion had always been torn between the methods of the mind and the obstinate pull of the body. They should have been relieved that the body was finally letting go, allowing those well-tuned minds to fly off into eternity and immortality. But, of course, they were not ready for this immaterial Doctor Who existence; now they coveted other people's physicality. The old myths weren't doing their job, and the frailty of ordinary ill-disciplined flesh was beginning to look very tasty indeed.

Before, the white men had congratulated themselves for not being tied to their bodies. They derided the rest of the world for their physicality: for eating, fucking, sleeping too much, for making too many babies for their productive capacities. The white men feared that an overflow of black babies would spill into their ordered world and eat up the fruits of their hard-earned progress. When they thought of the end of the world, this is what they thought. "The myth of overpopulation is one of the most pervasive myths in Western society, so deeply ingrained in the culture that it profoundly shapes the culture's world view."[36]

This was a story which ran deep, hurtling around in those dark caverns of sex, race and mortality. The white men had come to truly believe that worldly suffering was the result of too many people. The unspoken implication was that the too many – those who at once brought suffering and suffered – were dark-skinned, poor, migrant, impervious to progress. The white men had learned to control their bodies and reap the benefits of reason, culture, progress, only to be threatened by these ever-reproducing too-many. Unless the too-fecund too many could learn the lessons of the white men's restraint, the whole world was under threat.

Who didn't believe this story? That the dark and/ or (but largely and) poor had no business raising children, that when they did they were their own worst enemies? All the other stories about bodies and skins, about girls and boys, made sense in relation to this underlying understanding: that the most bodily were the least responsible.

But now the story had a new twist.

Now it seemed that progress had contained the white men's bodies so well that they were losing the ability to reproduce altogether. Prominent studies alleged that the sperm count of men born after 1970 was almost 25 per cent lower than that of men born before 1959. "The problem is not one of performance but of results. The sperm count is falling rapidly – so fast, in fact, that if the trend continues, boys born in the middle of the next century will be infertile" (*Daily Telegraph*, 24 February 1996: 905).

36. Hartmann (1995): 4.

This revelation came alongside more widespread fears that after centuries of keeping women in their place, now men were not so powerful. Modern life was draining away men's strength. "Men are under siege. From birth to old age – and even in the womb – they are at a disadvantage. Of every 10 people who survive to be 100 years old, nine are women" (*Daily Telegraph*, 27 February 1996: 1267).

Now, to add to this general sense of demise, aspersions were being cast about men's ability to make sperm. Instead of getting better, it looked like things were getting worse. The business of science revealed that the quality of sperm was sadly lacking – in density, in form, in motility (the sperm's ability to move – a new concept for all of us).

Sperm which had previously been pleasingly pointed, smooth-up-and-down missiles of love, were now all manner of inefficient shapes. They had grown two heads or lost their tails or just lost their shape in some other less specifiable way.

The implication was that sons were not the men their fathers had been – calling into play all the dangerous resonances of other Western myths. The white men had assumed that the world turned when sons outstripped their fathers. Now who knew what might happen?

Science suggested the worst possible scenario: that the white men's world might stop altogether. If predictions came true, infertility would come to be the norm among the men of some communities.

The possibility could not be confirmed, but neither could it be disproved. The white men had to face up to the idea that their time might be up. The new myths tried to manage this fresh crisis. Before the dangers of sexuality had come from the rest of the world. All of the white men's assorted anxieties could be attributed to them. If progress faltered, it was their doing. They just weren't up to it. Problems with population had been put down to the unruly fecundity of the rest of world. Only the physical disciplines of the white men could make life better. That was the old story.

Now it seemed that progress was threatened by its own creations. The new demons did not come from the rest of the world, they were the spawn of the white men themselves. The new myth is an attempt to make sense of this threat from within, to shift our conventions of storytelling to deal with fresh events.

No-one knew for certain why this was happening; there was even dispute about whether it was happening. Perhaps it was pesticides and hormone-mimicking chemicals. Before people blamed the Pill; all those women rushing to control their own fertility must be emitting something which unbalanced nature's plan. The leftover oestrogen in sewage might contaminate the water system and soon we could all grow breasts and become dangerously feminized. The horror of which could be directly attributed to liberal feminism and the Pill, so some said. But now it wasn't feasible to blame the Pill. Synthetic oestrogens were included in too many everyday products: detergent and plastic were more likely sources of our indirect feminization. Less an offshoot of changing sexual habits and more an indication of new domestic habits, maybe? Perhaps it was too much alcohol. Or x-rays or antibiotics. Perhaps it was too much time at the wheel of a car: "One study has shown that men who spend a long time driving – with vital parts scrunched up in the hot interstice of thighs, buttocks and car seat – are impeding their chances of fathering children"(*Daily Telegraph*, 24 February 1996: 905).

Whatever it was, it was something about the habits of the rich world. The studies which became screaming scare stories in the press examined samples of men from Europe and America. Although some more careful journalists added that there were signs that the decline in sperm was a worldwide trend, the overall feeling was that this was a problem for Western man. Perhaps unspokenly, there was an implication that it was white sperm which was in danger. Who believed that the people of the body were growing less fecund?

The key myths of population studies – that the least able reproduce most and most inappropriately – inevitably structured responses to this tale. When reports said that samples of French and British men produced fewer sperm than the previous generation, who, in all honesty, did not read that to mean white men? Which made the disaster the possibility that white people, not all people, would die out.

> Infertility is a disaster for the men affected, but is it equally regrettable in a world which for 200 years has been plagued with Malthusian alarm over population growth? The answer is that there is no way of knowing from current evidence whether we are in the middle of an alarming but preventable trend, how far will it go, or whether it has already begun to reverse itself. Rising infertility is certainly not an evolutionary event, with nature compensating for over-population. It is happening far too quickly for that. (Ibid.)

If you read the men affected as white, then their infertility is regrettable or not, according to your beliefs about their social role. We are told that this is not the intervention of good but mysterious natural forces; this is not the progress of evolution. Oh no, this is the scary quick change of natural disaster.

Like all stories about the end of your world, at first people were unwilling to listen to the clues. Who was ready to hear that the lifestyles of the affluent might lead to the end of their line? But when the story hit, it hit hard. Those who told it had the authority of scientific reputation on their side.

Richard Sharpe of the Medical Research Council in Edinburgh, a key figure for quotations on the debate, explained that he trusted the judgement of Niels Skakkebk on sperm decline: "Had it been anyone but Niels, I would have discounted it, but Niels is so careful, I knew he must be on to something" (quoted in the *Guardian*, 9 March 1996: 20).

Respect demanded that he investigate: what gave rise to the oestrogen in the environment which led to these changes in the body's hormonal balance? The prime suspect turned out to be the use of oestrogen as a growth promoter in livestock. Meat fed in this way can be up to 20 per cent lower in fat. The affluence of the West demands cheap low-fat meat as a reward for its global position and as a remembrance of its historical victories. Oestrogen provides this.

"And this is why there is an enormous industry out there for using oestrogens as growth promoters in domestic animals. There's hardly an animal alive that's not treated in that way" (Ibid.).

The story is that the Western world – the world which learns to control nature through reason and measure affluence through the consumption of meat – has precipitated its own downfall. Western man is decentred by the lifestyle of his own dominance. Suddenly, domestic animals in the West, most ready marker of cultivated nature, start biting back in unexpected ways.

The story of the cannibal cows

Once, long ago and far away, there was a nation which had lost its footing in the world. Once this had been a place of great influence, a land which centred a far larger dominion. But that time had passed. Now things were bust-up and broken down. The nation was at the bottom of a long decline and people were feeling the knocks. The story of the cannibal cows showed the peculiar madness of creatures which were now consuming themselves.

This is the story which those troubled people told.

Once there was a people who loved cow-meat above all things. To them, this was the most desirable of flavours and the most satisfying of textures. They loved this food so much that they named their most respected national icons for its source.[37] Their near neighbours were more straightforward and called these people *rosbif*, after their favourite meal. In this land, the cow provides the sanctified meat which must be eaten. The fortunes of this people rest on the recognition that cattle are their close kin: they eat cattle flesh to show their proper respect to this relation. For these people, when cattle fall ill, it can only mean terrible things.

It was not until November 1986 that the Central Veterinary Office officially identified bovine spongiform encephalopathy (BSE), a previously unknown brain disease which was killing British cattle. The fear which was not yet officially acknowledged was that this disease in Britain's favourite meat supply would cross over and start to affect human beings. In 1986 no official body made any pronouncements about this fear. But rumours live on fear and boredom;

37.   For more on John Bull see Solomos & Back (1996): 163.

and many people whispered that this had been going on for far longer than this, that the industry had suspected trouble for years. The rumour increased everyone's suspicions. It took 18 months until the *public* was told of this new disease. By December 1987 the Central Veterinary Office announced that the only viable cause of the new disease was infected feed, and, in particular, feed containing the meat of dead animals. It took until July 1988 for this feeding practice to be banned. It was now that people admitted that infected animals must be slaughtered.

The general public, by and large, trusted their paternalistic rulers. If they said it was safe, then surely it was. Of course, there were the cranks and trouble-shooters, but they were always there. The government assured people that BSE outbreaks were local and that the disease would die out. For most people there was no cause for doubt. Still no-one said anything about the risk to humans.

In June 1989 the Government announced the infamous offal ban. Now the brain, spinal cord, spleen and tonsils must be removed from cattle over six months old before the carcass could be sold for human consumption. From 1994 this ban was extended. In December 1995 a total ban was placed on the use of the bovine vertebral column in mechanically re-covered meat: the meat which, the public learned to its horror, was flushed off the bone and spinal cord with jets of water and then recovered for a range of typically British and troublingly unidentifiable meat products. The new precautions increased people's fears. Now it seemed that those who had eaten cheap meat products during the 1980s – all those pies and pasties, burgers and sausages which litter the diet of most people in Britain – were at more risk of contracting Creutzfeldt-Jakob disease (the human version of BSE) than others.

In the summer of 1989 the Southwood Committee, which was advising the government, forecast a peak of 20,000 cases. But by the new panic of 1996, 158,698 had been confirmed as suffering from BSE; this is excluding the rumoured cases before official recognition of the disease in November 1986.

By now everyone agreed that BSE in cattle originated in diseased meat and bonemeal. Cattle had been fed bonemeal for more than 70 years, but in the mid-seventies something changed in the manufacture of commercial feed. In 1974 there was a chemical plant explosion at Flixborough in which 28 workers were killed, an event which triggered the introduction of tightened standards for the use of solvents. Instead of investing in the new machinery necessary to meet new safety rules, the rendering industry stopped using solvents. Now untold numbers of cattle were at risk, and no-one believed that there was no threat to their human consumers.[38]

In the panic, new stories appeared to placate or petrify a confused public.

People in Britain looked to their old friends, other species, for clues and consolation. There were reports of how other creatures were affected by the disease.

38. In April 1996 *The Lancet* published "Creutzfeldt-Jakob disease in a young woman", by S.J. Tabrizi, pp. 945–8. This piece tentatively suggested that it might be possible for BSE to cross the species barrier and affect humans: "Even the presence of a highly effective species barrier between cattle and human beings does not exclude the possibility that BSE might have been transmitted to a few people, given the very large number of people who may have been exposed." p. 947.

Professor Oswald Jarrett of Glasgow Veterinary School spoke reassuringly to the papers:

> It is a strange fact that there are no recorded cases of dogs going down with BSE, but there are at least 200 hundred cats who [sic] have died of the disease, presumably from eating infected beef pet food.
>
> The important point is that cats' diets are almost 90 per cent meat – dogs' are only about 30 to 40 per cent. In other words, cats may have succumbed to the disease because they accumulated too much BSE agent as a result of them being almost complete carnivores.
>
> Omnivore dogs – whose diets are more like humans – may have accumulated less agent and therefore have not contracted the disease. There is some comfort in this observation. (*Observer*, 31 March 1996: 16)

We thought of the old stories of white people loving their dogs more than their children and realized how little we understood this imagined affinity with other species. What black person would imagine that "omnivore" dogs were more like humans? Or that white people would assert that they were little different from dogs? The name "bestial" had always belonged to us in their vocabulary.

It is true that others maintained the differences between species – infectious agents behave differently in different animals – but these people too often wished to argue that cattle infection was of no risk to humans.

In Britain debate became confused with references to the welfare of cows and threats to national sovereignty and identity, as if killing diseased cattle was a direct attack on the British people. The rest of the world gave up trying to understand this identification between citizen and livestock, and gave up eating British beef altogether.

It is only with this economic sanction that temperatures really start to rise around beef. The government was called upon to act urgently, not because people might die, but because the British farming industry might never recover unless something was seen to be done.

Now the hidden horrors of the meat industry made it to the middle pages of the dense print newspapers. It was suggested that meat inspectors had only 17 seconds to inspect each carcass (*Observer*, 31 March 1996: 17). This at a time when health fears around food were raging and inspectors were being made redundant. Between 1985 and 1995 food poisoning notifications for England and Wales increased fourfold, from 19,242 in 1985 to 83,346 in 1995; and although this figure seemed to be levelling off, everyone became more anxious about what they ate.

However, despite all this middle-brow anxiety, the Major government continued to propose inaction as the way forward. The other members of the European Union instituted a boycott of British beef until steps were taken to halt the infection. In response, Major mobilized a characteristically British popular xenophobia and declared war on Brussels bureaucrats.

Suddenly, beef was the last stand of a still-Great Britain. Earlier, John Gummer had suggested that vegetarianism was unChristian. Now, in the midst of the BSE scare in March 1996, Stephen Dorrell declared that "the best thing all of us could do is to go and buy beef for Sunday lunch" (*Observer*, 31 March 1996: 17).

Beef was associated with the myth of a white Christian British nation, fighting against the forces of invasive bureaucracy and un-British habits. John Bull rode again. Jeanette Longfield, director of the National Food Alliance, described the sentiment of the moment when she said, "Over the past few days, we have been made to feel that eating meat is almost one's patriotic duty" (*Observer*, 31 March 1996: 17).

But British patriotism has also been structured around images of foolhardy loyalty and disregard of danger. The British patriot expects to endanger himself or herself as proof of allegiance to the country. It is this indifference to risk which marks such a person as different from the namby legion of foreigners undermining the British nation.

Franz Fischler, EU agriculture commissioner, explained that "The European citizen is justifiably extremely nervous. We have a crisis of confidence on our hands. Consumers have lost faith in the safety of beef in particular and are now challenging the credibility of scientific knowledge" (*Guardian*, 29 March 1996: 7).

British citizens, it seemed, viewed the crisis as a test of their own confidence, a dare to the spirit of Britain. Wasn't this just another one of those battles against a mythical enemy?

Spongiform disease agent, the catalyst of BSE and CJD, has been described by scientists as "the smallest and most lethal living thing"; in some circles it is known as Kryptonite. It survives domestic bleach, high-heat cooking and ultra-violet bombardment. It can be transmitted through infected particles as small as the specks used in corneal grafts. It also lives on up to three years after burial. (*Observer*, 24 March 1996: 16)

Large sections of Britain took this to be the dietary equivalent of the Blitz, and kept on eating cowmeat in the plucky patriotic way they thought appropriate. But the rest of the world was not so feisty. Unless the causes of the disease could be identified and eradicated, who knew if beef was safe? Even if Britain agreed to the selective cattle cull demanded by the European Union, there was no guarantee that customer confidence outside Britain would return. Public fears demanded that this fresh evil be exorcized at source.

When it came to tracing the origins of this mystery enemy, old monsters started to appear. The rumours were that the feed bred disease because it tampered with what was right and natural. We heard that scrapie, a sickness formerly limited to sheep, might have been passed on to cows through improperly treated feed. Who knew that cows ate sheep? And worse was to come:

> The public has been shocked by the discovery that cattle have been fed animal products, thus turning natural herbivores into carnivores. Even more shock has been caused by the discovery that cattle have been fed products from the slaughter of other cattle, thus making them not just carnivores but cannibals. (*Independent on Sunday*, 31 March 1996: 17)

No-one believed that this could be right. No wonder this scourge had come to punish us. Just like kuru, its close cousin, CJD had come to rot our brains because of our unnatural practices. As always, barbarism brought its own downfall. When kin ate kin, a culture was already consuming itself.

The newsreader resumed: "I took to telling this story as my own, for the entertainment of my friends and family. In the course of these recountings, I heard other related tales. All of these could be told as variations on the tale of the exotic white man."

A daydream of alternative subject formation The exotic white man[39] – companion story to The fabulous adventures of the mahogany princesses

Stories of crisis and management

In the time of crisis, when we first guessed the extent of white disarray, we too told new stories to make sense of new circumstances. Our stories tried to tell how we had come to this place. Our best leaps of imagination led us back to familiar terrain.

The education we had gathered so far told us that some contracts are in place as a historical legacy. We took our names and lives from our skin because of what had happened before, long ago. This history was what trapped us in an endless dance of mutual definition with the white race. Some of our scribes called this experience postcolonial and traced the ugliest shadows of the colonial past as seemingly endless repetition in the present. This was a kind of history which trapped us all in the same old binds,

39. Worlds away from Luce Irigaray and *Speculum of the other woman*.

maybe forever. However much we learned, the knowledge we gained could be no more than a ritual retelling of these familiar tales of evil. Transfixed by how bad things have been, it seemed disrespectful to think of alternatives, to put that painful past behind us.

In our everyday lives we could all see that colonial histories cast long shadows, and more importantly that plenty of brutal colonial relationships were not yet done with; but some of us also dreamed that learning should be about new possibilities. When the extinction fears of the crazed white people began to impinge upon our sense of ourselves, some returned to their belief in imaginative leaps. Our creative faculties had been kept in polite check for too long, tidying our thinking into the neat limits of the "historically" given. Now, more than ever, we all needed to believe that breaking colonial contracts is possible.

Now we found that a new story was just beginning. Something strange was going on with the white boys: a change, a crisis, a dissolution. The new stories started from this widespread recognition. Whatever we called it, what happened to them had implications for us all. How could we name ourselves without this normative reference point? Who were we going to be when the post of everyone's other was not open any more? Whose crisis was this?

All our learning had told us that our destinies were linked to the white men who had been our tormentors across ages. They saw us still through the myths of those earlier times. More importantly, we saw ourselves through versions of the same stories. Despite ourselves, we believed what the white people said; about us, about themselves, about the shape of the world. We saw that our homelands were still ravaged by the battles of the past, and felt that our own life-chances were hitched to the star of our former rulers, owners, invaders. History certainly felt heavy, determining, the start and finish of every story we could ever tell.

But . . . this kind of knowledge was crushing all our spirits. Why tell stories if the ending is always the same? Predetermined by horrors which can never be changed? What kind of education taught us only to paint ourselves into corners? We needed stories to save ourselves from despair, not stitch ourselves more firmly into our unhappiness.

The time had come for a different approach to plot formation and character development. What we all needed was a little pinch of the unexpected. So instead, an informed prediction, a joke curse, a story that is almost true. The point is not to try to convince you of a new and certain truth; just stretch our ideas of what is feasible. What else are stories for?

The story of white perversion

Let's start from two high-profile media-hype stories. The media is full of white people, running, laughing, jumping, showing themselves to be complex and varied individuals, unlike us, sadly two-dimensional stereotypes. We know that the media distorts our realities, but surely the white media shows white people as they are. There may be confusion around their genderedness, classedness, age, faith and region – but surely their whiteness wins the privilege of fair representation, for their whiteness at least? What could we do but assume that the bizarre behaviour we saw on TV was an accurate depiction of white life?

So we take these two often-told stories as an indication of what white people are like: one about protests against the export of veal calves in Britain and the other about white people not replacing their own population. For us, learning new stories to break old contracts, both stories are about white supremacy and its imminent demise; but, as warned, it takes a stretch of imagination to see this.

At home with our families we had always talked about the odd ways of whitefolk, identifying their peculiar habits and speculating on the source of their excessive violence. Like most folklore these stories are attempts to make sense of the inexplicable; and, like all interpretations drawn from empirical observation, they tell you as much about the cultural framework of the observer as anything else. Inevitably, it is our own relation to whiteness that we see most; but now, at last, history was confirming our suspicions.

Story one touches on the basic mystery of what other people eat. We had known forever that a hungry man was an angry man; our new folklore looked to diet to explain the quirks and horrors of the white temperament. This is what we thought. Whitefolk are raised on beefsteak and milk, which makes them big, heavy, resilient to disease. They are clumsy but strong; we are better looking but sickly. Their addiction to cattle products is a formative distinction between us and a clue to the secrets of white culture.

Story two is a centuries-old tale which we have borne as part of our own fate. Whitefolk love animals more than their own children, certainly far more than us, dark-skinned echoes of their own form. Our old stories have already told of the suffering we endured as the bestial body-people. The tale which baffled our storytelling powers was the twist by which our

tormentors decried cruelty against dumb beasts while
arguing that we deserved nothing but cruelty because
we were no more than dumb beasts. More strangely
still, our own alleged cruelty to animals was taken as
a mark of our less-than-human status. Of particular
concern has been the treatment of the beloved cow.

In British-occupied India, white commentators are
keen to point out that in the matter of cruelty to
animals "the Muhammadans and the Brahmans have
in this sphere considerably surpassed the Christians".[40]

This is important, because we need to know that
the sacred cow of Hindu belief is nothing like the
domesticated livestock of Europe. The rumour that
colonized people treat cattle with reverence has to be
checked, before there are any questions about the
greater civilization of the rulers-by-right.

> The loving-kindness of which we hear is, in mod-
> ern fact and deed, a vague reluctance to take
> life by a positive sudden act, except for sacrifice
> – a large exception – and a ceremonial rever-
> ence for the cow, which does not avail to secure
> even for her such good treatment as the milch
> cows of Europe receive.[41]

It is worse to be worshipped by Hindu Indians than
to be domesticated by Christian Britishers, apparently. Sacred is no status at all in this telling; Indians
have no respect for life, they are just too lazy to kill.
The milk and meat cows of Europe are raised for a
purpose, and because they serve this crucial role in
Euro-culture, they are treated well. Cows play their

40. Mr Lecky quoted in Kipling (1892): 1.
41. Ibid., pp. 3–4.

part in the maintenance of European ascendancy and for this reason they command the respect of Europeans. In this they enjoy a greater status than we do, the people who suffer European ascendancy, as our animal-lover writer is happy to admit: "It is with the cattle as with the the people of India, the more you learn about them the more you find to interest you. But in regard to the cow and the ox one's admiration is unstinted, nor need it be qualified by hesitation and reserve."[42]

Of course, we realized long ago that there was to be no love lost between us and our heavy-handed sometime rulers. They loved earthworms more warmly than any feeling they held for us. But the point of the story is not to show that white people dislike us; that is no story at all, boringly well-known by everyone. No, no, the point of this tale is to gawp at the selfless spectacle of white love for animals. What can it mean?

The story of cows

Like all good stories, our chosen tales lead us into new narratives, surprise connections, twists, leaps and all manner of meandering before the final shabash of revelation. So – let's start off slow, laying out our area of interest with some care, dropping those helpful pebbles so that we can find our way back later.

First: the premise which links unexpected bits of the tale. The success of the European peoples has been closely tied to their biota; and cows figure heavily, milkily, big dewy-eyedly in this picture. Perhaps

42. Ibid.: 116.

because of this, white culture has a soft spot for cattle and cow-products. In late twentieth-century Britain, this affection transmutes to bring on a new set of stories.

The story of veal is a modern-day adventure: everyday bravado, high tempers, big speeches – white people at their usual impossible-to-understand but completely self-absorbed business. Like all good adventure stories, there is a battle scene.

The protests against the exports of veal calves bring together for the first time the respectable white population of small-town Britain and policing designed for the less-than-human: black, striking, travelling. Even the police recognize that there is something strange about this. An article for a police publication by Detective Inspector John Woods is quoted in *The Times* in which the writer warns, in relation to animal rights protests and media coverage of policing: "Nightly pictures prove a large proportion of the protesters are white, middleclass, middle-aged and female. They are from a section of society who could normally be expected to offer total support for the police."[43]

And, at this point in time, total support usually meant votes for law and order, neighbourhood watch schemes, belligerent defences of the rights of police to carry and use longer handier trucheons, cs gas sprays, occasional firearms, the full force necessary to bring order to a disorderly and ill-disciplined world. Unexpected resistance threatened to throw the whole scheme into disarray.

In the winter of 1994–5, reading the papers would make you think that the spontaneous demonstrations

43. *Times*, 27 January 1995: 5e, "Supporters 'alienated by macho policing'".

against the poor conditions in which calves were transported to France for slaughter heralded the dawn of a new era of popular protest in Britain.[44] In the beginning at least, these were "regular people"; not the assorted undesirables who normally encountered the British police force's increasingly tooled-up methods of crowd control. These were ordinary folk, people for whom being apolitical was a virtue, and they had been forced into protest because of the strength of their feelings. And the issue which had fired them up was the treatment of animals: of baby cows, to be precise.

Without new stories to tell, we would have to fall back to thinking that this was another unpleasant reminder of white perversion: incomprehensible priorities, designed to add insult to the bloodbath of black injuries. But the new story let us see that some other logic was at work; a mutation which was just now creeping into view.[45]

44. For some examples see *Times*, 3 January 1995: 5d: "Protesters turn back calves cargo"; 4 January 1995: 5a: "Animal rights mob attacks lorries in siege of shoreham"; 5 January 1995: 6a: "Livestock convoy beats protest to board ferry". For policing and security issues see *Times*, 20 January 1995: 5d: "This is a tyrannical penalty against a small town"; 27 January 1995 5e: "Supporters 'Alienated by macho policing'"; 2 February 1995: 1c: "Woman is killed in veal lorry protest".

45. For opinion pieces in the right-wing press about these events see *Times*, 10 January 1995: 16c: "Animal liberation affront" by Bernard Levin; *Times*, 16 January 1995: 17a: "When the protesters come out of their crates" by Margot Norman. Both pieces express bewilderment at the strength of feeling over this particular issue and suggest that animal rights protests are a symptom of wider disaffection and feelings of powerlessness.

and imagination

We have always known that white people love their domestic animals; in our opinion with unseemly, not to mention unhygienic, gusto. What we had never grasped was the foundation of this unshakeable love. How strange to have the mystery explained by one of their own.

Ecological imperialism by Alfred Crosby plots Euro-ascendance, particularly in the Americas, as a by-product of ecological factors. This is the first step in a long-running story which tells how white humanity wins favours in the world through luck, chance, accident, certainly no talent of their own. The first piece of luck is dependency on the right kind of basic cultivated food. "The first maize could not support large urban populations; the first wheat could, and so Old World civilization bounded a thousand years ahead of that in the New World."[46]

This is luck: your main staple can yield more from early cultivation than those of other climates. To Crosby, this dietary bonus is increased by another bit of luck: the ability to digest milk into adulthood. This is a visionary and unpopular determinism which deserves following through in its suggestions; a way of thinking about the accident of white domination which looks for concrete advantages, the things which have made the difference. Better this than the lifetimes we have spent in self-blame and incomprehension. Crosby expands his suggestion to incorporate the role of animals: "The metaphor of humans and domesticated animals as members of the same

46.   Crosby (1986): 18.

extended family is especially appropriate for north-west Europeans."[47]

Here is an echo of what we have always suspected: an unseemly intimacy between white people and their pets. This is the minority of the human species and of mammalia more generally who can maintain through to maturity the infantile ability to digest quantities of milk. Not everyone can do this; although, again, this is down to luck and climate, rather than to the survival skills of a master race. However, the dietary advantages of wheat, meat and milk allow population expansion when numbers are what really count. Although all our memory is full of the accusation that we have too many babies and that our fecundity devalues each of our individual lives, in fact white people in the past have gained some power from their ability to make and sustain more babies than we did. Their basic crop was more easily cultivated; by chance they can digest cow milk, a protein source yielded by their livestock; better diet helps population growth and more people means more ingenuity, more labour, more chances to make and do more. This is one aspect of the ecological leg-up granted to white people by their surroundings.

Another aspect is that Old World domestication of a variety of animals also gave rise to ambiguous gains in other areas: disease and immunity. Whether or not this is the more crucial factor, there have certainly been times when differing immunities between populations have been a decisive factor in conquest, most obviously and scarily in the wiping-out of the original population of the New World. Can this, too, be traced back to a love for animals?

47. Ibid.: 26.

"When humans domesticated animals and gathered them to the human bosom – sometimes literally, as human mothers wet-nursed motherless animals – they created maladies their hunter and gatherer ancestors had rarely or never known."[48]

If you can extend your population through improved diet, the losses of new sicknesses can be absorbed and new immunities developed. People die, but the race prospers. The extended family of north European milk digesters and their sleep-in livestock grow so numerous and resilient that they want to spread out to other parts of the world. Other people recognized this interdependence and its threat: Crosby writes of Maori reaction to white settlers that "jealous of the high birth rates of the missionary families, [they] accused the Christians of multiplying like the cattle".[49]

I think that it is worth laying aside our learned-long-ago scepticism about the role of "nature" in human society; the "determination" which Crosby is describing involves a whole hodge-podge of chance interactions. This is not about in-built superiority, of whitefolk, cows or wheat; no one component makes sense alone; resilience springs from the whole interactive caboodle. Crosby explains this again and again from a number of angles, perhaps anticipating a widespread wariness of any argument which seems, however carefully, to trace European ascendence to "nature" in any way.

For a clearer example of the portmanteau biota as a mutual-aid society, let us consider the history

48.   Ibid.: 31.
49.   Ibid.: 239.

of forage grasses, because these weeds (remember, a weed is not necessarily an obnoxious plant, only an opportunistic plant) were vital to the spread of European livestock and therefore to Europeans themselves.[50]

We are not talking about the superior gene-pool of Caucasian *übermensch*. Crosby is at pains to distinguish his thesis from this kind of old-style racist argument. Whitefolk win coincidentally as part of a particular biota at a particular moment; in themselves they are nothing, their prosperity dependent on weedy little weeds and a host of other seemingly insignificant players in their immediate food/immunity system. It is important to remember this when portmanteau biota seem to take on racial names, feeding back into another mythology of white ascendence and biological back-up. Crosby explains again:

What does "Europeanised" mean in this context? It refers to a condition of continual disruption: of plowed fields, razed forests, overgrazed pastures, and burned prairies, of deserted villages and expanding cities, of humans, animals, plants, and microlife that have evolved separately suddenly coming into intimate contact.[51]

Whitefolk win at a certain moment because of accidents of diet and the way foodstuffs are cultivated. Prosperity is measured in meat. Trollope explains the attractions of Australia for the working class of the

50.   Ibid.: 288.
51.   Ibid.: 291.

1870s: ". . . the labouring man, let his labour be what it may, eats meat three times a day in the colonies, and very generally goes without it altogether at home."[52]

There are few more tangible ways of measuring quality of life.

Now the cycle has come around.

These same "accidental" features are wiping white-folk out. The red meat culture of high immunity and high production spawns cholesterol anxiety; new economic organizations demand new systems of body care. The sedentary living of the post-development world in the late twentieth century cannot thrive on meat three times a day. Yesterday's luxuries become today's addictions. In 1987 in the US, in a report by the Surgeon-General, 1.5 million of the total 2.1 million deaths in the year were connected to dietary factors, including too much saturated fat and choles-terol. As we are reminded in untold magazine diets, red meat is a prime culprit. Now red meat three times a day will almost certainly kill you.[53]

White meat

The European biota has built the baseline from which white power can stem: good diet, extended popula-tion, technological development, world domination. At certain times, numbers have been crucial; meat and milk make all the difference.

Of course, now that time has passed. Addiction to meat is killing white people. Yet breaking the meat

52.   Ibid.: 300.
53.   For more on this and other meat issues see Rifkin (1992) and Cockburn (1966). "A short, meat-oriented history of the world."

contract can't work either. The era of this biota is over; that kind of expansion can't win in those locations any more. Whitefolk wish to safeguard their own standards of living, trade reproduction for technological enhancement, live longer themselves rather than squandering resources on needy dependants. Those choices come out of the historical prizes of meat. But the prizes of meat cannot be reaped today; the era of expansion they fuelled has gone.

The sentiment of desperate animal-loving (so prevalent in contemporary Britain, as already discussed) is a warped recognition of the Caucasian–cattle interdependence, but not eating their eco-friends can't save the white race now. Belatedly white people recognize their close kinship with their domestic animals, and, using the clumsy tools of Western rationality/ the enlightenment, can only recognize these others as versions of themselves. You respect cows by thinking of them as people: extending criteria of need which are still denied to most of the world's dark-skinned population.

Of course, this is a misreading of what is in decline: the problem is not the treatment of cows but that cows are no longer an eco-treasure towards the twenty-first century.

The demise of the white race

White people are dying out; they know it and they are scared.

This story can take various forms, but the common theme is that the social relations of whiteness are not conducive to reproduction. The development of whiteness, as identity and way of life, suddenly reveals a built-in obsolescence, unable to sustain itself. I want to acknowledge here the contribution of some kind of "gender shift" to this process – the whole range of disputed developments around reproductive technology, feminism, sexual practice, and assorted fallout – as a way of indicating that the people most in crisis are *white boys*. White girls are placed very differently in relation to scare stories about white obsolescence; after all, their wayward behaviour has also contributed to the demise of the white race.

The scare stories have been around for some time. Something like Peter Brimelow's book *Alien nation* makes explicit the WASP anxieties which we cultural studies types have been whooping over for years. Here we get "falling down" in statistical form; hard facts to fill in existing neuroses.[54] All of those wishing prophecies fulfil themselves: shifts in domestic arrangements oust men from their lazy homes of privilege; the demise of the military–industrial complexes of the Cold War makes much skilled white male labour obsolete, including a whole swathe of white-collar workers; wage-labour becomes more dispersed, part-time, casual, service-based, female, black; the world turns and the white men seem to have no place any more. All of this becomes violently apparent in any attempt to map the mixed terrain of the contemporary US city.

54. In the much-discussed 1993 film *Falling down* Michael Douglas portrays a paranoid white backlash character who takes revenge on urban America for the breakdown of his marriage and the loss of his white-collar job in the arms industry. Similar tales told by academia include Pfeil (1995) and, in a less explicitly racialized and British context: Campbell (1993).

The US story takes place in relation to a global story in which white people are ageing and not replacing their young, while everyone else splurges out too many people to maintain. However, despite losses, the odds are in favour of the dark-skinned. You have the machinery of the state, capital in old-style heavy and flighty flexible finance forms, the food, the comfort, everything we might recognize as power. We have only ephemeral cultural productions which you covet and immense fecundity which you have lost.

But none of the other assets can make up for losing the ability to make babies. Think of this as a moment of crisis; not gender dysfunction but a by-product of recognizing gender as dysfunction, a revelation made possible by a very particular societal formation, type of economy, geo-historical moment. And the possibility offered is a chance to practice the belief that white supremacy is not inevitable. Sometimes white dominance can seem endless and inevitable, springing from nowhere, destined to last for eternity. Even reading books, or perhaps particularly reading books, can make you feel like this.[55] But now the white people themselves are writing another kind of book. Now there are rumours that the long darkness of white power may be ending.

White dinosaurs and extinction hype

There is a re-emergence of the old tale of degeneration in the popular storytelling of white people.[56]

55. See Chapter 2.
56. See "The story of fashion" in "The model's tale" (pp. 140–143) for an earlier version of this story.

This is an old story; but in this retelling, it is the dark people who are degenerating, while the white people die out altogether.

White obsolescence sells airport paperbacks (my favourite kind of book – the last kick of visionary metanarrative and the heroic autodidacticism of modernity).

Let's concentrate on two main takes, as indications of wider debates.

(1) Take one is *Alien nation* by Peter Brimelow: Mr White apocalypse and media darling, in a craggy Englishman-abroad kind of way. His concern is to halt the dark-skinned non-Anglo immigration and to maintain the Anglo way of life in the US. This is old-style racist paranoia: there are more and more of these bestial people and they are going to swallow us up, steal what we have and give nothing back in return. Nothing much new about this – except the hype and the future projection.

Brimelow goes for the gullet in his account of impending catastrophes: "There is a sense in which current immigration policy is Adolf Hitler's posthumous revenge on America."[57]

He explains that in the aftermath of the Second World War the "US political elite" (his phrase to connote decision-makers in a wrapped-up undemocratic power structure) responded to the horrors of Fascism with a concern to abandon racism and xenophobia in the new world they hoped to build. To Brimelow it is this concern which culminates in the Immigration Act of 1965, technically the Immigration and Nationality Act Amendment.

57. *Times*, 22 April 1995: 18a.

And this, quite accidentally, triggered a renewed mass immigration, so huge and so systematically different from anything that had gone before as to transform – and ultimately, perhaps, even to destroy – the one unquestioned victor of the Second World War: the American nation, as it had evolved by the middle of the 20th century.[58]

Those unquestioned good guys of the United States, in their open-hearted desire to be fair to everyone, have unwittingly opened the door to their own destruction. The Brimelow line is hardly original; it echoes a whole cacophony of white backlash sentiment from North America and other parts of the wealthy developed world. Like all good pundits, Brimelow plays off this existing popular understanding; that's his angle, saying out loud what everyone (supposedly) already knows and feels.

"Race and ethnicity are destiny in American politics. The racial and ethnic balance of America is being radically altered through public policy. This can only have the most profound effects. Is this what America wants?"[59]

Brimelow articulates some kind of widely felt gut feeling among (white) Americans, it seems. Why else the hype? He makes that peculiar kind of racist sense which bills itself as both everyday commonsense and beyond reason, the unarguable populist strategy which says both that this is what everyone with any sense

58. Ibid.
59. *Times*, 22 April 1995: 18d.

knows and that these sentiments stem from primal depths which cannot be articulated or disputed.

". . . essentially, a nation is a sort of extended family. It links individual and group, parent and child, past and future, in ways that reach beyond the rational to the most profound and elemental in the human experience."[60]

Brimelow describes the nation as a unit which functions through affective bonds – with an implication that these bonds are being broken apart in the United States. However, despite all the bluster about speaking unwelcome truths, Brimelow is hard pushed to say what exactly he (and the rest of long-suffering and sensible America) is frightened of. His explicit concern is that whites are becoming a minority: white people in the US are living longer and having fewer children, assorted dark-skinned groups (and particularly "newcomers") are having plenty of children and have a much younger population to start with. "So the true impact of immigration is the proportion of immigrants *and their descendants* in the American population."[61]

Brimelow explains the significance of this trend, in case we do not recognize the enormity of this shift:

So what impact will all this have on America? In one word: profound. . . . The Government officially projects an ethnic revolution in America. Specifically, it expects that by 2050, American whites will be on the point of becoming a minority. My little son Alexander will be 59.[62]

60. *Times*, 22 April 1995: 18f.
61. *Times*, 24 April 1995: 18d.
62. *Times*, 24 April 1995: 18e.

However, what exactly this profound change means remains unclear. This, presumably, is a call to that set of relationships beyond reason which joins families, nations, societies and historical eras in a network of interdependency. The fear is that "our" own nearest and dearest will live with the consequences of white minority status, yet what these consequences are is never said. The prospects are too horrific to contemplate, yet sensible people know what they are, despite fudging from official bodies.

"The Census Bureau is apparently afraid to estimate the fateful day when American whites actually cease to be a majority."[63]

Clearly, Brimelow feels that the loss of white majority status is a big deal and that predicting just how close it is will cause public (i.e. white) outcry. And given his talent for riding the hype machine, his hunch is probably right. White people are probably quite worried about the non-replacement reproduction levels of their population, and the expression of this worry can take a number of dangerous forms.

(2) Take two is more liberal, and takes in a broader sweep. In *Preparing for the twenty-first century* Paul Kennedy describes a global population in which whitefolk get older and sparser, while the dark-skinned continue to multiply and die young. Kennedy is fearful for the "environment" rather than any more explicit invocation of white privilege – but those fecund black masses still give him the willies.

Kennedy begins with an analogy between the Europe of the late eighteenth century and more contemporary accounts of crisis in the West and beyond – the jumping-off point is Malthus and a sense that the

63. *Times*, 24 April 1995: 18e.

mismatch between population growth and technological development is a continuing dilemma and
dynamic in the world.

> As the better-off families of the northern hemi-
> sphere individually decide that having only one
> or at the most two children is sufficient, they
> may not recognize that they are in a small way
> vacating future space (that is, jobs, parts of inner
> cities, shares of population, shares of market
> preferences) to faster-growing ethnic groups both
> inside and outside their national boundaries. But
> that, in fact, is what they are doing.[64]

Poorer, darker people have more children and are
younger all round; older, paler people have a more
technologized and comfortable lifestyle, but are running out of people. Kennedy reckons that the interplay
between these sets of trends is what will determine
the future of the human race. Whether we survive
(for Kennedy this seems to mean everyone, not only
or primarily whitefolk), how well we all live – these
things depend on the management of the different
population crises of the rich and poor worlds. Towards
the twenty-first century, all our destinies are tied.

"The environmental issue, like the threat of mass
migration, means that – perhaps for the first time –
what the South does can hurt the North."[65]

Kennedy is indicative of more recent eco-sensibil-
ities in the West. No longer the preserve of the freaky
margins of white life, green populism has meant that
towards the new millennium Doomsday is figured in

64.   Kennedy (1994): 45.
65.   Ibid.: 96.

terms of ecological disaster: a nightmare which has taken over from self-inflicted nuclear annihilation as number one topic for progressive primary school project work and popular paperback apocalypse. Kennedy echoes many of the same concerns raised by Brimelow; he is also worried about the impact of demographic changes. However, unlike Brimelow's explicit fear that Anglo culture and dominance are coming to an end, Kennedy sees oncoming disasters as crises of sustainability. The problems he foresees are global, although he acknowledges that their horror is that events in the unlucky South of the world now are shown to have repercussions for the formerly complacent North.

I'm interested in the way that Kennedy presents white obsolescence as an ecological disaster – or at least as a byproduct and/or contributory factor in these dangerous trends. He does let us know that ageing is not the only problem facing the peoples of the developed world:

> While life expectancy for older white men and women has increased (much of the rise in healthcare spending has gone to those over seventy-five), that for black women and especially black men has fallen. Because of this widespread poverty, Oxfam America – famous for its aid to developing countries – announced in 1991 that it would also focus, for the first time ever, upon the United States itself.[66]

The much-talked-about "greying" of America is heavily skewed towards the white population (this is

66. Ibid.: 303.

Brimelow's point). Not only are poorer, darker sections of US society not keeping up with this mixed blessing of affluence; some communities are *dying younger* – in a sick reminder that poverty is often a key linking feature of diaspora identity, an unwanted affinity between scattered peoples and left-long-ago homelands. To Kennedy this is an echo of global trends which are destructive for everyone; such wide disparities in resource allocation are not so much unjust as unsustainable. And right now arguments about sustainability and globally felt ecological costs seem more effective than familiar calls for justice. Kennedy tries to put things in terms of everyone's interests: "A population explosion on one part of the globe and a technology explosion on the other is not a good recipe for a stable international order."[67]

But, as with Brimelow, it isn't clear what disaster he is describing here. After all, stability is an ambiguous concept – and many people wish that many things would *not* stay so insistently the same.

Despite the many thoughtful and thought-provoking ideas raised by Kennedy's book, in the end he too wishes that those dark-skinned people would not have so many babies, an argument which is hard to make without some echo of racist logic. He wishes that the dark women of the poor world would get "feminism", learn the positive dysfunctions of gender.

> In general, women in developing countries with seven or more years of education (and presumably from the better-off classes?) marry approximately four years later than those without education, have higher rates of contraceptive

67.   Ibid.: 331.

use, *and* enjoy lower maternal and child mortality rates – so both they and their offspring have better chances in life. This clearly implies that a change in the status of women would significantly reduce population growth in the developing world. But how likely is that in those parts of South Asia, Africa, and the Muslim world where gender restrictions are so pronounced?[68]

Isn't this the kind of first-world white feminist line we all learned better than in the 1980s? The kind of thing which fuels so much postcolonial study? The twist in this rendition is that here the first world declares its own interest: the spread of this enlightenment is good for white survival.

Brimelow and Kennedy write from very disparate perspectives, yet in their different ways they are both voicing concern over changes in the complexion of the world population. Either way, these stories say that the demise of the white race is bad for the planet; we will never manage without them.

Looking on the bright side

In response to all this hysteria what I am suggesting is the need to practise perverse imagining, to try to see the possibilities hidden in scary events. The less powerful you are, the more important this is.

Also, how can we learn if we don't entertain other possibilities?

Admittedly, this is a hard one to repackage as victory. If it was just numbers we would have won

68. Ibid.: 342.

long ago. But with a stretch of imagination, maybe we can see beyond the horror stories.

Here are some unlikely ideas about what might happen; perverse imaginings.

(1) Forever everyone has been hoping for miraculous technological innovation: feed your numbers and lots of other stuff becomes possible.

(2) The resource-rich people-short world will need care; the answer to who will nurse the formally strong signals a karmic victory. What goes around comes around.

(3) As one world order collapses, exhausts its own logic, begins to eat its own, maybe population size will again become a significant advantage.

Kennedy, in fact, outlines this possibility, summarizing a range of debate:

> . . . while there may be short-term costs associated with looking after and educating lots of young children, over the longer term there will be a larger population of productive workers between fifteen and sixty-four years old. Given the ingenuity and inventiveness of human beings, the more of them there are, the better; if on average there are two or three really creative people in every hundred, better to have a population of 100 million than 1 million.[69]

69. Ibid.: 31. For more on this see *Independent on Sunday*, 28 August 1994: 15a: "Too small a world?", and *The Independent*, 5 September 1994: 13a: "Overpopulation is not Africa's problem".

More likely, there will be no victory, just a shift – a new collection of wounds. For the dark world the challenge is to imagine ourselves without the demeaning counterpoint of whiteness, to stop being transfixed by the ogres of the past.

White-on-white violence

You don't have to look too far to find signs of white crisis these days. The bombing of the federal government building in Oklahoma on 20 April 1995 has been another event to shake the white psyche. *The Times* of 24/4/95 tells us that the "Search for alien scapegoats leads Americans to their own backyard: On Thursday night, America went to sleep with the depressing assumption that the nation had been attacked by evil foreigners. On Friday it awoke to the terrifying news that the worst terrorist attack on US soil was probably the work of Americans."[70]

This is another take which doesn't fit my meat story. It seems that white obsolescence brings up these contradictory responses: both anxious care of the metaphorical family of domesticated animals and white-on-white violence. Although early media coverage stressed that the bombers were "Americans", not "foreigners", it soon became apparent that here "American" was an easy code for a certain kind of US citizen, redneck patriot of the American heartland, the reliable white backbone of a violently divided nation, until then.

"The news that the suspects were almost archetypal products of America – an army veteran from

70. *Times*, 24 April 1995: 12a.

upstate New York linked with a Michigan farmer and his brother – left the media, and America as a whole, temporarily stunned."[71]

The framework of us-and-them, the logically same and those dangerous others, can't explain the obsolescence of the white race. This is death from within, self-destruct, not victim of attack.

Recent strains of white violence almost recognize this. The new white disaffection – the whole whinging syndrome of WASP victimage – cannot be pinned on the trespasses of an alien enemy. Again, the logic of the same is hard to escape: the root of this pain cannot be "us", it must be "them", different, other, elsewhere. But the familiar argument twists to accommodate new fears and new situations: "our representatives are our enemies". The fictions of democratic representation obscure this important battle between "people" and "state", apparently. "Anyone who talks about communism doesn't get it. The enemy is fascism in the White House." So – bomb people like us; the bizarre spectacle of white self-destruction as a protest against white self-destruction.[72]

I do think that something shifts with Oklahoma; the tearful declarations about America's loss of innocence with this event are, surely, indicative of something. Frightening as this bombing was, these levels of violence are not unknown in human history or, even, in contemporary events. What freaks people in this instance is the relationship between perpetrators and victims. For white America, it seems, Oklahoma has become a symbol of a warped aggression, dir-

71. *Times*, 24 April 1995: 12c.
72. For more on the paramilitarized backlash of white men in the US, see Gibson (1994).

ected inwards, towards its own. In the dysfunctional family of whiteness, rogue sons are running riot. Far more than teenage high-jinks, these boys act like they have got nothing left to lose: a nihilistic anti-heroism more usually associated with dispossessed populations. Since when has the violence of the powerful been terrorism? When white America starts killing its own in acts of terrorism (as opposed to venting its righteous aggression in racial violence, sex crimes, domestic beatings, child abuse, profit-motivated crime, road rage and military occupation) something is cracking in the house of the powerful. For the rest of us this is a realization of the truly irresponsible violences of a dying people. Old enemies stay dangerous and become more ruthless and unpredictable.

In response to these events, the question for us all, Anglos and others, troubled whiteys and expectant dark-skins, is: will we survive white obsolescence?

I can only understand events around veal exports as an irrational politicization: what kind of recognition of common interests is this? Surely even whitefolk cannot believe that this is the most significant issue of injustice in contemporary Britain, the one worth risking life and limb for, the struggle which will lead to universal freedom, or even the more modest goal of self-empowerment. So I can only read veal as a veil for some other unspeakable fear, a sense of coming catastrophe. And I think it makes sense to view Oklahoma as part of the same crisis: related deaththrows from an agitated people. The white world senses its loss of ascendency, but can respond only with desperate actions which contribute to the demise.

In our interconnected world of eco-horrors and high-tech networks, more than ever the actions of the rich white world (still now holders of capital, sources of information, entertainment and arms, all-round big influences in many people's lives) have repercussions for us all. I'm not interested in reforming white subjectivity, families, populations; but I am interested in surviving the fallout from the death of the white race . . . a challenge to all our imaginations.

In this fifth section of our tale, we learn of the extent and depth of the changes which surround us. The place, the shape, the very substance of bodies are shifting. Alongside these shifts in the status of flesh, we see other changes in the shape of the globe. Now, it seems, no one can tell for certain where the future will lie. In the next and final section, we turn, at last, to this future and practise living with its uncertainty.

Further reading

To explore the experience of education, see *Young, female and black*, by Heidi Safia Mirza.

For an extended account of the strange practice of travel-writing, see *Imperial eyes*, by Mary Louise Pratt.

For more on histories of race science, see *The idea of race in science*, by Nancy Stepan.

For more discussion of the re-emergence of race science, see *The bell curve wars*, by Steven Fraser.

To pursue the role of biological environment in white ascendancy, see *Ecological imperialism*, by Alfred W. Crosby.

CHAPTER 6

The entertainer's tale

In this, the last set of tales, at last we begin to sense a world beyond the constraints of yesterday. Here we learn of our gift to entertain and the uncertain benefits of being at once object of scrutiny and focus of attention. These are the stories in which we talk and sing and dance and talk some more – and hope to survive to see the future.

My story is not quite like those of my sisters. It is true that I, too, have led a varied life spanning great distances. But the shape of my life has taken a different turn.

I grew up in a land where it was expected that my people would be entertainers. No-one ever said that the role of entertainer would lead to the sacrifice of the more everyday benefits of citizenship, but, in effect, this was the bargain. Growing up, I saw the adults in my life belittled publicly, forever denied the proper respect due the fully grown. Whatever they did, their struggles somehow became spectacles.

When I grew, I tried to escape this fate of entertainer to my tormentors. Let them amuse themselves; it was time for us to live. And, like my sisters, I worked hard to achieve my goals, to make my family proud, to become more than the stilted vision of white people had allowed. I wanted respect, and that meant cutting away the distractions of glamour and frivolity. But, privately, I knew that my talents were the talents which had long been ascribed to my people and, secretly, I longed for an audience which would not compromise my dignity.

Now that I have heard my sister's story, I believe this may be possible.

The spectre of white obsolescence brings up possibilities for all sorts of people. Now we have heard the news, nothing can look the same again. All the names we call ourselves, the assumption that we make sense in relation to this other thing, cannot hold any more.

Perhaps this means feeling less bad?

Before we felt bad a lot of the time, it seems. Even when the stories started to change and people began to play around with the positive possibilities of negative ascriptions, the names we called ourselves still held the disparaging taint of victimage. After all, these names had been the names of suffering and disrespect for centuries. They were names which only seemed to make sense in that particular and undesirable matrix of power. However much we looked on the bright side and put our best feet forward, the danger was that only the bad old histories would show. However you packaged it, sometimes it felt as if those names could only mean one thing – and that one thing could never be good.

Even in the most optimistic moments, when new stories were being written, this fear crawled around our feet, tripping up our best intentions. What if our names could only be understood to mean helpless, worthless, lesser? What if that was what people saw, no matter what we did? What if there was no way of remaining ourselves and becoming free? What if, what if, what if?

Doubt makes people wary: stops things happening, freezes everything in dangerous hesitation. Its residue clipped the wings of the most far-flying new tale, a leftover stain on the shiny new possibility of the next episode. In one version, acknowledging the power of history means discounting the future because everything seems already decided.

Before white obsolescence, understanding our place in the world was an endless process of charting this determining history. We began to see what was happening and why, and started to dream of vengeance rather than surrender; but imagining another story seemed a disrespect to our ancestors. Our history made us what we were and trying to leave it behind would leave us with no name at all, invisible people.

Like all fears, this one left us nowhere. Look back and you are stuck in endless pain. Look forward and you have no way of being. We were equally scared of being visible and invisible. Either seen in the wrong way or not seen at all. And, of course, the fears became our fate.

Before, when we tried to understand what our names meant, we looked at what sense others might make of our actions. It was the name you were called in the street which told you who you were. So the important point to remember was that changing stories was about changing everyone's minds. We all had to come to a different agreement about what those names meant. Otherwise nothing had changed at all.

One version of this cautionary tale warned us that our enemies beat us by telling more convincing and entertaining stories. They knew how to appeal to their audience, to address their concerns, to push the right buttons of response. We, on the other hand, were in danger of speaking to ourselves, grabbing no-one's attention but our own. To live better lives, we had to become more entertaining.

Everyone's favourite big daddy of cultural theory recommended this approach. He argued that white ideas about black people were represented through a grammar of race: a lexicon consisting of images of deep ambivalence, but largely of dehumanizing implications. We were subhuman slaves, or dangerous natives, or laughable entertainers. Of course, everyone had always known the dangers of being seen as chattel or beast. It was the unease of our friendly entertainer persona which unsettled. Wasn't this one of the few ways in which we could make good? Apparently not.

> A third variant is that of the "clown" or "entertainer". This captures the "innate" humour, as well as the physical grace of the licensed entertainer – putting on a show for The Others. It is never quite clear whether we are laughing with or at this figure: admiring the physical and rhythmic grace, the open expressivity and emotionality of the "entertainer", or put off by the "clown's" stupidity.[1]

There it is, that deep ambivalence – except that it wasn't ambivalent to us. If our potential good points could be used against us so easily, that was straightforwardly bad, no two ways about it. Least ambivalent of all was the entertainment offered by our women.

"The sexually available 'slave-girl' is alive and kicking, smouldering away on some exotic TV set or on the covers of paperbacks, though she is now the centre of a special admiration, covered in a sequinned gown and supported by a white chorus line."[2]

Although this is an argument (made at a certain time for a certain purpose, like all arguments) about dominant representations, not all representations, it is easy to read the implications as bad. This underlying grammar runs deep, as much in the heads of the

1.   Hall (1981): 40.
2.   Ibid.: 41.

audience as in anything pictured before their eyes. We believed the argument about the grammar of race because it felt so true and familiar. We recognized those stories, and with shame we saw those names as versions of ourselves. However many new stories we told, it still felt as if those pictures of slave, native and clown were us. And the unwelcome events of our lives reinforced this belief.

The grammar of race story was always told as part of a package; and in the package great changes were eminently possible, if not already on their way. The point about telling stories about constraining interpretations was that it let you know where the story needed altering. We learned that there was a need for an anti-racist commonsense, and looking at what had worked for our enemies was meant to guide us in our own counter-attack.

Because this version of the state of play was described by a certain sort of much-needed and doted-upon father figure, the diligent children of the rest of the world quickly set to work on the tasks which had been set. Lots of books answered the riddle, and they were shelved together in the new places of knowledge.

From elsewhere, this gets described as a black British cultural studies which is

> concerned with issues of black appropriation of modern black performance as construction of identity, crossover texts, ambivalence, and the critique of sexism and homophobia in black communities. Thus, it is both "victim studies" and "performance studies" at the same time.[3]

3. Manthia Diawara in Henderson (1995): 203.

In truth, there isn't much of this stuff about; we can all guess the names which are not mentioned here and they take less than a page. But the shift from victim to performer in all our self-understandings is important. Now there is a chance that knowing more will also help you to do more, not just become stuck in endless contemplation of how bad things are. After the long legacy of white constructions of black entertainers, now the ability to perform reopened everyone's options. We had felt how bad the world could be and studying had revealed some reasons for our plight; it took imagination to remember that none of this was fixed or eternal, that new things could happen, even now, so late in the day. The smart black scholars started to devote their energies to this.

> It is through performance that we move away from stereotypes and fixed images of black people, toward great men and women, ordinary people, bad guys and good guys. It is also through per- formance that black people provide the most important critique of modernity, which continues to reify black lives. Performance is a political representation that enables the actor to occupy a different position in American [European, global] society, and to interpellate the audience's approval of the new and the emerging images of black people.[4]

Let's be clear what we are talking about here. This is not the performance of specialization; the people doing it are not named "performers". This is not about saying, "I am an actor – and my art demands

4. Ibid.: 209–10.

your respect." This is no boring showing-off in enclosed spaces. Not that game where I switch the lights out for no particular reason and you have to look at me for two hours while I do what I practised earlier. This is not what we are talking about at all, and that kind of talk about performance adds almost nothing to the new story we are hoping for.[5]

This is about learning to live brand new lives. Here performance is what everyone does everyday already. Another word for the strange but fortunate resilience of the human spirit and will to survive.

Here are some of the entertainers we can be.

The story of the new generation black scholar[6]

This is the story of a woman who performs a new set of tricks. For her, the trials of getting an education are transformed into a chance to show off her best side. This is her tale.

"I, too, used to believe these promises which you repeat. I have devoted long years to study, kneeling at the white man's feet, mastering his manner of argument. I thought, as you think, that this learning would protect me. What I hoped for was a chance to win on their terms, to argue myself into existence. I thought that if I was a scholar, then no-one could dispute my claims to equality.

It's true, my experience was bad. My fellow students ridiculed me, laughing at a diligence which to

5. The performance studies which grows out of theatre studies in Britain tends to be concerned with a different set of issues and remains tied to the agenda of organized theatre.
6. For another version of this story, see Bhattacharyya (1996).

their eyes appeared pointless. After all, their books taught them that my people were not built for scholarship. My teachers disliked my work, scolding me for the fractures in my writing, the spaces in which I tried to leave room for the gap between my life and their stories. In the library I cried at the volume of disrespect recorded in the tightly bound pages. But still, I ploughed on. After all, how could I disprove these ideas unless I studied them?

Now that my youth has long past, my diligence has reaped some reward. Now I teach others about the shapes of the world and work hard to dismantle that long history of disrespect.

I am employed according to a new set of demands. Before people had to shout and fight for the issues affecting our people to merit study; the keepers of knowledge did not believe that this was part of understanding the world. Then black people became educated by distancing themselves from blackness. This is what Fanon calls losing the jungle; and he thinks that no-one can ever do this successfully. Whatever you *do*, your body will always conjure up the jungle again.

But in this new story blackness becomes a necessary performance for proper education to take place. You need a touch of the jungle to understand how the world works. This isn't just about what gets taught: there is an expectation that it will change how things are taught too. Black teachers are good because they demonstrate the lesson by how they are, through the performance they give.

Paradoxically, this throws the forget-the-jungle white-masked people out of a job. Of course, there are plenty of places where white-masking is still the only option. Places where the suggestion of blackness causes panic. But in the particular performance of privileged intellectual (or not so intellectual) life, the part to play is skin. And, handily, along come a range of debates about the assumption of identity and everyday performance. Now this stuff seemed central to our understanding of the contemporary world.[7] So suddenly there are jobs for people demonstrating this tricksy skill of identity formation in difficult circumstances. In steps the new age black scholar, ready to provide endless commentary on these processes of late-twentieth-century life. From now on, we will all be employed to perform the special show of ourselves . . .

Maybe.

It is too easy to pretend that performance is the new choice for dark-skinned people living by pale-skinned rules. After centuries of trouble, the idea that make-believe and bravado can save you is sweet indeed.

But wait just one minute. Isn't performance one of those shared traits across black cultures? Something we have had to learn because of our long centuries of trouble?

Think about friend Fanon explaining our assumption of racialized identity.[8] When he writes, 'Out of the blackest part of my soul, across the zebra striping

7. For more on this, see standard works such as Rutherford (1990).
8. Famous Franz Fanon, Martiniquan psychiatrist and revolutionary fighter for Algeria, has been much discussed in recent years. His most famous works, *Black skin, white masks*, *Studies in a dying colonialism* and *The wretched of the earth*, address the pathological behaviour which attends the colonial experience and the effects on us all of these powerful sicknesses.

of my mind, surges this desire to be suddenly *white*. I wish to be acknowledged not as *black* but as *white*'[9], isn't he performing to show that being black is a question of performance? He has already told us earlier that this work will follow no recognized method; that he leaves to botanists and mathematicians, those dealing with the more predictable aspects of the world, the plants and numbers which didn't answer back. He promises to be derelict in his quest to uncover the effects of white civilization on black people (p. 14). Not only in method, but also in manner of address, this is not what we expect from learned doctors pursuing philosophical questions. When Fanon writes of his zebra stripes, he is not making an argument, he is making a speech. Half the book is like this, demonstrating its point in its manner. We are dragged into the impassioned monologues until we are ready to believe what he says. By the time he has described the humiliation of the white child's racist fear – 'Mama, see the Negro! I'm frightened!' (p. 112) – playing all the parts in that too-familiar pantomime, what reader cannot understand the point he is making?

> the occasion arose when I had to meet the white man's eyes. An unfamiliar weight burdened me. The real world challenged my claims. In the white world the man of color encounters difficulties in the development of his bodily schema. Consciousness of the body is solely a negating activity. It is a third-person consciousness.[10]

9.   Fanon (1969): 63.
10.   Ibid.: 110.

Racism makes its victims see themselves through the eyes of others, the others who torment and judge them. When people named by their skin try to transcend their bodies and claim their humanity, the look of the white other makes their flesh heavy again with racialized expectation. As our stories have told, the look is always backed up by more solid and wounding machineries of white disrespect, but the consciousness of the body described here is a sense of being objectified through sight. That's how this particular hegemonic head-fuck works on its victims, says Fanon; you feel so conspicuous that your body becomes a dead weight which you struggle to control. The burden of representing the whole history of fantasy-savages, and the downside of metaphysical equations to boot, stops you in your tracks, fills you with doubt and anxiety, polices every move you make. Impossible not to perform to such an omnipresent white eye, as Fanon explains again, 'I took myself far off from my own presence, far indeed, and made myself an object.'[11]

Surviving this constantly surveyed situation means adapting yourself to its demands. Instead of reaching towards the subjecthood of equality, an aspiration which stumbles on white incomprehension, here socialization demands acceptance of an outside structure. Unless you become the object of white culture, how can you learn to live in your body? Forgetting your body leaves you vulnerable to unexpected humiliation: not only children in the street, but more dangerous forces as well; nothing for it but to play to your audience and step into your allotted role of object. This is the desperate performance of necessity.

11.   Ibid.: 112.

> When the Negro [or the "Asiatic", or the "Oriental", or the "Indian", or the "Aborigine"?] makes contact with the white world, a certain sensitizing action takes place. If his psychic structure is weak, one observes a collapse of the ego. The black man stops behaving as an *actional* person. The goal of his behaviour will be The Other (in the guise of the white man), for The Other alone can give him worth.[12]

For Fanon, the performance of black identity is a sad affair, continually playing to a white audience which cannot appreciate, affirm, love, no matter how practised the performance. In this he echoes other talk about being colonized, our relation of deference, hiding, pleasing to an audience of cruelly variable attention. Memmi, another big man in the quotation stakes, asks, 'How could the colonized deny himself so cruelly yet make such excessive demands? How could he hate the colonizers and yet admire them so passionately?'[13] and ends up answering through his

12. Ibid.: 154.
13. Memmi (1967): 10. Albert Memmi, a Tunisian, wrote this book in 1957. The American edition, published in 1965, is "dedicated to the American Negro, also colonized". Although Memmi had published novels before this, *The pillar of salt* and *Strangers*, it was *The colonizer and the colonized* which brought him international attention. Memmi writes of this work that "I undertook this inventory of conditions of colonized people mainly in order to understand myself and to identify my place in the society of other men" (p. viii), and that although he writes from a Tunisian perspective, his readers across the world have convinced him "that all the oppressed are alike in some ways" (p. ix). The lasting influence of this book has been its suggestions about the subject formation of the colonized across contexts.

analysis of the relations of colonization. The evils of colonization addle the minds of the colonized, imposing the worldview of the colonizer. The colonized cannot help but want contradictory things: to at once be like the colonizer and to be rid of the colonizer. This, Memmi explains, is the destiny of the colonized: 'The two historically possible solutions are then tried in succession or simultaneously. He attempts either to become different or to reconquer all the dimensions which colonization tore away from him.'[14]

These goals can be achieved only with the overthrow of colonization; only then is it possible for the colonized to pursue the privileges which mark the humanity of the colonizer and to redevelop the lost heritage of their culture. The implication is that, to defeat the colonizer, the colonized must learn not to perform for the reaction of this audience; this is the moment when the colonized recognize their kinship with each other, the moment which marks the final untenability of the colonizer's position.

Much of what Memmi is talking about is the role of that confused entity: the colonized educated in colonizing culture. Like Fanon, he is interested in this position of false privilege and the special pain of all those promises which can never be kept. In both analyses, mental health and eventual happiness can come only when these half-way creatures give up their doomed love for the white colonizers and make the psychic journey back to their own.

Much later, when the world is shaped by structures which are both different and too much the same, these boy-based stories of surviving racial subjugation leave a legacy of performative resistance behind them. Once you learn these stories – really

14. Ibid.: 120.

learn them, so that your own skin crawls with zebra stripes – the skin you're in can never be quite the same again. After this, the various dances of masked and unmasked blackness must take place self-consciously. Listen to the stories properly and you might learn a new mode of becoming a black subject. Hidden in both tales is the chance that the performance could be twisted to more pleasurable ends, even that most pleasurable end of freedom.

I, the new age black scholar, inherit this possibility of twisting a new positive performance out of our histories of domination. Even my employers recognize this, however grudgingly. My job as teacher is to display myself as a certain kind of black subject. If I mask myself with whiteness too successfully, then the demands of the job are not being met. There are plenty of real unmasked white faces providing the educational exemplar of the white subject. My role is to be conspicuously black.

> We live in a world characterised not just by difference, but by a consuming and erotic passion for it. Gone are the metanarratives by which modernist thinkers sought to interpret the world through simplistic Enlightenment universalisms. But gone too are the forces of modernism and cultural imperialism that have operated in the past to constitute a homogenous world after images constructed in eighteenth century European bourgeois thought, hence making it possible for those of postmodern sensitivity at the same time to fear and marvel at the difference which is thereby revealed to them.[15]

15.   Kahn (1995): 125.

I am, it seems, a product of this new era – but I learn my trade from earlier performers."

The story of the caged songbird

Once, in a land far from here, a young girl grew up with the voice of a songbird. She was an amenable little thing, and never refused any request for a song. The grown-ups marvelled at her precocity. "She can sing anything, that one – wiggle her hips like a real cabaret star. The way she looks at you you'd think she knew what the words meant."

But, of course, she didn't. She was just a little girl who could sing. It was her talent for performance which transformed her into a vamp and a clown, an unlucky lover and a dangerous other woman. Her body changed its shape to fit the voice.

As the girl grew older, people nudged her parents: "You should encourage that talent. You could make some money there. There's little enough going here."

And although her parents wished for education, normality, some sort of secure everydayness, they saw the reason in this advice. But the girl herself was fearful about the stories she heard about the life of the singer. What if she became the tragic figure of the songbird? What kind of cartoon life was that?

"Most people remember Bessie as crude, tough, or ill-mannered; irresponsible; passionate, kind, or generous."[16]

She was old enough now to see that when people loved her singing this was the fantasy they saw. People loved her voice because it conjured up these

16.   Albertson (1975): 23.

delicious contrasts for them – hard and soft, rough and sweet – and that fantasy fitted their fantasy of all women like her. To them, these women could take sex and could take pain. Unlike the delicate flowers of white femininity who demanded so much and bruised so easily, these were women who survived the knocks of life.

"Bessie sang of mean mistreaters and two-timing husbands with tragi-comic optimism, offered advice to the dejected, and made it quite clear that she herself was not immune to such problems."[17]

The girl could see why people liked this story. Life is hard; everyone needs to know that survival is possible. And of course, the idea of the woman who can take some punishment has its own erotic charge. But wasn't there a cost to becoming this fantasy figure? The young girl learned to hide her talent, for fear of becoming exotic myth.

Then one day the girl heard a much older woman sing, a woman who looked like family. Just the kind of woman the girl was fearful of becoming. Yet somehow, something in her voice quelled the girl's fear. Later, she asked her to explain.

The older woman explained to her that there had always been kinship between performers. Singing was a special calling after all. She told the girl about the stories surrounding Ma Rainey: "A host of misconceptions grew up about her life: it was said that she kidnapped young Bessie, taking her on the tent show circuit and teaching her own art to her pupil."[18]

Kidnapping lesbians, stealing pretty children to train in their art. The envy in the tale was so thinly

17.   Ibid.: 45.
18.   Lieb (1981): 2.

veiled that even the girl laughed to see it. Whatever the singers had, it was enough to raise a rumour-mongering jealousy in others. Singers were such famously bad girls, such inappropriate and visible show-offs.[19] Perhaps this mythic independence was worth any woman's while, perhaps the risk was worth the pay-off?

To prove her point, the older woman told the girl another story about singers, a proper mythic tale about masculine endeavour in strange lands.

The sirens are creatures of far-off lands: the half-woman, half-beast beings of white boy fantasy.[20] Mythically seductive, with the uncannily beautiful voices of the sea, they are also deadly. The sweetness of their song calls passing travellers into the sea, drowning as they rush to hear more. There isn't much chance of entertainment here: listen and you're dead.[21]

Until Ulysses, of course. He brings tricky Euro intellect to bear, stealing other people's wisdom for his own ends, and learns how to resist and experi-ence the sirens' song. So he stops up the ears of his servant-sailors, has himself strapped to the mast and gets past the deadly charms of the sirens. Hero that he is, he completes his journey, gets back home, and

19. "Adorno claims that a woman's voice cannot be recorded well, because it demands the presence of her body. A man's voice is able to carry on in the absence of his body, because his self is identical with his voice; his body disappears": Engh, in Dunn & Jones (1994): 120.

20. "She [the siren] had allowed the masculine force of the bisexual primal state to resurface; hence she personified the regressive, bestial element in woman's nature. She was not the cultured pearl of modern, passive femininity but the dangerous, brutal, atavistic child of the sea's cold watery womb." Dijkstra (1986): 258.

21. See Homer (trans. 1992): 170.

becomes the stuff of myth. And the sirens, apparently, die of despair. Because one white boy got by?

> The sirens. Yes, they really sang, but not in a very satisfactory way. Their song merely suggested the direction from which the perfect song might come. Yet through their imperfect song – a song as yet unborn – they lured the navigator towards the space where singing really begins.[22]

The older woman explained this old bad-news story to the girl, laughed off her worries, taught her to see what wasn't said.

The boy couldn't resist. Everything he did confirmed the strength of the sirens, showed that these bird-women truly were irresistible to (European?) men. The point is not whether or not he gets by. What matters is how unsettling he finds the song. Can he keep control, his sense of self, the disciplined will which makes him the man? And no, he can't. Not without physical constraint and the obedient labour of his crew. A loosened knot, a loss of speed – the man is lost. Is this the self-mastery which founds European civilization?

Winning by trickery is no victory at all. By his actions Ulysses admits that he is scared and tempted by this distracting entertainment. The ambivalence runs deep.

All of which proves that our singing, the singing of us more and less than women, is powerful. Our enemies may defeat us with their greater resources, but they never feel truly safe, never stop wanting to succumb.

22. Blanchot (1982): 59.

This is the secret possibility of all our singing: that it changes what it means to be human, flips open new options for anyone who hears.

> Some have said that it was an inhuman song – a natural sound ... but on the borderline of nature, at any rate foreign to man; almost inaudible, it evoked pleasurable dreams of an endless descent which, in normal circumstances, can never be realised. Others suggested that it had a more mysterious charm; that it simply imitated the song of normal human beings; but since the sirens, even if they sang like human beings, were only beasts (very beautiful beasts, admittedly, and possessing feminine charm), their song was so unearthly that it forced those who heard it to realise the inhumanness of all human singing.[23]

"Without singers, who will know this lesson?"

Not waiting for an answer, the scholar quickly moved on to her next tale.

The story of the exotic dancer

Once there was a young woman of incredible grace. Her body moved as if it held no weight and wherever she went people could not help but stare. The young woman chose to nurture her talent and diligently studied the physical disciplines of dance. She wished to explore what the human body could do and in her quest consulted the wise sources of many cultures. With effort she came to understand that grace was anything but unthinking. When she understood

23. Ibid.: 59.

this, her teachers declared that she was ready to perform, "because now you see how precarious your control of your body is".

The woman felt anxious. Before she had held her body easily, moving it with the easy pleasure of what comes naturally. Now she felt conscious of every twitch and tremour. But her training had taught her the discipline of obedience, and she went to look for work. The first advert she answered brought her to a lonely back street. The white man who came to the door looked her up and down approvingly. "They like your sort around here. We don't get to see enough of that tasty brown flesh. Can you do the dance of the seven veils?"[24]

The dancer flicked over her repertoire before she heard the question properly. She had studied her discipline carefully and she knew well the history of the dance of the veils. She also knew that the man was not asking about the breadth of her dance knowledge. But she wanted to work, so she kept her answer vague. "I'm a trained performer – I can learn any dance you want me to."

The man chuckled nastily to himself: "Trained to please, eh? That's what the punters like." Then he frowned suddenly. "Do your family know what you do? We don't want any trouble here, you know. We've heard what your menfolk are like – protective of their girlies, aren't they? Don't be thinking I'll keep them off when they come to ship you back to get married."

"I haven't any family now – only a sister, and she's moved down south with her boyfriend. I promise

24. For more on this dance and the figure of Salome as a racially degenerate type, see Dijkstra (1968): 386–7.

you, you'll have no trouble at your place. At least let me audition for you as I'm here?"

Stepping onto the raised platform which passed for a stage, the dancer imagined her seven veils.

> The story of Salome and her mesmerizing Dance of the Seven Veils has become a standard trope of Orientalism, a piece of domesticated exotica that confirms Western prejudices about the "Orient" and about "women" because it is produced by those prejudices, is in fact an exercise in cultural tautology.[25]

Salome is another distracting entertainer: her dance of unveiling is sublimely indescribable, as good as dancing gets. She, too, performs for a despotic ruler – but the boon she chooses for her service is not peace for her people, but the head of John the Baptist. As others have noted (Garber), her story is linked to that of Medusa, and hidden in her vengeance is the implication that if you look too hard you might lose your head.

In the story, no-one is quite sure what Salome's dance looks like. We know that it is mesmerizing, and legend takes this to mean that the dance at once veils and reveals, transfixing the audience with the difficulty of seeing.[26] When Western dancers try to recreate this indescribable sight, of course they look

25. Garber (1992): 340.
26. Dijkstra writes of the Oscar Wilde version of the Salome story: "Wilde's play pitches sight against sound. Both may be primary senses, but for Wilde the battle between sight and sound represented the struggle between materialism and idealism, between the feminine and the masculine" (1968): 396.

to the East. They try "to copy the harlots of Cairo, who, pretending that a bee had gotten into their clothing, contrived to strip themselves garment by garment, all the while dancing frantically".[27]

So, in translation, Salome's dance becomes a performance of the body struggling to become free of material constraint, the twitching of flesh which itches to be revealed. In the story reworked through Western performance, Salome mesmerizes because she demonstrates the body's need to be confirmed through sight, and for sight to confirm the body. She refuses her veils and reveals her flesh. Instead of being sublimely indescribable, the story becomes one in which sight fixes the previously unseen and no troubling mystery remains.

As the girl started her dance, she did think about this shameless stripping away of someone else's sense of propriety. She knew that she had learned to love Salome because of this image, the idea that being naked made a woman strong, not weak. This was why generations of women had warmed to the Western performance of the story: "To women in the audience . . . Salome was perhaps an alter-image, through which it was proper to express their erotic longings, their will to power, and their suppressed fury toward men."[28]

But the performer in the girl knew that Salome held her audience by what she did not reveal. The seven veils play-acted revelation, as if the thing which mattered was being shown; but in the end, no amount of hard looking could see what mesmerized. That remained elusive, gone with the performance.

27. Jowitt (1988): 65.
28. Ibid.: 123.

So when she danced the girl thought of a story she had once heard, a story about the process of becoming which is never quite finished and complete.

The story of the storyteller

> Stories are always a complex production with many tellers and hearers, not all of them visible or audible. Story-telling is a serious concept, but one happily without the power to claim unique or closed readings. . . . The aesthetic and ethic latent in the examination of story-telling might be pleasure and responsibility in the weaving of tales. Stories are means to ways of living.[29]

The fabulous adventures of the mahogany princesses

In recent years it has often seemed as if all attempts to make sense of the troubled meanings of skin and genitals have returned again and again to pictures and words. Getting to the magic word "politics" depends on guessing the right thing to say, the best picture to draw. Spending so much time arguing about representation has drained everyone's resources; we have all forgotten other ways of thinking and fighting, it seems. This is my answer to those troubled years of watching what I said.

For us, telling stories has become a way of life. Living is hard and confusing and narrative promises

29. Haraway (1989): 8.

to guide us through. Of course, things get left out, misplaced, but the stories help us to keep on. Fictional tracks for unplanned journeys, that last memory of progress binds us still. Please don't shout white boy teleology. This isn't quite the linear track of Western science; that has its uses, but it isn't the right story for our everyday. Nor is it the overview of their panopticon god. We aren't waiting for the jailer of destiny to serve up the final sentences: there is no one watcher who can fix the ending here.

These are stories to live by, open to adaptation by ordinary contexts and unexpected giggles. Slip yourself into your role of choice. Try things out: see what fits, what helps you fly. If you find yourself in a story which doesn't help you to live, give it up. Stories with no chance of a happy ending aren't worth telling. Save your breath for the adventures to follow.

Before we go too far, it's important to believe that you know what I am talking about; maybe not in this form, but still the same thing. Think of the words of our favourite brothers:

> The early eighties . . . saw the gathering of critical mass through collectivist activities whose emergent agendas began to impact upon public institutions during the mid-eighties around the key theme of *black representation*. But to call it a "renaissance," while capturing the atmosphere of optimism and renewal, implies an authenticating myth of origins which Black Britain did not really have at its disposal: which is to say, if such myths did not exist they would have to be reinvented, using whatever materials came to hand.

> Having come to voice, what and whose language do you speak? What or whose language speaks you?[30]

This is the same will to enter the story, to be seen, to make sense: even if the bargain costs us dear, ties us to forms which can never be ours. It's too late to turn back, the plot is already in motion. Not being in the story isn't an option.

Think about representation, our bane and our obsession: why is this a good way to think about how "race" and "gender" work? Why isn't it? Where did class go? Here are some thoughts:

(1) This kind of social analysis seems to be inevitably about pictures for us; place this kind of body in this kind of landscape and try to judge the effects. We think you can understand "race" and gender by looking; you can see the different sorts there are and gauge what happens around them. How we make sense of what we see has an effect on our response, and our response feeds back into the scary real world of events.

(2) The drawback is that we get fixated on looking. Looking becomes the main social relation, the one that counts, the activity which shapes the world. All our energy goes on looking different and looking differently. The things we can't see we have no hope of understanding.

(3) Some dangers aren't about how things look. There is no picture to show how this works, what it looks like, where it lives. It makes a

30. Mercer (1994): 14.

difference to what we see, but we can't see how, where, when. Even looking at the ugliest pictures is easier than this not knowing. As the shiver of the world hits our shoulders, the distracting activity of tampering with pictures comes as a welcome relief.

It is too late to give up on representation now; too many of our hurts are refracted through this frame. Better to push the logic until the contract snaps. Better to leap into adventure, changing stories like party outfits.

First things first

Fabulous: the stuff of fable, folklore at its most heartwarming and educational. The kind of story which tells it like it is, but also shows you how it could be. A story where none of the characters are real, but you know them all. Remember Aesop: "his complexion so swarthy, that he took his very name from it; for Aesop is the same as Aethiop . . . such an impediment in his speech, that people could hardly understand what he said."[31] Named by our skin, we inherit his form. Garble our best truths through fantasy, telling stories which seem at once too obvious and too obscure. Not founded on fact, we mix supernatural characters and legendary tales, idle talk and false statements – halfway between possibility and deception, the special visionary lies of the undervalued. Instead of certainty, here morals are about confounding expectation: the things worth knowing are not straightforward to tell.

31. Richardson (1975): xvi.

Adventures: what every life should hold. Experience as thrill not threat. Battles of the good against evil, quests for lost treasures, a twisting plot which stays surprising. There is risk and danger, of course, the inevitable gambles of the still living. Daringly speculative, hazardously active, adventure turns away from past pain to what is about to happen.

Mahogany: dark brown polish with the time running out. Cut down, chopped up, from tropical forest to draughty dining-rooms, only the shiny surface is left. No amount of benefit socials can make things how they were before. Better instead to love the colour, texture, smooth hardness, slippery feel.

Princesses: fantasy creatures fallen out of fairytales, waiting to be discovered, appreciated, swept off their feet out of drudgery into luxury. Built to be adored, we have fallen on hard times. No calls to let down our hair, climb the mountain of mattresses. When we shout "Rumplestiltskin", no-one respects our ingenuity.

Yesteryears

Long ago, in the land of fairytales, the mahogany princesses lived their lives of wild adventure with no fear but nature, no enemy but death. Their bodies were not yet the imagery of lascivious fantasy. The light bounced off the burnish of their skins, and they savoured the sensation of warmth. Not yet somebody else's picture, their bodies were still a source of non-scopic pleasures. In this world flesh is about touch, smell, taste. Looking isn't the main thing to do and skin is for stroking.

Across the seas the white men dream of what the world might hold. Standing quite still and turning their heads, they imagine the reach of their territory. Looking makes them the centre of the world. They are the vantage spot, the place from which order emanates. Puffed up with this suggestion they crane their necks further, and imagine all the things which they could have.

"It was easiest of all to believe that what was good for Europe must be even better for the "natives'. By now the white man had worked himself into a high state of self-conceit."[32]

Sold on the new range of narcissistic fantasy, the white men stretch out to print their mark on the world. The endless repetition of blockprint stamped on the delicate sari length covering all our bodies.

Adventure No. 1

This is a story for times of despair and exhaustion. A dream of that magical time before history: the idyll broken by destructive events and charted occurrence.

Here the princesses are still invisible to their enemies; subject to no-one, not yet conquered. The story mixes up all these freedoms, from military occupation, economic impossibility, identity formation. As if that whole other world of pre-colonial civilization was blighted by the first white man's glance.

In this other time, when some other logic prevailed, the mahogany princesses were happy and doubt-free. They achieved easily, collecting success as their due. From our jumpy shell-shocked world, this looks like

32. Kiernan (1986): 26.

a time of innocence. Unaware of the colonial complexes to follow, the princesses bounce around the world charged with expectation.

This is the story we whisper to our children at bedtime. Taking off the battles of the day, heads hitting the pillow, that moment when we sense their connection to what we all used to be. Soft words into nearly sleeping ears, breathing the hope that we could be those things again.

To work this story has to link certain key themes; these are the plot points which must be remembered.

(1) There are ways of being beyond the ugliness of colonial relations. In this story we assume a before – the state of grace from which we have sadly fallen – but it is as much about possibility as nostalgia.

(2) The time before – the place outside the damaging relations which form our consciousness – offered untold possibilities and achievements. We don't have to be constituted through a paralyzed face-off in which we always lose. Beyond Hegel, Fanon, circular determination. The endless face-off of master/slave, colonizer/colonized, us only in relation to them, is a sickness of our time, not all time.

(3) For the mahogany princesses, this is importantly about a time before the regime of the scopic. We were not always constituted through someone's glance; maybe looking doesn't have to be the point.

The colonizing gaze is taut with envy

Frozen in the white gaze, the mahogany princesses shiver. Suddenly surface is what matters. They still touch – fill their mouths with flavour, breathe deeply the smells of experience – but they are caught in the nets of representation. Looking becomes the route to knowledge. Information is what you can see. Increasingly the mahogany princesses imagine themselves as the two-dimensional mirage of someone else's look. Self as picture sucks away the pleasures of self as flesh. The things which can't be shown lose their power to the demonstrable.

The scopic pressures distort the lovely bodies of the princesses. Their skins take over their beings. They are engulfed by surface. Colour becomes a sensation so intense it hurts. What is visible is all there is; nothing else seems so stark, so conspicuous. Texture is the way light is reflected, warmth is the promise from a pleasing curve. Sight sucks out the essence of other ways of being. What used to seem thick and solid becomes less substantial than a picture; sensations float away without the shared currency of visible proof.

Adventure No. 2

This is more painful altogether; much too close to our everyday ambivalence for any comfort. This is the story we sing to each other, a hen-night special to boost our broken self-esteem. In those moments aside, over chopping boards and bubbling pots, the chorus comes back. Helping each other dress, coiling the heavy hair slicked with coconut, smoothing dusty skin back into its shine, we remind each other how this trap works.

When we look for knowledge, we find a thousand stories of how we have lost. The pain comes not from being written out of their histories, but from being written in so insistently. Endless pictures, lascivious anecdotes, the background character in all their life-stories. Their most important stories are told through us. We are the shapes of their best dreams and worst fears. They look at pictures of us to recognize themselves, to see inside, to balance the thrill between feeling bad and feeling good. What we see doesn't come into it at all.

Looking at their pictures makes us feel like monsters: our sense of self shifts to fit what we see, all around, everywhere, from way back when to next week, month, year. They are the scopic masters, squashing everything jealously into two-dimensions. The weight of invasion flattens our volume out, the heavy breath of subjugation. Nothing left but the limp skins of their fantasy.

This story smarts with its telling: that moment of loss, the beginning of the end, the long descent to today. The plot needs these interludes of suffering. All superheroes endure ordeals on their journeys to victory. Dwelling on these downsides serves a variety of purposes.

(1) We see more clearly how the past haunts our lives.
(2) The reminder that we are living diminished lives prompts us to regain size, shape, weight, form. To imagine ourselves as something more than someone else's picture.
(3) Most importantly, things are not what they seem. This is the lesson which could change the future. The mahogany princesses are demeaned by a culture which secretly loves them better than itself. The centuries of ugliness are rooted

in fear, the destruction comes from a child's half-formed jealousy at sensing things beyond reach. The worst things in the world spring from weakness masquerading as strength, a terror of what others have. This story reminds us that even our persecutors are awed by our gifts, stunned by our beauty, desperate to climb inside our bodies.[33]

Half-devil – half-child

The children of the sun feed the hungry white gaze: all the flavours of their previous lives offered up in one delectable image. Children's drawings, family heirlooms, holiday gifts; guzzled in to the visitors' appetite. And still more – today's breakfast, dinner, tea, favourite clothes, tomorrow's hopes – all fallen in to the void. Even before birth future generations became pledged to keeping the picture show going. So much work and so little to show. Whatever they shovelled in seemed to get lost, leaving no traces of the offered comforts but that one same image. No fat, no warmth, no love, nothing saved. Just a picture of fear and desire.

Adventure No. 3

This is a story about physical endurance: giving beyond reason, careless of scarcity. We tell this story to recall the mixture of innocence and largesse which we once were. Excess was possible, we thought, more than enough to go around.

33. See Young (1995).

Whole worlds of resources were sucked into the West's hunger. Nothing held back, no extra tucked away for later. These gifts are registered nowhere, subsumed in achievements which show no acknowledgement. Instead, all that shows is that same old fantasy: the one which registers psychic fear and vengeful desire, but no economic relation, no one-way traffic in goods and services. We tell this story to remind ourselves of what the pictures don't show. At those dangerous moments when we almost believe what we see, when only images seem true, this story asks, "Who is the child in this game of manipulation?" We are used up feeding an infantile fury which is never appeased. This story acknowledges this relation of care as a way of managing bitterness.

(1)   The pictures of ourselves hide our efforts, talents, resources.
(2)   Cutting close ties always leaves pain. Remembering how intertangled our lives have been explains the confusion that follows.
(3)   Now it is time to reclaim that pre-betrayal generosity as strength and possibility, not a foolish mistake to be put right by experience. So concerned not to be suckered again, we forget to live at all.

A daydream of alternative subject formation: The exotic white man[34]

Not my object, my thing, my fantasy. I'm looking, but I can't fix him in my sights.

34.   Still worlds away from Luce Irigaray and *Speculum of the other woman*.

More and less human than us, he reddens easily. The scuffs of living come up tender on his skin. Not a story of the past, but still some map of pain. His surface cracks under pressure, grabs destruction from heat, weeps mucous tears. No lubricant to ease this brittleness; being wet just means being more sore.

Even as he flakes away and falls apart, the white man can't see himself. The world's audience can't recognize another's glance. Unaware, he lets it all hang out. Flaunts his paunch, scratches his crotch, wipes body ooze on his surroundings, convinced the marks don't show. Settling down for the performance, sinking into smugness, slumping as if the body belongs to someone else. Certainly no picture. Who'd look at that?

This weakness is touching. A clumsy child, finger in nose. So vulnerably oblivious. My job is to soak up the mess without accusing the source. Endless care and no more tears. My charge is too innocent for accountability, too pre-responsible for blame. The piss-stains on the carpet are nobody's fault. People with no sense of self deserve protection. I meet the bargain and hold the trust. The fiction of the one-way look, a master lie to live by.

I'm laying out the pieces; one by one, side by side. I touch, sniff, lick each fragment, curating carefully. The contract has come back round and I'm paying what I owe, the care that I have received. Who knows you better than me, recorder of your delicate places, vessel of your wounds. I hold what your life could never be. In me your fears are carried back as trophies, what hurts belongs to someone else. Trust me because I remember what you have been.

Looming in out of vision, she felt that she had won. Impossible to focus at this range; no barriers until, too late, they were broken. She knew that in his mind's eye he held a picture-reminder of her, a prompt for the frightening moments when looking didn't work. She knew that he remembered those other spaces where she was his object: that it was this memory of mastery which got him hard, guided him across her warmth. To him touch meant colour, form, responses filtered back through the thing he knew. Sensation as picture.

This was his weakness. She held his expectation, stroked and petted. Touched carefully, knowing he thought in pictures and stories, that her special skills were lost in his translations.

> The artist is somewhat prone to see the for-eigner as a comic creature. Our features were odd, our pinkish colour somewhat revolting, our kinder moments endearing. And this was how we were seen, odd creatures from far away who were sometimes quite charming, and sometimes hatefully cruel. In this book we shall have to take ourselves as others found us.[35]

Boy flesh: unfamiliar meat. Less pliant, less movement. The polite words flick by: wiry, gaunt, artistic, sensitive androgyne, gawky manchild. Of course, that wasn't it. Nothing like the thrill of the new. She wanted to remake him as an image of herself. Her mirror, her object; vessel to her dreams, mould to her body. In him she saw a slip, a twist, an inside-out version of the world she knew. The same, the same, the same. Same picture, same story. A confirmation of her hopes and fears screening out the possibility

35. Burland (1969): 11.

of anything different. What he lacked was proof of what she had. Against him she puffed up, splayed out, shone.

Sometimes he turned his head as if pulled by recollection. Some other place from before or to come. A home elsewhere. She dried up in the breeze from that movement, the thought that she didn't centre the world. The idea of a place beyond their two cracked her heart wide open, and out flew the safety of her name.

Territorial battles

In the struggles over land, people forgot to look. Flesh ripped and no-one remembered the lures of warm brownness. The princesses waited for darkness, regained powers which had been lost to pictures; found their teeth had bite, their nails could claw.

The violence snapped the brittle contract of desire. Better not to look at that tantalizing flesh. Better to give up those favourite pin-ups. Sometimes it is too noisy for titillation. Delectation needs a moment's peace, a sense of leisure. Now you can't be sure it costs nothing to look. The edges are blurring, things you can't quite see creep up from behind, beyond, underneath. The lookers are scared to stand still in case they are eaten. No time for head-swivelling. Nothing in view to recentre that eye.

Adventure No. 4

This most heroic moment, fought just yesterday, seems the most distantly mythic. Such a well-known narrative, good against evil, the weak kicking back, ultimate victory. A countless collection of individual sacrifices – everybody's uncle, cousin, village beauty, school sportstar – each told as proof of the master narrative of "we whipped their arses, they didn't think we could, after so long, so long, but we did and now we are home".

All over the world the mahogany princesses lap up the flavour of that victory, a nourishing supplement to spice up more everyday battles. This becomes our most formative story; an oedipalized break from interdependency to . . . interdependency? These are the stories of holidays and public events. Big crowd-pleasers, sure to get them dancing. We know how to deal with the proud and defiant heritage of our homelands.[36]

But this story conceals other lessons to be saved.

(1) That violence: the wrench that makes you, but from which you never recover. The desolation you wake up to. A story helps us encounter that unsettling rupture and move on.

(2) Only victory songs which recall the costs of victory can help in what follows.

(3) All wounds need mourning; maybe most of all the ones you don't know you suffer.

"Disremembered and unaccounted for, she cannot be lost because no one is looking for her, and even if they were, how can they call her if they don't know her name?"[37]

36. See Chatterjee (1993b) for a warning against these celebrations.
37. Morrison (1987): 274. A book which was a big event for mahogany princesses everywhere.

Journeys West

After the battle dusts settled, there was no moment of longed-for calm, no well-deserved relief. The princesses lifted their heads slowly and looked around, as the white men had taught them. What was left to survey? Smashed up, ripped out, cracked open. Shattered, splintered, torn, trashed. Not much to look at. Bits and pieces which didn't quite make a whole, injuries from no particular source. Plenty of pain.

The princesses scrunched up their lovely eyes and tried to imagine a better future. Spinning out, stretching into possibility: nostrils flared, fingers spread, reaching for all the things that might be. For a moment they float, on the edge of a new deal, a fresh space, the old contracts are almost broken. Eyes shut, we're almost there, sugar sweet, cotton soft. The hum of life takes over. Bodies feel like luxury items. The princesses throw back their heads and laugh.

Wallop. History smashes back. Dead weights on your back, rubble in the streets. The journey to this point, the ways things make sense. Yesterday's traces fill our todays. Cut out the past and there's nothing left. Of course, we follow where we can, what we know. Shifting our dreams to whatever seems likely.

Adventure No. 5

This story is about troubled journeys and permanent exile, about packing our bags and starting afresh. Like all women who love too much, we are addicted to destructive relationships. Run half-way around the globe to be close to those we've worked so hard to leave. In days wracked with homesickness, heads turned back to dreams we have left, being here is the punishment we choose, no-one but ourselves to blame. This is the story of our journey to this place, pulled by history, not addicted to pain.

(1)   We are here for a reason, living out a logic of pathology set in motion long ago.

(2)   The ripples of past relationships always shake up the present. Nothing is ever completely over. Smart is learning to live with the repercussions.

(3)   The sense of travel makes us what we are: nostalgic for back-homes which some have never seen, living with our bags packed, always ready to up and leave, holding on to nothing too heavy or bulky or breakable.

Contemporary adventures

Stepping out into unpredictable streets, it's hard to tell how people react to princess-skin. The old possibilities are there somewhere. The promise of warmth, the spread of colour; bodies smooth as appleskin, solid as hardwood. Pebble beach women who bruise their playmates, pushing hard to get back to touch.

Are all those things still true?

As time goes on, the princesses lose their burnish. Not so shiny happy. The past sinks away into water ghost hauntings; no sense of distance only a fear of depth. Princesses become everyday, hardly worth an objectifying turn of the head.

The millennium approaches and the exotic resides in the heartlands of the metropolis. There is no fantastic distance through which to imagine mammoth appetites, monstrous bodies. The edge of humanity folds in and suddenly these people are pushed right up against the white gaze.

At bus-stops and supermarkets, in the cities and suburbs of rundown cold old Britain, the daughters of the sun are here. The dark bodies which peopled the excesses of the orientalist imagination scatter over the landscape of contemporary Britain. Fulfilling the fearful expectations of human imagination, things change, and keep right on changing.

The earth shifts and new monsters appear out of the cracks in its surface. Some mate with the horrors of yesterday and their mutant offspring emerge as fresh terrors for an unsuspecting humanity. The mahogany princesses glance backwards towards the mythic homelands of their mothers, then take a breath and prepare to fight.

Their battles straddle the worlds of yesterday and today: at once colonial fantasy and scourge of the white nation. The eyes that watch are hungry for contact: closer, closer, touch, taste. The dark women move through this network of scrutiny as best they can, alert or numb, slipping between impossible options.

Choosing our routes is an endless adventure; an exercise in balancing risk and possibility. The mahogany princesses, mixed-up children of a changing world, weigh up their choices and jump right in.

Being a girl

Girl is the opposite to boy; this story splits the world in two, endlessly, seemingly for all time. Either one or not-one, presence or absence, subject or object. If you're not one then you must be the other.

Boy is central, pivotal, tall, strong and hardly ever visible. Far too good for everyday. Girl is everything else, background, container, water, nature, earth and home. The most taken for granted and the least seen. Here gender is the zero-sum game filling up the world, assigning roles, determining response. The first name we learn, our entry into language, the social, human living. All other relations happen after this first one; echoes of this two of non-communication. Apparently.

In the arena of skin the white boys win again. Central, pivotal, tall, strong and hardly ever visible. So far so familiar. The powerful hog the privilege of the norm and the rest of us squeeze in behind, around, wherever there is room. Boys stride and girls cower, light skin preens while dark skin waits. In the economy of two there are only winners and losers, tops and bottoms bonded in a hermetic contract with no outside. The mahogany princesses fall out of both contracts: too much skin to be simply girl, too feminine to be just dark. If the world is full of ones and their others then white/black is an echo of man/ woman is an echo of master/slave is an echo of culture/nature is an echo of coherence/confusion. We recognize the winning team again and again; the couplets must be true. But where are the mahogany princesses in this map of the world? Doubly marked, unspeakable in two, more than the other of white or boy: how do we choose what to be? Do we frock up? Primp our way into girlhood? Or swagger our way alongside gender and live in the names of skin? Of course, the answer is both and neither, whatever will work for right now. It is still impossible to tell which comes first, which hurts most, which is most precious, formative, scratched deep on the inside.

Try to picture a mahogany princess: what do you see first, her colour or her shape?

The picture may not be important to you, but it is to her. The pictures you have of yourself structure what you can do, tell you how to go about getting some of the things you want.

Passing

Some pictures are pre-make-over: the before of the process of becoming a new and miraculous after. The point is to identify the weak points and conspicuous features which need toning down.

You might choose to be a girl: wear a dress, curl your hair, talk sexuality, domestic violence, personal politics. You might paint your face and go for ultra-femininity, dangerous dagger heels or sweet-enough-to-eat prettiness. You might collect the stories of international sisterhood, link up all those details about petty slights and major mutilations which punish girls and run straight to the women's caucus. You don't lose your skin, but you tone down its colours to fit in and get things done.

You might choose to let skin take over: wear ethnicity, authenticity, tradition, talk colonialism, racist violence, pride and heritage. You might wear clothes as extensions of your skin, back-home outfits cut to please grandmothers or those looks which white girls never wear. You might collect all those histories of slavery and colonialism, the scary disregard for the value of human life in a dark skin, then and now, and put your energies into black self-organization. You are still a girl, but you put that to one side for a while and concentrate on defending your community.

We learn these stories as dangerous cop-outs to be avoided at all costs; lose sight of the complexities of identity and things will never get better. We don't value disguise these days. We've forgotten the ballerina skills of those deceptions, the disciplines which played with perception and changed possibilities.

The most risky disguise is taking the centre; by yourself, on the enemy's terms. The least elegant passing, the walking-on-daggers bargain which never stops cutting. Desperate measures for desperate times, wiping out everything we used to be. This story is a cautionary tale.[38]

Difference

We pretend that we have learned better than to try to pass. No point trying to be what you are not, so instead we work hard at being ourselves. Everyone is looking for their own spaces, and ours is the tapestry fun palace, the sunken-bath land of exotic mysteries. Instead of camouflaging our most conspicuous features, we are building them up, showing them off. Flaunting what we have to those who don't. Preening for each other in mutual appreciation. We can't escape the world of pictures. Memory no longer extends to the time before. Now skin really is the main thing we are, the way we imagine ourselves. Feeling better depends on altering the picture, the criteria of visual values. It's too hard to see beyond that scopic contract any more. Other ways of being are forgotten; they don't feel real to us.

38. See sad and familiar stories in bell hooks (1993), particularly ch. 7.

The only option is to rework the pictures to show off our best sides.

Imagination

Eager to learn, heads in books, scrabbling up the schooling of our parents' sacrifice: too many of the lessons stop us dead in despair. Bolted down by circumstance and held tight by the knowledge of how things are. The kind of education which wears you out, grinds you down, makes you lie down, give up, hide. Knowing hurts so much that living seems impossible; and anyway, not worth the effort.

All the stories so far serve a purpose, but trap us where we are. Forgetting the exuberant pleasures of narrative, we play over and over the unhappy endings which it is too late to change. I want to stop; to take the lessons and move on, up, out, away.

The stories worth telling join the unbearable past to the exuberant future just a breath away. Everything is not yet lost. Now, in the middle of the film, battered by the events of yesterday and just now, the plot twists ahead seem unimaginable. Take a breath and jump right in.

After so many hours of storytelling, the girl sighed to a pause. Time to reflect for a moment.

"Is that it?", snapped the king, surprised by the sudden silence. "No conclusion, no manifesto, no plan of action? What kind of story is that?"

The girl sighed again and resumed:

"The parent stories of my tale, *The Arabian nights* and *Capital*, both come to abrupt and arbitrary endings. One ends at the mysterious point where love overcomes violence. When the king no longer wishes to kill her, Scheherazade can end her stories. The other is one of those notorious life-works which expands beyond the limited lifetime available to the teller. The end section entitled 'Classes' seems to re-open the whole story all over again, stopping suddenly with the apology, 'Here the manuscript breaks off'. Both cycles end with the chance of a new beginning, an opportunity to play the cycle through differently, with different outcomes. You listen to the story to imagine what else might be possible.

So, here we break off."

Of course, this is the oldest of fairytale strategies: to leave things hanging, up in the air and in the hands of the listener. But sadly, in these times of forgotten stories, listeners are not always so attentive.

To return to the beginning of the cycle: the rifts of the world long for stories to distract and mend. Narrative remains our oldest strategy of negotiation and reconciliation: we tell tales to our would-be friends and pray that they can learn how to listen.

In this long and rambling tale, we have seen the costs of some ways of telling. The scopic regimes of the world's waning masters have made us forget other ways of getting the picture. The span of attention required to piece together a narrative cannot compete with the instant it takes for a visual fix, however metaphorical.

Alongside this habit of instant knowing, the world learns to judge value through exchange. We learn that there are dangers to being not seen and to being too seen: the dark women of our tales suffer from their invisibility and from their conspicuousness. We learn that somehow neither the experience of inhabiting the fantasies of exoticism and anthroporn nor the experience of working too hard without recognition of value can register the weight of fleshly need.

In fact, we learn, the mixed-up bag of Western ascendency called modernity rewrites the connections between minds and bodies in a way which makes fleshly need hard to recognize. In this time, human accomplishment comes to mean overcoming the various limits and constraints of the body; instead, these limitations become the property of the sections of humanity who have no access to accomplishment on these terms. We, those abused people of the body, are vilified for our improper relations to flesh.

For many years the world is split between accomplished but anxious minds and suffering but undeserving bodies. However, late in the tale an unexpected twist appears. Now the privileged people of the mind find that their bodies are complaining, kicking back against so many years of disregard. This happens against a backdrop of global changes; so now no-one is quite sure where power and privilege lie. This is our space, still riddled with old evils, but where many things are not yet decided.

For us, too-visible objects of these previous regimes, the challenge is to survive into the future. We live in worlds cluttered with material hurdles, the everyday pains of our sedimented histories, but the best stories help us to see where we are and move on.

Further reading

For more on performance, see *Let's get it on*, by Catherine Ugwu.

For more on stories and teaching, see *The alchemy of race and rights*, by Patricia Williams.

To think more about white masking, see *Black skin, white masks*, by Franz Fanon.

Bibliography

Abrahams, R.D. & J.F. Szwed. 1983 *After Africa: extracts from British travel accounts and journals of the seventeenth, eighteenth, and nineteenth centuries concerning the slaves, their manners, and customs in the British West Indies*. New Haven and London: Yale University Press.

Adorno, T. & M. Horkheimer. 1979 *The dialectic of the enlightenment*. London: Verso.

AEKTA. 1995 Clothing Industry Action Research Project. 1993–5 annual report. Birmingham: AEKTA.

Aesop's fables. trans. V.S. Vernon Jones. 1994 Ware: Wordsworth Editions.

Afshar, H. & M. Maynard. 1994 *The dynamics of "race" and gender*. London: Taylor & Francis.

Ahmed, A. 1992 *In theory: classes, nations, literatures*. London: Verso.

Albertson, C. 1975 *Bessie, Empress of the blues*. London: Abacus.

Allen, C. 1975 *Plain tales from the Raj: images of British India in the twentieth century*. London: Andre Deutsch and BBC.

Allen, T.W. 1994 *The invention of the white race*. London: Verso.

Allison, R. 1988 *The Soviet Union and the strategy of non-alignment in the Third World*. Cambridge and New York: Cambridge University Press.

Alpers, S. 1991 The museum as a way of seeing. In I. Karp & S.D. Levine, *Exhibiting cultures: the poetics and politics of museum display*. Washington DC and London: Smithsonian Institute Press.

Amnesty International annual report. New York: Amnesty International, 1997.

Andersen's fairy tales. 1993 London: Wordsworth Editions.

Anderson, D.M. & D. Killingray. 1991 *Policing the empire: government, authority and control, 1830–1940*. Manchester: Manchester University Press.

Anderson, D.M. & D. Killingray. 1992 *Policing and decolonisation: politics, nationalism and the police, 1917–65*. Manchester: Manchester University Press.

Anderson, R.M., C.A. Donnelly, N.M. Ferguson, M.E.J. Woolhouse, C.J. Watt, H.J. Udy, S. MaWhinney, S.P. Dunstan, T.R.E. Southwood, J.W. Wilesmith, J.B.M. Ryans, L.J. Hoinville, J.E. Hillerton, A.R. Austin, G.A.H. Wells. 1996 Transmission dynamics and epidemiology of BSE in British cattle. *Nature*, **382**, 29 August.

Anzaldua, G. 1987 *Borderlands/La Frontera: the new mestiza*. San Francisco: Aunt Lute Books.

Apter, E. 1992 Female trouble in the colonial harem. In *Differences*, Spring, **4**, 1.

Arabian nights' entertainments. ed. R.L. Mack. 1995 Oxford: Oxford University Press.

Aram-Veeser, H. 1994 *The new historicism reader*. New York: Routledge.

Arens, W. 1979 *The man-eating myth: anthropology and anthropophagy*. New York: Oxford University Press.

Armstrong, N. & L. Tennenhouse. 1989 *The violence of representation*. London and New York: Routledge.

Arnold, M. 1960 *Culture and anarchy*. Cambridge: Cambridge University Press.

Ashford, M. 1993 *Detained without trial: a survey of Immigration Act detention*. London: JCWI.

Attali, J. 1988 *Noise: the political economy of music*. Manchester: Manchester University Press.

Back, L. 1996 *New ethnicities and urban culture: racisms and multiculture in young lives*. London: UCL Press.

Back, L. & A. Nayak. 1993 *Invisible Europeans? Black people in "new Europe"*. Birmingham: AFFOR.

Back, L. & V. Quaade. 1993 Dream utopias, nightmare realities: imagining race and culture within the world of Benetton advertising. *Third Text* 22, Spring.

Bagrow, L. 1964 *History of Cartography*. London: C.A. Watts & Co.

Baker, H.A. 1993 Scene . . . not heard. In R. Gooding Williams, *Reading Rodney King: reading urban uprising*. New York and London: Routledge.

Banerjee, A.C. 1985 *History of India*. Calcutta: A. Mukherjee & Co.

Barkan, E. 1992 *The retreat of scientific racism*. Cambridge: Cambridge University Press.

Barker, F. et al. 1985 *Europe and its others*. Colchester: University of Essex.

Barnes, R. & J.B. Eicher. 1992 *Dress and gender: making and meaning*. Providence and Oxford: Berg.

Baskett, G.C. 1995 "Selections from Arabian nights". In A. Galland, *Arabian nights entertainments*. Oxford and New York: Oxford University Press.

Basu, T., P. Datta, S. Sarkar, T. Sarkar, S. Sen. 1993 *Khaki shorts saffron flags*. New Delhi: Orient Longman Ltd.

Batsleer, J., T. Davies, R. O'Rourke, C. Weedon. 1985 *Rewriting English: cultural politics of gender and class*. London: Methuen.

Beckles, H. McD. 1989 *Natural rebels: a social history of enslaved black women in Barbados*. London: Zed.

Behague, G.H. 1994 *Music and black ethnicity: the Caribbean and South America*. New Brunswick and London: Transaction.

Behdad, A. 1994 *Belated travelers: orientalism in the age of colonial dissolution*. Cork: Cork University Press.

Benjamin, W. 1986 *Reflections*. New York: Schocken Books.

Benjamin, W. 1992 *Illuminations*. London: Fontana.

Berger, J. 1972 *Ways of seeing*. London and Harmondsworth: BBC and Penguin.

Bettelheim, B. 1991 *The uses of enchantment*. Harmondsworth: Penguin.

Bhabha, J. & S. Shutter. 1994 *Women's movement: women under immigration, nationality and refugee law*. Stoke-on-Trent: Trentham Books.

Bhattacharyya, G. 1996 Black skin/white boards: learning to be the "Race" lady in British higher education. *Parallax*, Issue 2, February.

Billig, M. 1995 *Banal nationalism*. London: Sage.

Blanchot, M. 1982 *The sirens' song*. Brighton: Harvester Press.

Bland, L. "Cleansing the portals of life": the venereal disease campaign in the early twentieth century. In M. Langan & B. Schwartz. *Crises in the British state 1880–1930*. London: Hutchinson, 1985.

Bock, G. & S. James. 1992 *Beyond equality and difference*. London and New York: Routledge.

Bottomore, T. 1991 *A dictionary of Marxist thought*. Oxford: Blackwell.

Boyle, P.G. 1993 *American-Soviet relations*. London and New York: Routledge.

Braham, P., E. Rhodes, M. Pearn. 1981 *Discrimination and disadvantage in employment: the experience of black workers*. London: Harper & Row with OU.

Bridenthal, R. & C. Koonz. 1977 *Becoming visible: women in European history*. Boston: Houghton Mifflin Company.

Bridges, G. & R. Brunt. 1981 *Silver linings: some strategies for the eighties*. London: Lawrence & Wishart.

Brues, A.M. 1977 *People and races*. New York and London: Macmillan.

Bryson, N. 1983 *Vision and painting: the logic of the gaze*. Basingstoke and London: Macmillan.

Burgin, V. 1982 *Thinking photography*. London: Macmillan.

Burland, C.A. 1969 *The exotic white man*. London: Weidenfeld & Nicolson.

Burnett, J. 1974 *Useful toil: autobiographies of working people from the 1820s to the 1920s*. London: Allen Lane.

Burnham, J. 1985 *Suicide of the West*. Washington, DC: Gateway.

Burton, Sir R. & F.F. Arbuthnot. 1993 *The Kama Sutra* (translation). London: Diamond Books.

Burton, R. 1995 *The perfumed garden* (translation). Ware: Wordsworth Editions.

Butler, J. & J.W. Scott. 1992 *Feminists theorize the political*. New York and London: Routledge.

Byatt, A.S. 1995 *The djinn in the nightingale's eye*. London: Vintage.

Cadbury, E. & G. Shann. 1907 *Sweating*. London: Headley Bros.

Campbell, B. 1993 *Goliath: Britain's dangerous places*. London: Methuen.

CARF. 1996 *Calendar of race and resistance* no. 34. October/November 1996, 2 August 1996.

Carter, E. & S. Watney. 1989 *Taking liberties*. London: Serpent's Tail.

Cashmore, E. 1990 *Making sense of sport*. London and New York: Routledge.

Cashmore, E. & E. McLaughlin. 1991 *Out of order? Policing black people*. London and New York: Routledge.

Chakrabarty, D. 1994 Postcoloniality and the artifice of history: who speaks for "Indian" pasts? In H. Aram-Veeser *The new historicism reader*. New York: Routledge.

Cham, M.B. & C. Andrade-Watkins. 1988 *Black frames: critical perspectives on black independent cinema*. Cambridge, Mass. and London: MIT Press.

Chambers, I. & L. Curti. 1996 *The post-colonial question: common skies, divided horizons*. London and New York: Routledge.

Chartier, R. 1989 *The culture of print: power and the uses of print in early modern Europe*. Cambridge: Polity.

Chatterjee, P. 1993a *The nation and its fragments* Princeton, N.J. and Chichester: Princeton University Press.

Chatterjee, P. 1993b *Nationalist thought and the colonial world: a derivative discourse*. Minneapolis: University of Minnesota Press.

Checkland, S. 1983 *British public policy 1776–1939*. Cambridge: Cambridge University Press.

Chew, N.N. & T.T. Minh-Ha. 1994 "Speaking nearby". In L. Taylor, *Visualizing theory*. New York and London: Routledge.

Christensen, K.E. 1988 *The new era of home-based work*. Boulder, Col. and London: Westview.

Churchill, W. 1992 *Fantasies of the master race: literature, cinema and the colonization of American Indians*. Monroe, Maine: Common Courage Press.

Clarkson, L.A. 1985 *Proto-industrialization: the first phase of industrialization?*, Basingstoke and London: Macmillan.

Clifford, J. 1995 On ethnographic authority. In J. Munns & G. Rajan, *A cultural studies reader: history, theory, practice*. London and New York: Longman.

Cockburn, A. 1996 A short, meat-oriented history of the world, from Eden to the Mattole. *New Left Review*, no. 215, January/February, pp. 16–42.

Collins, P.H. 1991 *Black feminist thought: knowledge, consciousness, and the politics of empowerment*. New York and London: Routledge.

Commission for Racial Equality. 1987 *Living in terror: a report on racial violence and harassment in housing*. London: CRE.

Commission for Racial Equality. 1988 *Learning in terror: a survey of racial harassment in schools and colleges*. London: CRE.

Coplan, D.B. 1994 *In the time of cannibals: the word music of South Africa's Basotho migrants*. Chicago and London: University of Chicago.

Corbey, R. 1995 Ethnographic showcases, 1870–1930. In J.N. Pieterse & B. Parekh, *The decolonization of imagination: culture, knowledge and power*. London and N.J.: Zed Books.

Corbin, A. 1992 *The village of the cannibals: rage and murder in France, 1870*. Cambridge: Polity.

Craik, J. 1994 *The face of fashion*. London: Routledge.

Crary, J. & S. Kwinter. 1992 *Incorporations*. New York: Zone.

Crosby, A.W. 1986 *Ecological imperialism: the biological expansion of Europe, 900–1900*. Cambridge: Canto, University of Cambridge Press.

Curtin, P., S. Feierman, L. Thompson, J. Vansina. 1995 *African history: from earliest times to independence*. London and New York: Longman.

Dabydeen, D. 1984 *Slave song*. Mundelstrup and Oxford: Dangaroo.

Dabydeen, D. 1988 *Coolie odyssey*. London and Coventry: Hansib and Dangaroo.

Dabydeen, D. & B. Samaroo. 1987 *India in the Caribbean*. London: Hansib Press.

D'Aguiar, F. 1993 *British subjects*. Newcastle upon Tyne: Bloodaxe Books.

Dahl, L. 1984 *Stormy weather: the music and lives of a century of jazzwomen*. London: Quartet Books.

Davidoff, L. 1995 *Worlds between: historical perspectives on gender and class*. Cambridge: Polity.

Davies, C. & S. Lloyd. 1976 *Peace, print and protestantism, 1450–1558*. London: Hart-Davis MacGibbon.

Dawood, N.J. 1973 *Tales from the thousand and one nights*. Harmondsworth: Penguin.

Decosta-Willis, M., R. Martin, R.P. Bell. 1992 *Erotique noire/black erotica*. London: Doubleday.

Derrida, J. 1982 *Margins of philosophy*. New York and London: Harvester Wheatsheaf.

Derrida, J. 1988 *Limited Inc*. Evanston, Ill.: Northwestern University Press.

Dijkstra, B. 1968 *Idols of perversity: fantasies of feminine evil in fin-de-siecle culture*. New York and London: Oxford University Press.

Doogan, K. 1992 *Flexible labour? Employment and training in new service industries*. Bristol: SAUS.

Drake, S. 1980 *Galileo*. Oxford: Oxford University Press.

Duncan, C. 1991 Art museums and the ritual of citizenship. In I. Karp & S.D. Levine. *Exhibiting cultures: the poetics and politics of museum display*. Washington DC and London: Smithsonian Institute Press.

Dunn, L.C. & N.A. Jones. 1994 *Embodied voices: representing female vocality in Western culture*. Cambridge: Cambridge University Press.

Dyer, R. 1997 *White*. Routledge.

Eagleton, T. 1991 *Ideology: an introduction*. London: Verso.

Eby, C.D. 1987 *The road to Armageddon: the martial spirit in English popular literature, 1870–1914*. Durham and London: Duke University Press.

Edwards, E. 1992 *Anthropology and photography 1860–1920*. New Haven and London: Yale University Press in association with the Royal Anthropological Institute, London.

Edwards, H. 1969 *The revolt of the black athlete*. New York: Free Press.

Ellmann, M. 1993 *The hunger artists: starving, writing, and imprisonment*. Cambridge, Mass.: Harvard University Press.

Engh, B. 1994 Adorno and the Sirens: tele-phonographic bodies. In L.C. Dunn, N.A. Jones, *Embodied voices: representing female vocality in Western culture*. Cambridge: Cambridge University Press.

Ewing, E. 1974 *History of twentieth-century fashion*. London: B.T. Batsford Ltd.

Fanon, F. 1967 *The wretched of the earth*. Harmondsworth: Penguin.

Fanon, F. 1968 *Black skin, white masks*. London: MacGibbon & Kee Ltd.

Fanon, F. 1989 *Studies in a dying colonialism*. London: Earthscan Publications Ltd.

Farquhar, J. & D.C. Gajdusek. 1981 *Kuru: early letters and field-notes of D. Carleton Gajdusek*. New York: Raven Press.

Ferguson, R., M. Gever, T.T. Minh-ha, C. West. 1990 *Out there: marginalization and contemporary cultures*. New York and Cambridge, Mass.: The New Museum of Contemporary Art and MIT Press.

Fiddes, N. 1991 *Meat: a natural symbol*. London and New York: Routledge.

Figueira, D.M. 1994 *The exotic: a decadent quest*. Albany, N.Y.: State University of New York Press.

Fornas, J. & G. Bolin, 1995 *Youth culture in late modernity*. London: Sage.

Foster, H. 1988 *Vision and visuality*. Seattle, Wash.: Bay Press.

Foster, S.L. 1996 *Corporealities: dancing, knowledge, culture and power*. London: Routledge.

Foucault, M. 1977 *Discipline and punish: the birth of the prison*. London and Harmondsworth: Penguin.

Foucault, M. 1980 *Power/knowledge: selected interviews and other writings 1972–1977*. Brighton: Harvester.

Frankel, S.H. 1977 *Money: two philosophies*. Oxford: Blackwell.

Franko, L.G. 1983 *The threat of Japanese multinationals: how the West can respond*. Chichester: John Wiley and Sons.

Fraser, S. 1995 *The bell curve wars: race, intelligence, and the future of America*. New York: Basic Books.

Freud, S. 1938, *Totem and Taboo*, Harmondsworth: Penguin.

Fry, G.K. 1979 *The growth of government*. London: Frank Cass & Co. Ltd.

Fusco, C. 1988 *Young British and black*. Buffalo, N.Y.: Hallwalls/Contemporary Arts Center.

Gaar, G.G. 1992 *She's a rebel: the history of women in rock and roll*. Seattle, Wash.: Seal Press.

Gabriel, J. 1994 *Racism, culture, markets*. London and New York: Routledge.

Galland, A. 1995 *Arabian nights entertainments*. Oxford and New York: Oxford University Press.

Garber, M. 1992 *Vested interests: cross-dressing and cultural anxiety*. London and New York: Routledge.

Gargi, B. 1962 *Theatre in India*. New York: Theatre Arts Books.

George, N. 1985 *Where did our love go? The rise and fall of the Motown Sound*. New York: St Martin's Press.

Gerhardsson, B. 1961 *Memory and manuscript*. Uppsala: Gleerup & Munksgaard.

Gibson, J.W. 1994 *Warrior dreams: violence and manhood in post-Vietnam America*. New York: Hill & Wang.

Gill, A. 1995 *Ruling passions: sex, race and empire*. London: BBC Books.

Gilman, S. 1986 Black bodies, white bodies. In H.L. Gates, Jr, *"Race", writing and difference*.

Gilroy, P. 1993 *The black Atlantic: modernity and double consciousness*. London: Verso.

Giroux, H. 1992 *Border crossings: cultural workers and the politics of education*. New York and London: Routledge.

Goings, K.W. 1994 *Mammy and Uncle Mose: black collectibles and American stereotyping*. Bloomington and Indianapolis: Indiana University Press.

Goldberg, D.T. 1993 *Racist culture, philosophy and the politics of meaning*. Oxford: Blackwell.

Goodman, J. & K. Honeyman. 1988 *Gainful pursuits: the making of industrial Europe 1600–1914*. London: Edward Arnold.

Gould, S.J. 1977 *Ever since Darwin: reflections in natural history*. New York: W.W. Norton & Co.

Gould, S.J. 1981 *The mismeasure of man*. New York and London: W.W. Norton & Co.

Grafton, A. 1992 *New worlds, ancient texts: the power of tradition and the shock of discovery*. Cambridge, Mass. and London: The Belknap Press of Harvard University Press.

Gramsci, A. 1971 *Selections from prison notebooks*. London: Lawrence & Wishart.

Gray, C.H. 1995 *The cyborg handbook*. New York and London: Routledge.

Gray, J.E.B. 1961 *Indian tales and legends*. Oxford: Oxford University Press.

Greenblatt, S. 1980 *Renaissance self-fashioning: from More to Shakespeare*. Chicago and London: University of Chicago.

Greenblatt, S. 1991 *Marvelous possessions: the wonder of the new world*. Oxford: Clarendon Press.

Greenhalgh, P. 1988 *Ephemeral vistas: the expositions universelles, great exhibitions and world's fairs, 1851–1939*. Manchester: Manchester University Press.

Grimm, J.L.C. and W.C. Grimm. 1993 *Grimm's Fairy Tales*. Ware: Wordsworth Editions.

Grosz, E. 1994 *Volatile bodies: toward a corporeal feminism*. Bloomington and Indianapolis: Indiana University Press.

Grosz, E. & E. Probyn. 1995 *Sexy bodies: the strange carnalities of feminism*. London: Routledge.

Gupta, S. 1993 *Disrupted borders: an intervention on definitions and boundaries*. London: Rivers Oram Press.

Gurnah, A. & A. Scott. 1992 *The uncertain science: criticism of sociological formalism*. London: Routledge.

Hacking, I. 1995 Pull the other one. *London Review of Books*, 26 January.

Haddawy, H. 1992 *The Arabian nights*. London: Everyman.

Hale, J. 1994 *The civilization of Europe in the Renaissance*. London: Fontana.

Hall, S. 1981 The whites of their eyes: racist ideologies and the media. In G. Bridges & R. Brunt, *Silver linings: some strategies for the eighties*. London: Lawrence & Wishart.

Hall, S. 1991 The local and the global. In A.D. King, *Culture, globalization and the world-system*. London and Basingstoke: Macmillan, Education.

Hall, S., C. Critcher, T. Jefferson, J. Clarke, B. Roberts. 1978 *Policing the crisis*. Macmillan.

Hall, S. & B. Gieben. 1992 *Formations of modernity*. Cambridge: Polity and Open University.

Hall, S. & M. Jacques. 1989 *New times: the changing face of politics in the 1990s*. London: Lawrence & Wishart.

Hall, S. & T. Jefferson. 1976 *Resistance through ritual*. London: Hutchinson for CCCS.

Hamilton, R. & M. Barrett. 1986 *The politics of diversity*. London: Verso.

Hammond, D. & A. Jablow. 1970 *The Africa that never was: four centuries of British writing about Africa*. New York: Twayne Publishers.

Haraway, D. 1989 *Primate visions: gender, race, and nature in the world of modern science*. London: Routledge.

Haraway, D.J. 1991 *Simians, cyborgs and women: the reinvention of nature*. London: Free Association Books.

Harbsmeier, M. 1984 Early travels to Europe. In *Europe and its others*, vol. 1. Essex Conference on the Sociology of Literature. Colchester: University of Essex.

Harris, T. 1984 *On lynching: exorcising blackness, historical and literary lynching and burning rituals*. Bloomington: Indiana University Press.

Hartley, J. 1992. *The politics of pictures*. London: Routledge.

Hartmann, B. 1995 *Reproductive rights and wrongs: the global politics of population control*. Boston, Mass.: South End Press.

Hebdige, D. 1979 *Sub-culture: the meaning of style*. London: Methuen.

Helms, M.W. 1988 *Ulysses' sail: an ethnographic Odyssey of power, knowledge, and geographical distance*. Princeton, N.J.: Princeton University Press.

Henderson, M. 1995 *Borders, boundaries, and frames: cultural criticism and cultural studies*. New York and London: Routledge.

Herrnstein, R.J. & C. Murray. 1994 *The bell curve: intelligence and class structure in American life*. New York: Free Press.

Hoch, P. 1979 *White hero, black beast: racism, sexism and the mask of masculinity*. London: Pluto.

Hoggart, R. 1958 *The uses of literacy*. Harmondsworth: Penguin.

Homer. *The Odyssey*. trans. T.E. Lawrence. 1992 Ware: Wordsworth Editions.

hooks, bell. 1993 *Sisters of the yam: black women and self-recovery*. London: Turnaround Press.

hooks, bell. 1994 *Outlaw culture: resisting representations*. New York and London: Routledge.

Hopkins, E. 1995 *Working-class self-help in nineteenth-century England*. London: UCL Press.

Houshell, D.A. 1984 *From the American system to mass production 1800–1932*. Baltimore and London: Johns Hopkins.

Huizer, G. & B. Mannheim. 1979 *The politics of anthropology: from colonialism and sexism toward a view from below*. The Hague and Paris: Mouton Publishers.

Humphrey, C. & S. Hugh-Jones. 1992 *Barter, exchange and value*. Cambridge: Cambridge University Press.

Husband, C. 1994 *A richer vision: the development of ethnic minority media in Western democracies*. London and Paris: UNESCO and John Libbey & Co.

Hyam, R. 1992 *Empire and sexuality: the British experience*. Manchester: Manchester University Press.

Inden, R. 1990 *Imagining India*. Oxford: Blackwell.

Irigaray, L. 1985 *Speculum of the other woman*. Ithaca, N.Y.: Cornell University Press.

Jane, C. (trans.) 1960 *Journal of Christopher Columbus*. London: Anthony Blond and the Orion Press.

Jay, M. 1993 *Force fields*. London: Routledge.

Jewell, K.S. 1993 *From Mammy to Miss America*. London and New York: Routledge.

Johnson, R. *The Blue Books and education, 1816–96*. Birmingham: Centre for Contemporary Cultural Studies Stencilled Paper SP3.

Joint Council for the Welfare of Immigrants. 1995 *Immigration and nationality law handbook*. London: JCWI.

Jones, L. 1963 *Blues people*. New York: William Morrow & Co.

Journal of Christopher Columbus trans. C. Jane 1960 London: Anthony Blond and Orion Press.

Jowitt, D. 1988 *Time and the dancing image*. Berkeley and Los Angeles: University of California Press.

Kabbani, R. 1994 *Imperial fictions: Europe's myths of orient*. London: Pandora.

Kahn, J.S. 1995 *Culture, multiculture, postculture*. London: Sage.

Karp, I. & S.D. Levine. 1991 *Exhibiting cultures: the poetics and politics of museum display*. Washington DC and London: Smithsonian Institute Press.

Katz, M.N. 1990 *The USSR and Marxist revolutions in the Third World*. Cambridge: Cambridge University Press.

Katz, W.L. 1968 *Five slave narratives*. New York: Arno Press and the New York Times.

Kennedy, P. 1994 *Preparing for the twenty-first century*. London: Fontana.

Kessler-Harris, A. 1982 *Out to work: a history of wage-earning women in the United States*. New York and Oxford: Oxford University Press.

Kiernan, V.G. 1986 *The lords of human kind: black man, yellow man and white man in an age of empire*. New York: Columbia University Press.

King, A.D. 1991 *Culture, globalization and the world-system*. Basingstoke and London: Macmillan Education.

King, A.D. 1996 *Re-presenting the city: ethnicity, culture and capital in the twenty-first century metropolis*. Basingstoke and London: Macmillan.

Kipling, J.L. 1892 *Beast and man in India: a popular sketch of Indian animals in their relations with the people*. London: Macmillan and Co.

Kirschbaum, W.R. 1968 *Jakob-Creutzfeldt disease*. New York: American Elsevier Publishing Company.

Kohn, M. 1995 *The race gallery*. London: Jonathan Cape.

Koskoff, E. 1989 *Women and music in cross-cultural perspective*. Urbana and Chicago: University of Illinois.

Kristeller, P.O. 1979 *Renaissance thought and its sources*. New York: Columbia University Press.

Kulsum, N. 1832 *Customs and manners of the women of Persia, and their domestic superstitions*. London: Printed for the Oriental Translation Fund of Great Britain.

Kunzle, D. 1982 *Fashion and fetishism: a social history of the corset, tight-lacing and other forms of body-sculpture in the West*. Totowa, N.J.: Rowman & Littlefield.

Kurien, C.T. 1994 *Global capitalism and the Indian economy*. New Delhi: Orient Longman Ltd.

Lane, E.W. 1847 *The thousand and one nights; or, The Arabian nights' entertainments*. London: John Murray.

Langan, M. & B. Schwarz. 1985 *Crises in the British state 1880–1930*. London: Hutchinson.

Latour, B. 1993 *We have never been modern*. Hemel Hempstead: Harvester Wheatsheaf.

Law, J. 1994 *Organizing modernity*. Oxford: Blackwell.

Lawrence, T.E. 1935 *Seven pillars of wisdom*. London: Jonathan Cape.

Ledger, S. & S. McCracken. 1995 *Cultural politics at the fin de siecle*. Cambridge: Cambridge University Press.

Ledger, S. 1995 The new woman and the crisis of Victorianism. In S. Ledger & S. McCracken. *Cultural politics at the fin de siecle*. Cambridge: Cambridge University Press.

Levy, A. 1991 *Other women: the writing of class, race, and gender, 1832–1898*. Princeton, N.J.: Princeton University Press.

Lewis, R. 1996 *Gendering orientalism: race, femininity and representation*. London: Routledge.

Lieb, S.R. 1981 *Mother of the blues: a study of Ma Rainey*. Amherst, Mass.: University of Massachusetts.

Longhurst, B. 1995 *Popular music and society*. Cambridge: Polity.

Lorde, A. 1984 *Sister Outsider*. Freedom, C.A.: Crossing Press.

Lukacs, G. 1971 *History and class consciousness: studies in Marxist dialectics*. London: Merlin Press.

MacCannell, J.F. & L. Zakarin. 1994 *Thinking bodies*. Stanford, Cal.: Stanford University Press.

Mackenzie, J. M. 1995 *Orientalism: history, theory and the arts*. Manchester and New York: Manchester University Press.

Magnus, B. & S. Cullenberg. 1995 *Whither Marxism? Global crises in international perspective*. New York and London: Routledge.

Mahasweta, D. 1993 *Imaginary maps*. trans. by G.C. Spivak. Calcutta: Thema.

Majeed, J. 1992 *Ungoverned imaginings: James Mill's "The history of British India" and orientalism*. Oxford: Clarendon.

Malti-Douglas, F. 1991 *Woman's body, woman's word: gender and discourse in Arabo-Islamic writing*. Princeton, N.J.: Princeton University Press.

Marx, K. *Capital*. vols 1–3. 1983 edn. vol. 1 trans. S. Moore & E. Aveling, vols 2–3 trans. F. Engels; ed. F. Engels. Moscow: Progress Publishers.

Massey, D., P. Quintas & D. Wield. 1992 *High tech fantasies: science parks in society, science and space*. London and New York: Routledge.

McClary, S. 1991 *Feminine endings: music, gender, and sexuality*. Minnesota: University of Minnesota.

McClintock, A. 1995 *Imperial leather: race, gender and sexuality in the colonial contest*. London and New York: Routledge.

McKenna, D. 1996 *The homeworker's story*. Trades Union Congress homepage: http://www.tuc.org.uk/

McRobbie, A. 1989 *Zoot suits and second-hand dresses*. Basingstoke and London: Macmillan.

McRobbie, A. 1991 *Feminism and youth culture: from Jackie to Just Seventeen*. London and Basingstoke: Macmillan Educational.

Memmi, A. 1965 *The colonizer and the colonized*. Boston: Beacon Press.

Mercer, K. 1994 *Welcome to the jungle*. New York and London: Routledge.

Mernissi, F. 1994 *Dreams of trespass: tales of a harem girlhood*. Reading, Mass.: Addison-Wesley.

Miles, R. & A. Phizacklea. 1981 "The TUC and black workers, 1974–76", in P. Braham, E. Rhodes, M. Pearn. *Discrimination and disadvantage in employment*. London: Harper & Row with Open University.

Miles, R. 1987 *Capitalism and unfree labour: anomoly or necessity?* London and New York: Tavistock.

Minchinton, W.E. 1969 *Mercantilism: system or expediency?* Lexington, Mass.: Raytheon Education Company.

Minh-Ha, T.T. 1991 *When the moon waxes red: representation, gender and cultural politics*. New York and London: Routledge.

Minh-Ha, T.T. 1992 *Framer framed*. New York and London: Routledge.

Mirza, H.S. 1992 *Young, female and black*. London: Routledge.

Montellano, B. 1978 Aztec cannibalism, *Science*, 200:611–17.

Moraga, C. & G. Anzaldua. 1981 *This bridge called my back: writings by radical women of color*. New York: Kitchen Table.

Morley, D. & Chen, K.-H. *Stuart Hall: critical dialogues in cultural studies*. New York and London: Routledge.

Morrison, T. 1979 *The bluest eye*. London: Chatto & Windus.

Morrison, T. 1987 *Beloved*. London: Chatto & Windus.

Mothe, G. De La. 1993 *Reconstructing the black image*. Stoke-on-Trent: Trentham Books.

Mungham, G. & G. Pearson. 1976 *Working class youth culture*. London and Henley: Routledge & Kegan Paul.

Munns, J. & G. Rajan. 1995 *A cultural studies reader: history, theory, practice*. London and New York: Longman.

Nancy, J.-L. 1994 Corpus. In J.F. MacCannell & L. Zakarin, *Thinking bodies*, Stanford, Cal.: Stanford University Press.

Narayan, R.K. 1987 *The Mahabharata*. New Delhi: Vision Books.

Nava, M. & A. O'Shea. 1996 *Modern times: reflections on a century of English modernity*. London: Routledge.

Nebelsick, H.P. 1985 *Circles of God: theology and science from the Greeks to Copernicus*. Edinburgh: Scottish Academic Press.

Nelson, C. & L. Grossberg. 1988 *Marxism and the interpretation of culture*. Basingstoke and London: Macmillan.

Nochlin, L. 1991 *The politics of vision: essays on nineteenth-century art and society*. London: Thames and Hudson.

Noyelle, T. 1990 *Skills, wages, and productivity in the service sector*. Boulder, Col.: Westview.

Ogilvie, S.C. & M. German. 1996 *European proto-industrialization*. Cambridge: Cambridge University Press.

Oliver, P. 1990 *Blues fell this morning: meaning in the blues*. Cambridge: Cambridge University Press.

Omissi, D. 1994 *The sepoy and the Raj: the Indian Army, 1860–1940*. Basingstoke and London: Macmillan.

Oskar, P. 1979 *Renaissance thought and its sources*. New York: Columbia University Press.

Parker, A., M. Russo, D. Sommer, P. Yaeger. 1992 *Nationalisms and sexualities*. New York and London: Routledge.

Parry, J. & M. Bloch. 1989 *Money and the morality of exchange*. Cambridge: Cambridge University Press.

Paterson, T.G. & R.J. McMahon. 1991 *The origins of the Cold War*. Lexington, Mass: D.C. Heath & Co.

Patton, C. 1990 *Inventing AIDS*. London and New York: Routledge.

Paz, O. 1976 *The siren and the seashell*. Austin and London: University of Texas Press.

Pendergrast, M. 1993 *For God, country and Coca Cola*. London: Weidenfeld & Nicolson.

Perot, P. 1994 *Fashioning the bourgeoisie: a history of clothing in the nineteenth century*. Princeton, N.J.: Princeton University Press.

Pfeil, F. 1995 *White guys: studies in postmodern domination and difference*. London: Verso.

Phelan, P. 1993 *Unmarked: the politics of performance*. London and New York: Routledge.

Phillips, W. & C.R. Phillips. 1992 *The worlds of Christopher Columbus*. Cambridge: Cambridge University Press.

Phizacklea, A. & R. Miles. 1980 *Labour and racism*. London, Boston and Henley: Routledge & Kegan Paul.

Phizacklea, A. 1990 *Unpacking the fashion industry: gender, racism, and class in production*. London and New York: Routledge.

Phizacklea, A. & C. Wolkowitz. 1995 *Homeworking women: gender, racism and class at work*. London: Sage.

Pieterse, J.N. 1992 *White on black*. New Haven, Conn.: Yale University Press.

Pieterse, J.N. & B. Parekh. 1995 *The decolonization of imagination: culture, knowledge and power*. London and N.J.: Zed Books.

Poignant, R. 1992 Surveying the field of view: the making of the RAI photographic collection. In E. Edwards. 1992. *Anthropology and photography, 1860–1920*. New Haven and London: Yale University Press in association with the Royal Anthropological Institute, London.

Pratt, G.J.-J., Abu-Jamal, M. 1993 The Black Panthers: Heike Kleffner interviews. *Race and Class*, 35, July–September, no.1.

Pratt, M.L. 1992 *Imperial eyes: travel writing and transculturation*. London and New York: Routledge.

Rajan, R.S. 1993 *Real and imagined women: gender, culture and postcolonialism*. New York and London: Routledge.

Ribeiro, A. 1986 *Dress and morality*. London: B.T. Batsford.

Richards, D. 1994 *Masks of difference: cultural representations in literature, anthropology and art*. Cambridge: Cambridge University Press.

Richards, T. 1993 *The imperial archive: knowledge and the fantasy of empire*. London: Verso.

Richardson, S. (ed.) 1975 *Aesop's Fables*. New York and London: Garland Publishing.

Rifkin, J. 1992 *Beyond beef*. London: Thorsons.

Rodney, W. 1972 *How Europe underdeveloped Africa*. Washington, DC: Howard University Press.

Root, M.P.P. 1996 *The multicultural experience: racial borders as the new frontier*. Thousand Oaks, CA: Sage.

Rose, G. 1995 *Love's work*. London: Chatto & Windus.

Rosen, E. 1995 *Copernicus and his successors*. London and Rio Grande: The Hambledon Press.

Rowan, C. 1985 Child welfare and the working-class family. In M. Langan & B. Schwarz, *Crises in the British state 1880–1930*. London: Hutchinson.

Rowbotham, S. 1973 *Woman's consciousness, man's world*. Harmondsworth: Penguin.

Rushdie, S. 1996 *The Moor's last sigh*. London: Vintage.

Rushton, J.P. 1994 "Professors of hate". *Rolling Stone*, 20 October.

Rutherford, J. 1990 *Identity: community, culture, difference*. London: Lawrence & Wishart.

Said, E. 1978 *Orientalism*. London and Harmondsworth: Penguin.

Said, E. 1981 *Covering Islam*. London and Henley: Routledge & Kegan Paul.

Sanday, P.R. 1986 *Divine hunger: cannibalism as a cultural system*. Cambridge: Cambridge University Press.

Sassen, S. 1991 *The global city: New York, London, Tokyo*. Princeton, N.J.: Princeton University Press.

Saville, J. 1988 *The labour movement in Britain*. London and Boston: Faber & Faber.

Schick, I.C. 1990 Representing Middle Eastern women. In *Feminist Studies*, **16**, no.2, Summer.

Schlereth, T.J. 1992 *Cultural history and material culture: everyday life, landscapes, museums.* Charlottesville and London: University Press of Virginia.

Scott, G.R. 1995 *A history of torture.* London: Senate.

Seccombe, W. 1993 *Weathering the storm: working-class families from the industrial revolution to the fertility decline.* London: Verso.

Sedgwick, E.K. 1994 *Epistemology of the closet.* London: Penguin.

Senadhira, S. & H. Dawson. 1994 Raising India. *Beverage World*, **113**, issue 1560, February, pp. 46–8.

Sennett, R. & J. Cobb. 1993 *The hidden injuries of class.* London: Faber & Faber.

Seremetakis, N. 1994 The memory of the senses: historical perception, commensal exchange, and modernity. In L. Taylor, *Visualizing theory.* New York and London: Routledge.

Simmell, G. 1950 *The sociology of Georg Simmell.* Glencoe, Ill.: Free Press.

Skegg, D.C.G. 1966 Sacred cows, science and uncertainties. *Nature*, **382**, 29 August.

Sloterdijk, P. 1988 *Critique of cynical reason.* London: Verso.

Snead, J. 1994 *White screens black images: Hollywood from the dark side.* New York and London: Routledge.

Solomon, R.C. & K.M. Higgins. 1996 *A short history of philosophy.* New York and Oxford: Oxford University Press.

Solomos, J. & L. Back. 1996 *Racism and society.* Basingstoke and London: Macmillan.

Sontag, S. 1979 *On photography.* London and Harmondsworth: Penguin.

Sontag, S. 1988 *AIDS and its metaphors*. London: Penguin.

Spillers, H. 1985 *Conjuring: black women, fiction, and literary tradition*. Bloomington: Indiana University Press.

Spillers, H.J. 1987 Mama's baby, Papa's maybe: an American grammar book, *Diacritics*, Summer, **17**, no.2.

Spivak, Chakravorty, G. 1987 *In other worlds*. New York and London: Methuen.

Spivak, Chakravorty, G. 1988 Can the subaltern speak? In C. Nelson, L. Grossberg, *Marxism and the interpretation of culture*, Basingstoke and London: Macmillan.

Spivak, Chakravorty, G. 1993 *Outside in the teaching machine*. New York and London: Routledge.

Spivak, Chakravorty, G. 1995 Teaching for the times, in J.N. Pieterse & B. Parekh, *The decolonization of imagination: culture, knowledge and power*. London and N.J. Zed Books.

Sport for Immigrants. 1979 Council of Europe Report. Lisbon, 11–14 December.

Stafford, B.M. 1991 *Body criticism: imaging the unseen in Enlightenment art and medicine*. Cambridge, Mass. and London: MIT Press.

Stannard, D.E. 1992 *American holocaust: the conquest of the New World*. New York and London: Oxford University Press.

Stearns, M. & J. Stearns. 1994 *Jazz dance: the story of American vernacular dance*. New York: Da Capo Press.

Steel (ed.) 1994 *English Fairy Tales*. London: Wordsworth Editions.

Stepan, N. 1982 *The idea of race in science: Great Britain 1800–1960*. London: Macmillan.

Stephenson, P. 1979 The objectives of the promotion of the sports practice. In *Sport for Immigrants*, Council of Europe Report, Lisbon, 11–14 December.

Steward, S. & S. Garratt. 1984 *Signed, sealed and delivered: true life stories of women in pop.* Boston: South End Press.

Stocking, G.W. 1968 *Race, culture, and evolution: essays in the history of anthropology.* New York: Free Press.

Stocking, G.W. 1985 *Objects and others: essays on museums and material culture.* Madison, Wisconsin: University of Wisconsin Press.

Stocking, G.W. 1987 *Victorian anthropology.* New York and London: Free Press, Collier Macmillan.

Stoller, P. 1989 *The taste of ethnographic things: the senses in anthropology.* Philadelphia: University of Pennsylvania.

Street, B. 1992 British popular anthropology: exhibiting and photographing the other. In E. Edwards, *Anthropology and photography.*

Suleri, S. 1992 *The rhetoric of English India.* Chicago and London: University of Chicago Press.

Tagg, J. 1988 *The burden of representation.* Basingstoke: Macmillan.

Taylor, L. 1994 *Visualizing theory.* New York and London: Routledge.

Ten.8. 1992 *Critical decade: black British photography in the 80s.* Birmingham: Ten.8.

Tilton, R.S. 1994 *Pocahontas: the evolution of an American narrative.* Cambridge: Cambridge University Press.

Tinker, H. 1974 *A new system of slavery: the export of Indian labour overseas 1830–1920.* London: Oxford University Press.

Tinker, H. 1979 *Separate and unequal: India and the Indians in the British Commonwealth 1920–1950*. London: C. Hurst & Co.

Tseelon, E. 1995 *The masque of femininity*. London: Sage.

Ugwu, C. 1995 *Let's get it on: the politics of black performance*. London: Institute of Contemporary Arts.

Vincent, D. 1981 *Bread, knowledge and freedom: a study of nineteenth century working-class autobiography*. London: Europa Publications.

Virilio, P. 1991 *The aesthetics of disappearance*. New York: Semiotext(e).

Wagner, P. 1994 *A sociology of modernity: liberty and discipline*. London: Routledge.

Wahad, D.B., M. Abu-Jamal, A. Shakur. 1993 *Still black, still strong: survivors of the US war against black revolutionaries*. New York: Semiotext(e).

Waldinger, R., H. Aldrich, R. Ward and associates. 1990 *Ethnic entrepeneurs: immigrant business in industrial societies*. London: Sage.

Wallace, M. & G. Dent. 1992 *Black popular culture*. Seattle: Bay Press.

Ware, V. 1996 Defining forces: "race", gender and memories of empire. In I. Chambers & L. Curti, *The post-colonial question*.

Warner, M. 1994 *Managing monsters: six myths of our time. The Reith Lectures 1994*. London: Vintage.

Warner, M. 1995 *From the beast to the blonde: on fairy tales and their tellers*. London: Vintage.

Weld, T.D. 1968 *American slavery as it is: testimony of a thousand witnesses*. New York: Arno Press and New York Times.

Wiegman, R. 1995 *American anatomies: theorizing race and gender*. Durham and London: Duke University Press.

Will, R.G., J.W. Ironside, M. Zeidler, S.N. Cousens, K. Estbeiro, A. Alperovitch, S. Poser, M. Pocchiari, A. Hofman, P.G. Smith. 1996 A new variant of Creutzveldt-Jakob disease in the UK. *The Lancet*. **347**, 6 April.

Williams, E. 1944, 1994 *Capitalism and slavery*. Chapel Hill and London: University of North Carolina Press.

Williams, P.J. 1991 *The alchemy of race and rights*. Cambridge, Mass.: Harvard University Press.

Wilson, E. 1985 *Adorned in dreams: fashion and modernity*. London: Virago.

Wilson, E. & L. Taylor. 1989 *Through the looking glass: a history of dress from 1860 to the present day*. London: BBC Books.

Wilson, H.S. 1994 *African decolonization*. London: Edward Arnold.

Wittig, M. 1992 *The straight mind and other essays*. New York and London: Harvester Wheatsheaf.

Young, J.D. 1989 *Socialism and the English working class*. New York and London: Harvester Wheatsheaf.

Young, L. 1996 *Fear of the dark: "race", gender and sexuality in the cinema*. London and New York: Routledge.

Young, R.C. 1995 *Colonial desire: hybridity in theory, culture and race*. London: Routledge.

Index